Weight Watchers®
Favorite Homestyle
Recipes

Weight Watchers®
Favorite Homestyle
Recipes

NAL BOOKS

WEIGHT WATCHERS IS A REGISTERED TRADEMARK
OF WEIGHT WATCHERS INTERNATIONAL, INC.

NAL BOOKS
Published by the Penguin Group
Penguin Books USA Inc., 375 Hudson Street,
New York, New York 10014, U.S.A.
Penguin Books Ltd, 27 Wrights Lane,
London W8 5TZ, England
Penguin Books Australia Ltd, Ringwood,
Victoria, Australia
Penguin Books Canada Ltd, 10 Alcorn Avenue,
Toronto, Ontario, Canada M4V 3B2
Penguin Books (N.Z.) Ltd, 182–190 Wairau Road,
Auckland 10, New Zealand

Penguin Books Ltd, Registered Offices:
Harmondsworth, Middlesex, England

First published by NAL Books, an imprint of New American Library, a division of Penguin Books USA Inc.

First Printing, January, 1993
10 9 8 7 6 5 4 3 2 1

REGISTERED TRADEMARK—MARCA REGISTRADA

LIBRARY OF CONGRESS CATALOGING IN PUBLICATION DATA
Weight Watchers favorite homestyle recipes.
    p.   cm.
  Includes index.
  ISBN 0-453-01029-6
  1. Reducing diet. I. Weight Watchers International.
RM222.2.W31357   1993
641.5'635—dc20   92-25240
                                           CIP

Printed in the United States of America
Set in Caslon open face and Cloister roman
Designed by Kathleen Herlihy-Paoli
Photographer: Rita Maas
Food Stylist: A. J. Battifarano
Prop Stylist: Adrienne Abseck-Costanzo

With admiration, we dedicate this book to Weight Watchers members everywhere. You have come to us seeking help with your weight and have persevered and succeeded; your success has helped make Weight Watchers the largest, longest-established, and most respected weight-loss company in the world. Many of you have made significant life changes and have forged ahead to pursue a wealth of opportunities, walking through newly opened doors to health and happiness. This book is an affirmation of your achievement, a demonstration of your ability to savor wonderful meals that express your new attitudes about food. We thank you for sharing these recipes and your stories with us and the millions of others who will enjoy them.

Contents

Introduction

Five years ago, a recipe contest we conducted among our members and staff gave birth to a bestseller: *Weight Watchers Favorite Recipes* cookbook. This collection of winning recipes has sold more than one million copies, and continues to be an all-time favorite Weight Watchers cookbook. It has also prompted numerous requests from its fans for a sequel.

So in 1991 we decided to run a new contest, inviting our members, staff, and *Weight Watchers Magazine* readers to submit original recipes they've created that support their healthy eating habits and weight-loss or maintenance goals.

We were overwhelmed by the enthusiastic response: more than 5,000 entries were received from all areas of the United States and Canada, offering recipes from simple snack ideas to gourmet family fare. The process of reviewing and testing the entries was a challenging yet delightful experience, as one recipe after another showed us an extraordinary range of culinary creativity and delicious ingenuity in planning and cooking healthful, satisfying meals that follow the Weight Watchers Food Plan guidelines.

Most delightful, however, were the personal stories the entrants shared along with their recipes—inspiring tales and testimonials of success on the Weight Watchers Program.

We heard from Weight Watchers members and staff who juggle busy careers, family, school, a host of hobbies, and exercise time—and yet, as their recipes prove, still find time to be creative in the kitchen. We heard how their special recipes help keep them on track toward their goals. And over and over again, we heard words of gratitude for helping them achieve those goals.

In turn, we wish to express our sincere gratitude to all those who entered the contest and shared with us their stories and original recipes, and to all of our areas throughout North America which so enthusiastically supported the contest by distributing the entry forms.

The result is a delicious, down-home, kitchen-created, and Weight Watchers tested collection that we are very proud to bring from our family to yours: *Weight Watchers Favorite Homestyle Recipes*.

WEIGHT WATCHERS INTERNATIONAL

Tips, Tactics, and Techniques

Here are some of the ways we save time and work smarter in the kitchen.

REVIEWING THE RECIPE

When using a recipe for the first time, take a few minutes to read through the ingredients and directions. This could save you from getting halfway through the recipe and discovering that you're missing an important ingredient or that something needs several hours of marinating before cooking. Once you understand the recipe, assemble all the ingredients and utensils within easy reach. Cleaning up as you go frees you from a major wash-up at the end.

GETTING THE BEST RESULTS
∎

In this book, the weights of fresh fruits and vegetables are before any peeling, coring, etc. If a recipe calls for one pound of apples, cored, pared, and diced, begin with a full pound of apples; then prepare them according to directions.

MEASURING
∎

The success of any recipe depends greatly on accurate weighing and measuring. The accuracy of the Selection™ Information and nutrition analysis depends on correct measuring as well. Never guess at amounts, but use these guidelines.

Foods should be weighed on a food scale. To measure liquids, use a standard clear glass or plastic measuring cup placed on a level surface. For amounts less than ¼ cup, use standard measuring spoons. To measure dry ingredients, use metal or plastic measuring cups that come in ¼-, ⅓-, ½-, and 1-cup sizes. Working over wax paper, fill the appropriate cup and level it with the blunt edge of a knife or a spatula handle. Return any excess to its container. For amounts less than ¼ cup, use standard measuring spoons in the same manner.

Nonstick cookware, a real boon when you're interested in limiting your fat intake, allows you to cook without adding fat or having foods stick to the pan. You can spray an ordinary skillet or pan with nonstick cooking spray to gain the same advantage. This cooking spray, which adds few, if any, calories to food, is also helpful when measuring sticky ingredients like honey or molasses. A brief spray directed into the bowl of the measuring spoon will allow the sticky stuff to slide right out.

CONVENIENCE FOODS
∎

With time such a precious commodity, you can take shortcuts and still serve a home-cooked meal. Your own "planned-overs" are a great source of already-cooked food. Just measure serving-size amounts for the number of people you usually cook for or portions called for in your Food Plan and refrigerate or freeze them. The deli counter at the supermarket can supply ready-to-eat chicken, turkey, roast beef, ham, and other meats. We suggest that you avoid prepared mixtures, as they often contain hidden fats, sodium, and other undesirable ingredients or additives. For a quick stir-fry or salad for one, try the supermarket salad bar. Everything is already cut up, and you can buy a large variety without having perishable vegetables left over. It's a little more expensive to shop this way, but there's no waste. Scout the aisles for "quick-cooking" or "instant" versions of many products. Hot cereals, potato flakes, grits, polenta, and no-boil lasagna noodles are examples of commonly available time-savers. If you're sodium-sensitive, however, check the nutrition labels on these products; they sometimes contain more sodium than regular versions.

THE FREEZER ADVANTAGE
■

Storing portion-controlled soups, cooked meats, rice or pasta, stews, or other mixed foods in your freezer is a great way to be sure that you eat properly on no-cooking nights or have an appropriate lunch to take to work. Breakfast items like homebaked muffins are wonderful to bank against the lure of the office coffee cart. A recipe for 12 muffins bakes up in a jiffy and yields a dozen dividends. Thaw frozen ingredients or already-cooked foods in the refrigerator for several hours or overnight to prevent any spoilage. Or follow the manufacturer's directions for defrosting foods in the microwave oven.

SOME NOTES ON REFRIGERATING AND FREEZING
■

Always allow foods to cool slightly before chilling or freezing them, since placing hot food in the refrigerator or freezer may affect the efficiency of the appliance. Divide large quantities of food into smaller portions before refrigerating or freezing so that they will cool faster, reducing the chance of spoilage. Cover any food to be refrigerated or frozen in moisture- and vapor-resistant wrap.

OVEN TECHNIQUES
■

Always check as directed to determine whether a dish is done rather than relying exclusively on the cooking time indicated in a recipe.

Check the accuracy of your oven thermostat from time to time. Any discrepancy may affect the quality of your cooking. To determine whether the thermostat is registering correctly, place an oven thermometer on a rack centered in the oven. Set the oven temperature, wait 10 to 15 minutes, then check the thermometer. If the actual oven temperature doesn't match the temperature setting, adjust the setting higher or lower as needed to compensate for the difference.

To prevent heat loss and rapid changes in oven temperature, close the oven door promptly after putting food in and avoid opening the door unnecessarily.

Place baking pans in the middle of the center rack to permit air to circulate freely, helping food to bake evenly. Use one oven rack at a time. If you must use more than one rack at the same time, position the racks so that they divide the oven into thirds. Stagger the pans so that they're not directly above each other. Again, this helps air circulate well and maintains even baking.

Here's another baking tip: When using only some of the cups in a muffin pan, prevent the pan from warping or burning by partially filling the empty cups with water. When you're ready to remove the muffins, carefully drain off the hot water.

When broiling, unless a recipe indicates otherwise, use the standard distance of 4 inches from the heat source.

SUCCESSFUL MICROWAVING

■

Perhaps no other culinary innovation has had the tremendous impact on food preparation that the microwave oven has. Cooking and defrosting have never been faster or easier. And since the microwave oven cooks without heating up the kitchen, it's an especially appealing cooking tool in warm weather. A microwave oven at the office allows you to enjoy soup or leftovers that need a quick heating.

The recipes here make generous use of the microwave oven. They were tested in 650- to 700-watt microwave ovens with variable power levels. These levels control the percentage of power introduced into the oven cavity and automatically cycle power on and off. Lower power levels cook more slowly;

higher levels cook faster. The power levels may also vary depending on the brand of oven. Our recipes use these power levels:

High (100%)
Medium-High (60 to 70%)
Medium (50%)
Low (10 to 20%)

Adjust the recipes if the levels in your microwave oven differ from these. For a lower-wattage oven, increase the cooking time. For a higher-wattage oven, decrease the cooking time slightly.

When cooking in your microwave oven, be sure to use cookware that is specifically recommended, such as microwavable casseroles with matching covers. When food is arranged on a microwavable plate or in custard cups, try using an inverted microwavable pie plate or saucer as a cover.

READING THE RECIPES

■

To help you keep track of your choices on the Weight Watchers Food Plan, we've provided the Selection Information for each recipe—for example, "Each serving provides: 1 Milk; 2 Proteins; 15 Optional Calories." Be sure to recalculate the Selection Information if you make any changes to a recipe.

Each recipe also includes a per-serving nutritional analysis of calories, protein, fat, carbohydrate, calcium, sodium, cholesterol, and dietary fiber. These figures are based on the most up-to-date data available and are for the recipe *exactly as given*. Any changes you make to a recipe will alter the information. For example, the nutritional analyses for recipes containing cooked items such as rice, pasta, or vegetables assume that no extra salt or fat will be added during cooking. Adding salt or fat will alter the nutritional information shown for the recipe—whether or not the changes affect the Selection Information.

When you're preparing a recipe for more than one serving, mix the ingredients well and be sure to divide the servings evenly so that each portion will contain equal amounts of all ingredients.

Breakfast

Clearly breakfast is an important meal. Breakfast trends these days indicate a strong preference for inventive and delicious muffins that make excellent use of grains, fruits, and spices. In most cases, only a beverage is needed to make a full and wholesome meal. We recommend that you bake a batch of muffins and stash them in your freezer, where they will be ready to be whisked off to work, to become an instant snack with a cup of tea, or to be warmed for surprise guests to enjoy with coffee.

Blueberry Hotcakes and Chocolate Banana Pancakes are a new spin on the short stack; a fresh idea from south of the border is the Banana Burrito. Oats and pecans give a satisfying crunch to the Pecan Oatmeal Belgian Waffle.

Wonderful recipes for family breakfasts or brunch include Breakfast Pie and Savory Breakfast Puff. We hope these recipes inspire you too.

Honey Bran Muffins

Whats a woman to do when her favorite food is loaded with fat and calories? Cindi headed for the kitchen to devise a delicious compromise.

CINDI REDDING · EDISON, WASHINGTON

1¼ cups all-purpose flour
1 tablespoon double-acting baking
    powder
¼ teaspoon salt
3 ounces bran flakes

1 cup low-fat (1%) milk
⅓ cup honey
¼ cup vegetable oil
1 large egg, lightly beaten

1. Preheat oven to 400°F. Spray twelve 2½-inch nonstick muffin cups with nonstick cooking spray, or line with paper liners; set aside.

2. In medium bowl, whisk together flour, baking powder, and salt. In another medium bowl, combine remaining ingredients; let stand until cereal softens, 2 to 3 minutes. Pour wet ingredients into dry and stir until just moistened (do not beat or overmix).

3. Spoon batter evenly into prepared cups, filling each about two-thirds full. Bake 18 to 20 minutes, until muffins are golden brown and toothpick inserted in center comes out clean. Cool on rack.

MAKES 12 SERVINGS

EACH SERVING PROVIDES: *1 Fat; ¾ Bread; 50 Optional Calories*

PER SERVING: *156 Calories, 3 g Protein, 6 g Fat, 24 g Carbohydrate, 86 mg Calcium, 234 mg Sodium, 19 mg Cholesterol, 0 g Dietary Fiber*

Fruity Bran Muffins

Scrumptious snacks that are naturally sweet without added sugar, these muffins use whatever fruit you have on hand. Or try making them with zucchini.

DIANA POWELL · DELBURNE, ALBERTA, CANADA

1½ cups whole-wheat flour
2¼ ounces quick-cooking oats
3 tablespoons unprocessed coarse bran
1 teaspoon double-acting baking powder
1 teaspoon baking soda
1½ cups unsweetened applesauce

½ cup low-fat (1.5%) buttermilk
⅓ cup vegetable oil
2 tablespoons molasses
1 large egg
¾ cup raisins

1. Preheat oven to 375°F. Spray twelve 2½-inch nonstick muffin cups with nonstick cooking spray, or line with paper liners; set aside.

2. In large bowl, whisk together flour, oats, bran, baking powder, and baking soda. In medium bowl, whisk together applesauce, buttermilk, oil, molasses, and egg.

3. Make well in center of flour mixture. Pour in applesauce mixture and stir until just combined; fold in raisins. Spoon batter evenly into prepared muffin cups, filling each about two-thirds full.

4. Bake 18 to 20 minutes, until lightly browned and toothpick inserted in center comes out clean. Cool on rack.

MAKES 12 SERVINGS

EACH SERVING PROVIDES: *1¼ Fats; 1 Bread; ¾ Fruit; 25 Optional Calories*

PER SERVING: *187 Calories, 4 g Protein, 7 g Fat, 28 g Carbohydrate, 51 mg Calcium, 123 mg Sodium, 18 mg Cholesterol, 4 g Dietary Fiber*

Apple Spice Muffins

Kim is a homemaker and mother of four—including twin toddlers—so she's always in the market for easy-to-make food that tastes great. These muffins fit the bill, and they're a hit with the kids.

KIM MILLER · IDA GROVE, IOWA

1½ cups all-purpose flour
3 ounces quick-cooking oatmeal
1 tablespoon double-acting baking
    powder
1 teaspoon ground cinnamon
¾ teaspoon salt
¼ teaspoon ground nutmeg
¼ teaspoon ground ginger

2 small Granny Smith apples, pared,
    cored, and cubed
¾ cup skim milk
½ cup firmly packed dark brown sugar
¼ cup softened margarine
1 large egg
½ cup raisins

1.   Preheat oven to 375°F. Spray twelve 2½-inch nonstick muffin cups with nonstick cooking spray, or line with paper liners; set aside.

2.   In large bowl, whisk together flour, oatmeal, baking powder, cinnamon, salt, nutmeg, and ginger.

3.   In food processor, process apples, milk, sugar, margarine, and egg until apples are coarsely chopped.

4.   Make well in center of flour mixture. Pour in apple mixture and stir until just combined; fold in raisins. Spoon batter evenly into prepared muffin cups, filling each two-thirds full.

5.   Bake 20 to 25 minutes, until lightly browned and toothpick inserted in center comes out clean. Cool on rack.

MAKES 12 SERVINGS

EACH SERVING PROVIDES: *1 Fat; 1 Bread; ½ Fruit; 50 Optional Calories*

PER SERVING: *194 Calories, 4 g Protein, 5 g Fat, 34 g Carbohydrate, 96 mg Calcium, 306 mg Sodium, 18 mg Cholesterol, 1 g Dietary Fiber*

Date Bran Muffins

Ellen is a deputy attorney general for the State of California, a wife, and a mother of two. She lost weight even while enduring a stressful appearance in the California Supreme Court, and recently became a lifetime member.

ELLEN BIRNBAUM KEHR · LOS ANGELES, CALIFORNIA

1½ cups all-purpose flour
⅓ cup granulated sugar
1 tablespoon double-acting baking
    powder
¼ teaspoon salt
2 cups low-fat (1.5%) buttermilk

4 ounces wheat-bran cereal
¼ cup vegetable oil
1 large egg, lightly beaten
12 large pitted dates (4½ ounces),
    chopped

1. Preheat oven to 375°F. Spray twelve 2½-inch nonstick muffin cups with nonstick cooking spray, or line with paper liners; set aside.

2. In large bowl, sift 1 cup plus 2 tablespoons of the flour, the sugar, baking powder, and salt. In medium bowl, combine buttermilk and cereal. Let stand until cereal softens, 2 to 3 minutes; stir in oil and egg. Pour wet ingredients into dry and stir until just moistened (do not beat or overmix).

3. In small bowl, toss dates with remaining flour; stir into batter.

4. Spoon batter evenly into prepared cups, filling each about two-thirds full.

Bake 20 to 25 minutes, until toothpick inserted in center comes out clean. Cool on rack.

MAKES 12 SERVINGS

EACH SERVING PROVIDES: *1 Fat; 1 Bread; ½ Fruit; 50 Optional Calories*

PER SERVING: *200 Calories, 5 g Protrain, 6 g Fat, 35 g Carbohydrate, 75 mg Calcium, 287 mg Sodium, 20 mg Cholesterol, 4 g Dietary Fiber*

Fruity Muffins

Angela and her daughter amuse themselves by devising healthful recipes that taste so good that the rest of the family thinks they ought to be gaining weight. Instead, the pair has dropped nearly 100 pounds!

ANGELA REESE · BOTHELL, WASHINGTON

2 cups all-purpose flour
1 tablespoon double-acting baking
    powder
1 tablespoon fructose
½ teaspoon salt

¼ cup reduced-calorie tub margarine
1 cup low-fat (1%) milk
1 large egg, lightly beaten
1 cup fresh or frozen blueberries

1. Preheat oven to 400°F. Spray twelve 2½-inch nonstick muffin cups with nonstick cooking spray, or line with paper liners; set aside.

2. In medium bowl, sift flour, baking powder, fructose, and salt. Using pastry blender or 2 knives, cut in margarine until mixture resembles coarse meal.

3. In small bowl, whisk together milk and egg; pour into dry ingredients and stir until just combined (do not beat or overmix). Fold in blueberries.

4. Spoon batter evenly into prepared cups, filling each about two-thirds full. Bake 25 minutes, until golden brown and toothpick inserted in center comes out clean. Cool on rack.

Variation: Substitute 1 cup thinly sliced apples and 1 teaspoon cinnamon for the blueberries. Selection Information remains the same.

MAKES 12 SERVINGS

EACH SERVING PROVIDES: *½ Fat; ¾ Bread; 25 Optional Calories*

PER SERVING: *119 Calories, 3 g Protein, 3 g Fat, 20 g Carbohydrate, 84 mg Calcium, 251 mg Sodium, 19 mg Cholesterol, 0 g Dietary Fiber*

Blueberry-Orange Muffins

Sandra's recipe makes large, moist muffins. When she's not caring for her children, Sandra loves aerobics, swimming, cross-stitch, reading, and cooking.

SANDRA GRIFFITHS · RED DEER, ALBERTA, CANADA

2¼ cups all-purpose flour
⅔ cup granulated sugar
2 teaspoons double-acting baking powder
1 teaspoon baking soda
½ teaspoon salt
½ cup reduced-calorie tub margarine

¾ cup plain nonfat yogurt
1 small orange, peeled, seeded, and finely chopped, with juice
2 teaspoons grated orange peel
2 large eggs, beaten
1½ cups fresh or frozen blueberries

1. Preheat oven to 400°F. Spray twelve 2½-inch nonstick muffin cups with nonstick cooking spray, or line with paper liners; set aside.

2. In large bowl, whisk together flour, sugar, baking powder, baking soda, and salt; cut in margarine until mixture resembles fine crumbs.

3. In small bowl, combine yogurt, orange, and orange peel until thoroughly blended. Stir in eggs.

4. Make well in center of flour mixture. Pour in egg mixture and stir until just combined; gently fold in blueberries.

5. Spoon batter evenly into prepared muffin cups, filling each about two-thirds full. Bake 20 to 25 minutes, until lightly browned and a toothpick inserted in center comes out clean. Cool on rack.

MAKES 12 SERVINGS

———

EACH SERVING PROVIDES: *1 Fat; 1 Bread; ¼ Fruit; 75 Optional Calories*

———

PER SERVING: *199 Calories, 4 g Protein, 5 g Fat, 34 g Carbohydrate, 78 mg Calcium, 327 mg Sodium, 36 mg Cholesterol, 1 g Dietary Fiber*

Banana Spice Muffins

Julia loves muffins and wanted to incorporate them into her Food Plan. She enjoys these nutty treats with a cup of cocoa at breakfast, or as an afternoon snack.

JULIA ANNE MERCER · FORESTVILLE, CALIFORNIA

1¼ cups plus 1 tablespoon all-purpose flour
3 tablespoons firmly packed dark brown sugar
1½ teaspoons double-acting baking powder
¾ teaspoon ground cinnamon
½ teaspoon ground nutmeg
⅛ teaspoon ground cloves
1½ medium bananas, mashed
¼ cup low-fat (1%) milk
3 tablespoons reduced-calorie tub margarine, melted
1 large egg, lightly beaten
1 ounce chopped walnuts

1.   Preheat oven to 400°F. Spray six 2½-inch nonstick muffin cups with nonstick cooking spray, or line with paper liners; set aside.

2.   In medium bowl, combine flour, sugar, baking powder, and spices. In another medium bowl, stir together all remaining ingredients except walnuts. Pour wet ingredients into dry and stir just until moistened (do not beat or overmix).

3.   Spoon batter evenly into prepared cups, filling each about two-thirds full. Sprinkle evenly with chopped walnuts.

4.   Bake 20 minutes, until muffins are light brown and toothpick inserted in center comes out clean. Cool on rack.

MAKES 6 SERVINGS

EACH SERVING PROVIDES: *1 Fat; 1 Bread; ½ Fruit; 75 Optional Calories*

PER SERVING: *226 Calories, 5 g Protein, 7 g Fat, 36 g Carbohydrate, 90 mg Calcium, 181 mg Sodium, 36 mg Cholesterol, 1 g Dietary Fiber*

Pineapple Danish

Diane loves experimenting in the kitchen and bringing new recipes to her Weight Watchers meetings, where she works as a weigher and receptionist. This Danish freezes well for future use.

DIANE REAMS · WARRENSBURG, MISSOURI

2 slices reduced-calorie white bread, crumbled
½ cup part-skim ricotta cheese
Granulated sugar substitute to equal 2 teaspoons sugar
1 teaspoon reduced-calorie tub margarine, melted

½ cup drained canned crushed pineapple
1 teaspoon firmly packed dark brown sugar
⅛ teaspoon ground cinnamon

1.   Preheat oven to 375°F.

2.   Spray small individual ceramic casserole with nonstick cooking spray; set aside.

3.   In small bowl, combine bread, cheese, sugar substitute, and margarine; press into casserole.

4.   In same bowl, combine remaining ingredients until blended; spread evenly over bread mixture. Bake until golden, about 20 minutes. Cool.

MAKES 1 SERVING

THIS SERVING PROVIDES: ½ Fat; 2 Proteins; 1 Bread; 1 Fruit; 20 Optional Calories

PER SERVING: 370 Calories, 19 g Protein, 14 g Fat, 49 g Carbohydrate, 399 mg Calcium, 383 mg Sodium, 38 mg Cholesterol, 2 g Dietary Fiber

Oatmeal Scones

A former *habituée* of restaurants and bakeries, Cynthia patterned these delectable scones after the high-fat counterparts sold in her local bakeshop.

CYNTHIA PATTERSON · UPLAND, CALIFORNIA

2¼ ounces quick-cooking *or* old-fashioned oats
½ cup plus 1 tablespoon buttermilk baking mix
1 teaspoon double-acting baking powder

2 tablespoons firmly packed light brown sugar
½ cup whole milk
¼ cup plus 2 tablespoons golden raisins

1. Preheat oven to 425°F.

2. In medium bowl, whisk together oats, baking mix, baking powder, and sugar. Stir in milk and raisins until just combined. Drop dough by ¼-cup measures onto non-stick baking sheet, making 6 scones. Bake 8 to 10 minutes, until golden.

MAKES 6 SERVINGS

EACH SERVING PROVIDES: *1 Bread; ½ Fruit; 40 Optional Calories*

PER SERVING: *141 Calories, 3 g Protein, 3 g Fat, 27 g Carbohydrate, 89 mg Calcium, 215 mg Sodium, 3 mg Cholesterol, 1 g Dietary Fiber*

Pecan Oatmeal Belgian Waffle

Brenda is a full-time Weight Watchers field clerk who loves camping, fishing, waterskiing, walking, and bicycling with her husband. Her recipe can play many roles—as a breakfast, healthy dessert, or snack—and accommodate a variety of fruit toppings.

BRENDA CRIDER · BILLINGS, MONTANA

¾ ounce quick-cooking oats
1 tablespoon all-purpose flour
1 teaspoon granulated sugar
½ teaspoon double-acting baking
    powder
Dash salt

1 large egg, separated
¼ cup skim milk
¼ ounce shelled pecans, finely chopped
Fresh fruit and confectioners' sugar for
    garnish (optional)

1. Spray a nonstick waffle iron with non-stick cooking spray; heat according to manufacturer's directions.

2. In small bowl, combine oats, flour, sugar, baking powder, and salt. In 1-cup measure, whisk together egg yolk, milk, and pecans; stir into oat mixture until just combined (do not beat or overmix). Set aside.

3. In separate small bowl, with electric mixer on high speed, beat egg white until stiff; fold into oat mixture.

4. Pour batter into preheated waffle iron. Close and bake on High or according to manufacturer's directions, until golden brown, about 4 minutes.

Note: This recipe can be doubled, and freezes well.

MAKES 1 SERVING

THIS SERVING PROVIDES: *¼ Milk; 1 Fat; 1 Protein; 1 Bread; 50 Optional Calories (Add Fruit Selections as used, plus 10 Optional Calories per ½ teaspoon confectioners' sugar.)*

PER SERVING: *278 Calories, 13 g Protein, 12 g Fat, 30 g Carbohydrate, 221 mg Calcium, 440 mg Sodium, 214 mg Cholesterol, 2 g Dietary Fiber*

Blueberry Hotcakes

Linda considers herself a wife, mother, grandmother, artist, and author—in that order. These days she's losing weight along with her daughter and two daughters-in-law, and the quartet vows not to quit until they're downright gorgeous!

LINDA WILLIS · GRANTS PASS, OREGON

½ teaspoon cornstarch
1½ cups fresh or frozen blueberries
Granulated sugar substitute to equal
    4 teaspoons sugar
1½ ounces quick-cooking oats
⅓ cup buttermilk powder
3 tablespoons all-purpose flour

½ teaspoon double-acting baking
    powder
½ teaspoon baking soda
½ teaspoon granulated sugar
¼ teaspoon salt
¼ cup egg substitute

1.   To prepare blueberry sauce, in small saucepan, combine cornstarch and ¼ cup cold water until smooth. Add blueberries; cook over medium heat, stirring frequently, until thickened, about 5 minutes. Stir in sugar substitute; set aside.

2.   Heat nonstick electric griddle or 2 medium nonstick skillets until hot.

3.   In large bowl, combine remaining ingredients until just blended.

4.   Drop batter by ⅓-cup measures onto hot griddle, making 6 hotcakes. Cook until golden brown, about 3 minutes. Carefully turn and cook until other side is golden, about 3 minutes. Serve immediately with blueberry sauce.

MAKES 2 SERVINGS

EACH SERVING PROVIDES: *½ Milk; ½ Protein; 1 Fruit; 1½ Breads; 10 Optional Calories*

PER SERVING: *286 Calories, 15 g Protein, 3 g Fat, 52 g Carbohydrate, 318 mg Calcium, 761 mg Sodium, 14 mg Cholesterol, 5 g Dietary Fiber*

Chocolate Banana Pancakes

With her ribbon of stars celebrating 102 pounds lost and her goal weight achieved, Daria is known as "The General" at home. When she has KP duty the results are superb—like this sweet treat.

DARIA BARNES · BEL AIR, MARYLAND

1 packet reduced-calorie chocolate dairy shake (70 calories per serving as packaged)
1 medium banana, peeled and mashed

¼ cup egg substitute
3 tablespoons all-purpose flour
1 teaspoon double-acting baking powder
1 teaspoon vanilla extract

1. In medium mixing bowl, whisk together all ingredients and ½ cup water.

2. Spray large nonstick skillet or griddle with nonstick cooking spray; heat over medium-high heat. Spoon batter into skillet by thirds, making 3 pancakes, each 4 inches in diameter. Reduce heat to medium and cook until bubbles appear on surface, about 2 minutes. Using spatula, turn pancakes over and cook until cooked through, about 2 minutes.

MAKES 1 SERVING

PER SERVING: *300 Calories, 14 g Protein, 1 g Fat, 59 g Carbohydrate, 492 mg Calcium, 698 mg Sodium, 0 mg Cholesterol, 2 g Dietary Fiber*

THIS SERVING PROVIDES: *1 Milk; 1 Protein; 1 Bread; 2 Fruits*

Banana French Toast

An active church volunteer, painter, reader, cook, and seamstress, Pearl lost 77 pounds on the Weight Watchers Program and feels "like a new person."

PEARL KRZYKWA · GRAND RAPIDS, MICHIGAN

6 tablespoons plain nonfat yogurt
¼ teaspoon vanilla extract
Granulated sugar substitute to equal 1
    teaspoon sugar
½ cup egg substitute

4 slices reduced-calorie white bread
1 medium banana, sliced
¼ cup reduced-calorie maple-flavored
    syrup

1.   In small bowl, whisk together yogurt, vanilla, and sugar substitute. Set aside.

2.   Pour egg substitute into shallow bowl; dip bread in egg substitute, coating both sides and absorbing all liquid.

3.   Spray large nonstick skillet with nonstick cooking spray; over medium heat, cook bread until browned on both sides. Remove to heated platter, cover, and keep warm. In same skillet, quickly cook banana slices until golden on each side.

4.   Place 2 slices bread on each serving plate; top evenly with yogurt mixture, banana slices, and syrup.

MAKES 2 SERVINGS

EACH SERVING (2 SLICES) PROVIDES: *½ Milk; 1 Protein; 1 Bread; ½ Fruit; 25 Optional Calories*

PER SERVING: *239 Calories, 12 g Protein, 2 g Fat, 48 g Carbohydrate, 150 mg Calcium, 385 mg Sodium, 1 mg Cholesterol, 2 g Dietary Fiber*

Savory Breakfast Puff

Patricia is a chemistry-physics teacher married to a chemical engineer, and mother of two grown children. She writes, "I have been on every diet in the book and lost hundreds of pounds over the years, but only Weight Watchers really worked for me." Patricia loves to cook and create new recipes, like this one, which really puts the "good" in "good morning."

PATRICIA KIMBROUGH · HUTCHINSON, MINNESOTA

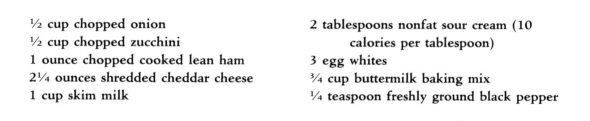

½ cup chopped onion
½ cup chopped zucchini
1 ounce chopped cooked lean ham
2¼ ounces shredded cheddar cheese
1 cup skim milk

2 tablespoons nonfat sour cream (10 calories per tablespoon)
3 egg whites
¾ cup buttermilk baking mix
¼ teaspoon freshly ground black pepper

1.   Preheat oven to 350°F. Spray 9-inch glass pie plate with nonstick cooking spray; set aside.

2.   Spray small nonstick skillet with nonstick cooking spray; add onion, zucchini, and ham. Cook over medium heat until onion is translucent, about 2 minutes.

3.   Spread onion mixture over bottom of pie plate; sprinkle cheese over top.

4.   In small bowl, combine milk, sour cream, egg whites, baking mix, and pepper until blended. Pour into pie plate. Bake until golden brown and puffy, 35 to 40 minutes.

MAKES 4 SERVINGS

EACH SERVING PROVIDES: *¼ Milk; 1¼ Proteins; ½ Vegetable; 1 Bread; 25 Optional Calories*

PER SERVING: *213 Calories, 13 g Protein, 9 g Fat, 20 g Carbohydrate, 239 mg Calcium, 525 mg Sodium, 22 mg Cholesterol, 1 g Dietary Fiber*

Breakfast Pie

From a busy mother of three who works as an elementary education aide comes an innovative breakfast that really starts the day off right.

PENNIE LINDEMANN · SPEARFISH, SOUTH DAKOTA

1 refrigerated 9-inch pie crust
6 ounces shredded part-skim mozzarella
    cheese
4 ounces cooked crumbled turkey
    sausage
¼ cup chopped mushrooms

1 tablespoon chopped onion
1 tablespoon chopped green bell pepper
4 large eggs
¾ cup low-fat (2%) milk
½ teaspoon salt
Dash freshly ground black pepper

1.   Preheat oven to 425°F. Prick crust several times with fork; line with aluminum foil and fill with dry beans or pie weights. Bake until lightly browned, 10 to 12 minutes. Place crust on rack to cool completely. Reduce oven heat to 375°F.

2.   Place half the cheese in baked pie shell; top evenly with sausage, mushrooms, onion, and green pepper. Sprinkle evenly with remaining cheese.

3.   In medium bowl, whisk eggs, milk, salt, and pepper; pour over filled pie crust. Bake 45 minutes, until knife inserted in center comes out clean.

MAKES 8 SERVINGS

EACH SERVING PROVIDES: *2 Proteins; ½ Bread; 65 Optional Calories*

PER SERVING: *213 Calories, 13 g Protein, 9 g Fat, 20 g Carbohydrate, 239 mg Calcium, 525 mg Sodium, 22 mg Cholesterol, 1 g Dietary Fiber*

Puffy Chive Omelet

Let this be one of your handiest recipes when you want a quick, no-fuss meal. If available, fresh chives are even nicer than dried; use about 2 teaspoons.

3 large egg whites
2 large eggs, separated
2 tablespoons low-fat (1%) milk

1 tablespoon grated Parmesan cheese
1 tablespoon dried chives
Dash paprika

1.   Spray 10-inch glass pie plate with non-stick cooking spray; set aside.

2.   In medium bowl, with electric mixer on high speed, beat egg whites until stiff but not dry.

3.   In another medium bowl, with electric mixer on medium speed, beat egg yolks until thick and lemon-colored. Using rubber spatula, gently fold yolks, and remaining ingredients, into egg whites, until completely blended. Pour into prepared plate; smooth top to distribute mixture evenly. Microwave on High 2½ to 3 minutes, or until just set, rotating plate once. (Looking through bottom of plate will help you see when omelet is set.) Omelet will puff considerably when cooking and will drop as it cools.

4.   Gently fold omelet in half and slide onto serving plate.

MAKES 2 SERVINGS

EACH SERVING PROVIDES: *1½ Proteins; 20 Optional Calories*

PER SERVING: *121 Calories, 13 g Protein, 6 g Fat, 2 g Carbohydrate, 82 mg Calcium, 199 mg Sodium, 215 mg Cholesterol, 0 g Dietary Fiber*

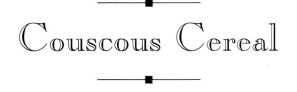

Couscous Cereal

Surprise! Couscous, the North African dinner staple, makes a terrific breakfast! As a 30-pound loser and Weight Watchers leader, Alice enthusiastically recommends her hearty hot cereal adaptation.

ALICE MOLTER · CLEVELAND HEIGHTS, OHIO

1 teaspoon margarine
1½ ounces couscous
2 tablespoons raisins

1 teaspoon honey
½ cup low-fat (1%) milk

1.   In medium saucepan, heat ⅓ cup water and the margarine until boiling. Stir in couscous; remove from heat; let stand, covered, 5 minutes.

2.   Stir in raisins and honey. Serve with milk.

MAKES 1 SERVING

THIS SERVING PROVIDES: ½ Milk; 1 Fat; 1½ Breads; 1 Fruit; 20 Optional Calories

PER SERVING: 321 Calories, 10 g Protein, 5 g Fat, 59 g Carbohydrate, 171 mg Calcium, 112 mg Sodium, 5 mg Cholesterol, 1 g Dietary Fiber

Banana Burrito

A quick pick-me-up you can fix in your microwave, this luscious burrito will please youngsters and the young at heart.

DOROTHY (DOODLES) YOUNG · SHAWNEE, KANSAS

One 6-inch flour tortilla
1 tablespoon creamy peanut butter
2 teaspoons reduced-calorie raspberry
    spread (8 calories per teaspoon)

1 teaspoon shredded coconut (optional)
½ medium banana

1. Lay tortilla on flat surface; spread evenly with peanut butter and raspberry spread. Sprinkle with coconut, if desired.

2. Place banana on edge of tortilla; roll up to enclose. Wrap loosely in paper towel. Microwave on High 35 seconds.

MAKES 1 SERVING

THIS SERVING PROVIDES: *1 Fat; 1 Protein; 1 Bread; 1 Fruit; 20 Optional Calories. (Add 5 Optional Calories if coconut is used.)*

PER SERVING: *232 Calories, 7 g Protein, 10 g Fat, 31 g Carbohydrate, 49 mg Calcium, 216 mg Sodium, 0 mg Cholesterol, 3 g Dietary Fiber*

International Breakfast

Tortillas for breakfast? Why not! Along with the flavors of Swiss cheese and apple pie, they give this dish its international status.

MARGARET VROOMAN · VANCOUVER, WASHINGTON

One 6-inch flour tortilla
1 small apple, pared, cored, and thinly
    sliced

¾ ounce shredded Swiss cheese
Dash ground cinnamon

1.   Spray small nonstick skillet with nonstick cooking spray. Add tortilla; cook over medium heat until browned and crisp, about 2 minutes.

2.   Turn tortilla; arrange apple and cheese on top. Cover and cook 1 minute longer.

3.   To serve, slide tortilla onto serving plate; sprinkle with cinnamon.

MAKES 1 SERVING

THIS SERVING PROVIDES: *1 Protein; 1 Bread; 1 Fruit*

PER SERVING: *212 Calories, 8 g Protein, 9 g Fat, 27 g Carbohydrate, 250 mg Calcium, 195 mg Sodium, 20 mg Cholesterol, 3 g Dietary Fiber*

Breakfast Blizzard

Looking for a quick, nutritious breakfast shake with substance, Sara hit upon this luscious combination. It's filling and keeps her going all morning long.

SARA BODDY · GOLDEN, COLORADO

¾ cup plain nonfat yogurt
½ medium banana, sliced
¼ cup apple or orange juice
¼ cup part-skim ricotta cheese
2 ice cubes

1 tablespoon wheat germ
1 teaspoon ground cinnamon
Granulated sugar substitute to equal
    1 teaspoon sugar

In blender, combine all ingredients; blend until smooth, about 45 seconds. Pour into 12-ounce glass.

MAKES 1 SERVING

THIS SERVING PROVIDES: *1 Milk; 1 Protein; 1½ Fruits; 30 Optional Calories*

PER SERVING: *295 Calories, 20 g Protein, 6 g Fat, 42 g Carbohydrate, 544 mg Calcium, 209 mg Sodium, 22 mg Cholesterol, 2 g Dietary Fiber*

Appetizers

To start a special dinner, to make a mini-meal with salad and fruit, to create a collection of appetizing choices on a buffet, or to be passed at your next party, here are a dozen fresh ideas.

Dips, a universal favorite, have been reinterpreted. Curry Dip, equally delicious with vegetables or fruits, would be wonderful preceding a meal of Chutney Baked Fish and Confetti Pilaf.

Everyone seems to have a love affair with pizza, and if you've got kids to feed, Pizza Cups will surely become their favorite snack.

A spectacular presentation, destined to be a showpiece at any gathering, is Party Bread Pot Fondue: A whole round loaf of bread becomes the container for a creamy, cheesy dip, surrounded by brilliant vegetables. For a special treat, when the veggies and dip are gone, wedges of the flavored bread are left to munch. Take this as a hostess gift; you're sure to be the center of attention, and you'll guarantee an appetizer that fits your Food Plan.

Curry Dip

An avid gardener, Emily devised this dip to complement her fresh home-grown broccoli, sugar snap peas, and cucumbers. Nonfat cottage cheese and yogurt stand in for most of the usual mayonnaise.

EMILY FRITTS · NORTH HAVEN, CONNECTICUT

1 cup nonfat cottage cheese
¼ cup plain nonfat yogurt
¼ cup reduced-calorie mayonnaise
2 teaspoons diced onion

1½ teaspoons curry powder, or to taste
1 packet low-sodium instant chicken
     broth mix
¼ teaspoon dry mustard

In blender, combine all ingredients until smooth and creamy. Use as a dressing or dip for fresh vegetables; as a sauce for fish or chicken; as a salad dressing; or as a sandwich spread.

MAKES 6 SERVINGS

EACH SERVING (¼ CUP) PROVIDES: *1 Fat; ½ Protein; 20 Optional Calories*

PER SERVING: *67 Calories, 6 g Protein, 3 g Fat, 4 g Carbohydrate, 42 mg Calcium, 196 mg Sodium, 7 mg Cholesterol, 0 g Dietary Fiber*

Ranch-Mustard Dip

Unwilling to admit her mission, the first time she went to Weight Watchers, Sue told her family she was going shopping. Now Sue's a lifetime member (since 1977) and proud of it.

SUE ROBERTS · FORT WORTH, TEXAS

1 cup drained whole pimientos
¼ cup plus 1 tablespoon reduced-calorie ranch dressing (16 calories per tablespoon)

2 teaspoons mustard
¾ cup plain nonfat yogurt
¼ cup nonfat sour cream (10 calories per tablespoon)

1. In food processor or blender, puree pimientos. Add dressing and mustard; process until combined.

2. Transfer mixture to medium bowl; whisk in yogurt and sour cream. Cover and refrigerate several hours.

3. To serve, pour into small serving bowl and surround with fresh vegetables for an appetizer; or pass as a sauce for chicken or fish.

MAKES 4 SERVINGS

PER SERVING: *67 Calories, 4 g Protein, 0 g Fat, 11 g Carbohydrate, 109 mg Calcium, 257 mg Sodium, 1 mg Cholesterol, 0 g Dietary Fiber*

EACH SERVING (½ CUP) PROVIDES: *¼ Milk; ½ Vegetable; 30 Optional Calories*

Hummus Dip/ Salad Dressing

Following the Weight Watchers Program and exercising regularly—including walking to and from work over the Brooklyn Bridge several times a week—helps Judy feel great while losing weight. She recommends her tasty Middle Eastern dip as a satisfying snack. "My teenage son loves it, too!" she writes, noting that's "no easy accomplishment."

JUDY GOULD · BROOKLYN HEIGHTS, NEW YORK

12 ounces drained cooked chick-peas
6 ounces soft tofu
¼ cup chopped onion
¼ cup low-sodium chicken broth
2 tablespoons reduced-sodium soy sauce
2 tablespoons dry white wine
1 tablespoon olive oil

1 garlic clove, minced
¼ teaspoon ground cumin
¼ teaspoon ground red pepper
3 cups assorted raw vegetables: carrot sticks, cucumber rounds, sliced yellow squash

In food processor or blender, combine all ingredients except vegetables; puree until smooth. Transfer to serving bowl and surround with assorted vegetables. (Or, add ¼ cup water and use as a salad dressing.)

MAKES 6 SERVINGS

EACH SERVING (ABOUT ⅓ CUP PLUS 2 TEA-SPOONS, AND VEGETABLES) PROVIDES: ½ Fat; 1 Vegetable; 1 Bread; 30 Optional Calories

PER SERVING: *154 Calories, 7 g Protein, 5 g Fat, 21 g Carbohydrate, 52 mg Calcium, 240 mg Sodium, 0 mg Cholesterol, 3 g Dietary Fiber*

Magical Hummus

"I call it magical because chick-peas can be counted as Breads or Proteins," writes Sarah, who enjoys her portion in a pita with lettuce, tomato, and non-fat yogurt.

SARAH COOK · AUSTIN, TEXAS

16 ounces drained cooked chick-peas
¼ cup thinly sliced scallions (green onions; use white part only)
¼ cup chopped fresh parsley
¼ cup tahini (sesame seed paste)
4 garlic cloves, minced

1 tablespoon reduced-sodium soy sauce
¼ teaspoon freshly ground black pepper
Juice of 2 lemons
Four 1-ounce pitas, cut into quarters
Chopped parsley for garnish (optional)

1. In food processor, process all ingredients except pitas and parsley until well blended. Transfer to serving dish; cover and refrigerate until ready to serve.

2. To serve, bring hummus to room temperature. Place dish on platter, surround with quartered pitas, and garnish with parsley, if desired.

MAKES 8 SERVINGS

EACH SERVING PROVIDES: *½ Fat; ½ Protein; 1½ Breads*

PER SERVING: *188 Calories, 8 g Protein, 6 g Fat, 28 g Carbohydrate, 71 mg Calcium, 180 mg Sodium, 0 mg Cholesterol, 3 g Dietary Fiber*

Party Bread Pot Fondue

Peggy created this recipe to help her resist temptation at a holiday gathering. Instead, she tempted everyone else! She offers this hint: "Be sure to get your portion measured out and set aside before it's gone!"

PEGGY BROWN · SEDALIA, MISSOURI

One 1-pound round, firm loaf of bread
1 cup reduced-calorie cream cheese, softened
1 cup nonfat sour cream (10 calories per tablespoon)
4½ ounces grated cheddar cheese
¼ cup reduced-calorie mayonnaise
½ cup drained canned chilies, chopped

2 ounces diced smoked ham
¼ cup thinly sliced scallions (green onions)
1 teaspoon Worcestershire sauce
5¼ cups assorted raw vegetables for dipping (broccoli florets, mushroom caps, bell pepper and carrot strips, etc.)

1. Preheat oven to 300°F.

2. Slice a 1-inch "lid" off top of bread; reserve. Hollow out loaf, removing 4 ounces of bread from center (reserve for other use).

3. To prepare filling, in large bowl, with electric mixer on low speed, beat cream cheese, sour cream, cheddar cheese, and mayonnaise until smooth. Stir in chilies, ham, scallions, and Worcestershire. Spoon filling into bread shell; top with lid. Wrap filled loaf tightly in foil.

4. Place wrapped loaf on baking sheet; bake 40 minutes, until filling is hot. Unwrap and place on serving platter; surround with assorted vegetables for dipping. After filling is eaten, cut loaf into 8 equal wedges; serve with any remaining vegetables.

MAKES 8 SERVINGS

EACH SERVING CONTAINS: ¾ Fat; 1 Protein; 1½ Vegetables; 1½ Breads; 80 Optional Calories

PER SERVING: 285 Calories, 14 g Protein, 12 g Fat, 31 g Carbohydrate, 226 mg Calcium, 618 mg Sodium, 32 mg Cholesterol, 2 g Dietary Fiber

Pizza Rounds

Losing may be made easier when you allow yourself snacks, says Jennifer. This special treat helped her shed 46 pounds.

JENNIFER CASE • REYNOLDSBURG, OHIO

6 ounces shredded cheddar cheese
½ cup chopped scallions (green onions)
¼ cup reduced-calorie mayonnaise
½ teaspoon curry powder

4 English muffins, split and lightly
    toasted
Dash white pepper

1.   Preheat oven to 400°F.

2.   In medium bowl, combine all ingredients except English muffins. Spread mixture evenly on each muffin half; place on nonstick baking sheet. Bake until cheese is melted, about 5 minutes. Cut into quarters; serve immediately.

MAKES 8 SERVINGS

EACH SERVING PROVIDES: ¾ Fat; 1 Protein; 1 Bread

PER SERVING: 173 Calories, 7 g Protein, 10 g Fat, 14 g Carbohydrate, 198 mg Calcium, 278 mg Sodium, 25 mg Cholesterol, 1 g Dietary Fiber

Pizza Cups

Thanks to Weight Watchers, the Walton family is eating more—yes, more—since eliminating excess snacks in favor of healthier meals. This recipe gets added zip from fennel.

CARYL WALTON · WILTON, IOWA

10 refrigerated buttermilk biscuits (1 ounce each)*
9 ounces ground turkey
½ cup tomato sauce
1 tablespoon minced onion
1 teaspoon dried basil
1 teaspoon Italian seasoning
½ teaspoon fennel seed
½ teaspoon garlic powder
¼ teaspoon freshly ground black pepper
2¼ ounces shredded part-skim mozzarella cheese

1.   Preheat oven to 400°F. Spray ten 1½- or 2-inch muffin cups with nonstick cooking spray. Using rolling pin, lightly flatten each biscuit; press onto bottom and up sides of prepared muffin cups. Set aside.

2.   In medium nonstick skillet, sauté turkey about 8 minutes, until browned, breaking up with a spoon. Drain and discard any accumulated liquid; stir in remaining ingredients except cheese.

3.   Spoon turkey mixture evenly into prepared cups; sprinkle evenly with cheese. Bake until cheese is bubbly and golden brown, about 12 to 15 minutes.

MAKES 5 SERVINGS

EACH SERVING (2 CUPS) PROVIDES: *2 Proteins; 2 Breads*

PER SERVING: *325 Calories, 17 g Protein, 16 g Fat, 28 g Carbohydrate,90 mg Calcium, 828 mg Sodium, 41 mg Cholesterol, 0 g Dietary Fiber*

*   *Keep biscuits refrigerated until ready to use. Separate dough into layers as soon as biscuits are removed from refrigerator; they will be difficult to work with if allowed to come to room temperature.*

Brilliant Beet Dip

The vibrant color of beets gives this dip a stunning look. Serve it in the center of steamed vegetables—like broccoli, mushrooms, and green and yellow squash. This dip also makes a great sauce for pasta or grains. Just add a bit of broth to bring it to a thinner consistency.

2 cups cooked or drained canned whole
    beets, cut into quarters
⅔ cup low-fat (1%) cottage cheese
2 tablespoons apple cider vinegar
2 tablespoons minced shallots

½ teaspoon dry mustard
½ teaspoon dried thyme, crumbled
½ teaspoon dried tarragon, crumbled
Dash salt

In food processor, puree all ingredients until smooth, stopping occasionally to scrape down sides of workbowl.

MAKES 4 SERVINGS

EACH SERVING (½ CUP) PROVIDES: *½ Protein;
1 Vegetable*

PER SERVING: *60 Calories, 6 g Protein, 1 g Fat, 8 g
Carbohydrate, 41 mg Calcium, 229 mg Sodium,
2 mg Cholesterol, 2 g Dietary Fiber*

Chinese Chicken Wings

Karen is an avid craftswoman, an accordion player, and a retired beautician. Since she's a diabetic, she adapted this sweet-and-sour recipe to minimize the sugar.

KAREN LOUISE WIETMAN • WRENSHALL, MINNESOTA

1½ pounds chicken wings, skinned
¼ cup reduced-sodium soy sauce
⅓ cup pineapple juice
1 tablespoon vegetable oil

1 tablespoon honey
1 teaspoon minced garlic
1 teaspoon minced pared ginger root

1. Cut chicken wings at joints and discard tips. Place wings in one layer in 13-by-9-inch baking pan.

2. In small bowl, combine remaining ingredients and 2 tablespoons water. Pour over chicken wings and toss to combine. Cover and refrigerate at least 3 hours, or overnight.

3. Preheat oven to 350°F. Drain off any marinade that chicken wings have not absorbed. Bake chicken until browned, about 30 to 40 minutes.

MAKES 8 SERVINGS

PER SERVING: *69 Calories, 9 g Protein, 3 g Fat, 1 g Carbohydrate, 6 mg Calcium, 122 mg Sodium, 24 mg Cholesterol, 0 g Dietary Fiber*

EACH SERVING PROVIDES: *¼ Fat; 1 Protein; 20 Optional Calories*

Spinach-Cheese "Croissants"

Celeste and her buddies meet for special Weight Watchers luncheons, where her mock croissants are a perennial hit. Thanks to recipes like this one, Celeste's "judgment jeans" zip without a hitch.

CELESTE ETZKORN · HURRICANE, WEST VIRGINIA

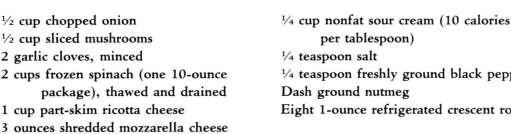

½ cup chopped onion
½ cup sliced mushrooms
2 garlic cloves, minced
2 cups frozen spinach (one 10-ounce package), thawed and drained
1 cup part-skim ricotta cheese
3 ounces shredded mozzarella cheese

¼ cup nonfat sour cream (10 calories per tablespoon)
¼ teaspoon salt
¼ teaspoon freshly ground black pepper
Dash ground nutmeg
Eight 1-ounce refrigerated crescent rolls

1. Spray medium nonstick skillet with nonstick cooking spray. Sauté onion, mushrooms, and garlic over medium-high heat, stirring frequently, until onion is translucent, about 2 minutes.

2. Remove from heat; stir in spinach, ricotta, mozzarella, sour cream, salt, pepper, and nutmeg until thoroughly combined.

3. Preheat oven to 350°F.

4. Separate dough; place 3 tablespoons spinach mixture on wide end of each roll.

Roll up to form croissant; place on nonstick baking sheet. Repeat with remaining rolls. Bake until golden, about 20 minutes.

MAKES 8 SERVINGS

EACH SERVING (1 CROISSANT) PROVIDES: *1 Protein; ¾ Vegetable; 1 Bread; 5 Optional Calories*

PER SERVING: *193 Calories, 9 g Protein, 10 g Fat, 16 g Carbohydrate, 192 mg Calcium, 408 mg Sodium, 18 mg Cholesterol, 1 g Dietary Fiber*

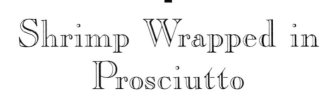

Shrimp Wrapped in Prosciutto

This makes a dazzling appetizer for a dinner party or centerpiece for a light lunch. The slightly salty ham is a perfect foil for the sweet shrimp, with the anise undernote of fennel throughout.

1 teaspoon fennel seeds
¼ cup dry white wine
3¾ cups diced fennel
¼ cup thinly sliced shallots
2 teaspoons olive oil
1 bay leaf

Salt and freshly ground black pepper to
   taste
6 shelled and deveined medium shrimp
1 ounce thinly sliced prosciutto
1 tablespoon Pernod

1. In small bowl, combine fennel seeds with 1 tablespoon of the white wine; set aside.

2. Preheat oven to 350°F. In medium saucepan with heatproof handle, combine fennel, shallots, olive oil, and bay leaf; place over medium heat. Add 2 cups water, remaining wine, salt, and pepper. Bring mixture to a boil; remove from heat. Cover and bake 35 minutes.

3. While fennel mixture is baking, prepare shrimp: Wrap each shrimp in one-sixth of the prosciutto and thread 3 pieces to a skewer. Arrange skewers on a platter; sprinkle evenly with Pernod and soaked fennel seeds. Grind fresh pepper over skewers and set aside 10 minutes.

4. Remove fennel mixture from oven; place saucepan over medium heat. Cook, uncovered, until liquid evaporates.

5. Grill or broil shrimp skewers 3 to 4 minutes, or until shrimp are opaque and prosciutto is crisp. Arrange fennel mixture evenly on each of 2 plates; top each with a shrimp skewer.

MAKES 2 SERVINGS

———

EACH SERVING PROVIDES: *1 Fat; 1 Protein; 4 Vegetables; 40 Optional Calories*

———

PER SERVING: *184 Calories, 12 g Protein, 6 g Fat, 13 g Carbohydrate, 141 mg Calcium, 420 mg Sodium, 51 mg Cholesterol, 2 g Dietary Fiber*

Calamari Cocktail

A bookkeeper who collects miniatures, Cindy also loves entertaining. Here's a light appetizer that's perfect with multicourse meals.

CINDY LEVERONE · MODESTO, CALIFORNIA

4 ounces cleaned cooked squid, sliced
    into rounds
¼ cup chopped celery
1 tablespoon chopped fresh flat-leaf
    parsley
1 teaspoon chopped fresh basil
2 teaspoons extra-virgin olive oil

2 teaspoons balsamic vinegar
1½ teaspoons fresh lemon juice
1 garlic clove, minced
⅛ teaspoon salt
⅛ teaspoon freshly ground black pepper
Parsley sprigs and lemon slices for
    garnish

1. In medium bowl, combine all ingredients except parsley sprigs and lemon slices. Cover and refrigerate at least 4 hours.

2. To serve, divide squid mixture between 2 seafood cocktail cups. Garnish with parsley and lemon slices.

MAKES 2 SERVINGS

EACH SERVING PROVIDES: *1 Fat; 1 Protein; ¼ Vegetable*

PER SERVING: *113 Calories, 11 g Protein, 6 g Fat, 4 g Carbohydrate, 39 mg Calcium, 184 mg Sodium, 165 mg Cholesterol, 0 g Dietary Fiber*

Soups

An incredible variety of vegetables, grains, cheese, and seafood become fair game for the stockpot. Fragrant with herbs, redolent with spices, robust with garlic, tangy with buttermilk, soups appear here for every occasion, heralding the start of a gracious meal or, with simple additions, becoming meals in themselves.

From elegant Sherried Tomato-Shrimp Bisque to intriguing Shrimply Delicious Buttermilk Soup to homey Cabbage Soup, you'll find a recipe to fit your mood and style.

Consider making Pumpkin Soup the opener for a fall harvest meal or even Thanksgiving dinner; pair Zucchini Egg Drop Soup with Chinese Chicken Wings and Zesty Oriental Cucumber Salad for an interesting Eastern flavor; serve Mary's French Onion Soup followed by Gruyère cheese, crisp apples, and French roast coffee; gather the family around a tureen of Vegetable Barley Soup with hunks of pumpernickel bread and a down-home Southern Banana Pudding. You'll want to keep your soup kettle handy.

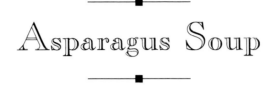

Asparagus Soup

The mother of four grown children, Sharon works as a bookkeeper for several churches, experiments with low-calorie recipes, and loves crafts, including tole painting. When summer comes, Sharon likes to putter in her flower garden.

SHARON CAMERON · ELYRIA, OHIO

2 cups low-sodium chicken broth
18 asparagus spears, cut into 1-inch
        pieces
½ cup frozen peas

¾ teaspoon dried tarragon
Dash salt
Dash freshly ground black pepper
2 carrot curls for garnish

1. In large saucepan, combine all ingredients except carrot curls. Bring to a boil; reduce heat to low and simmer 10 minutes. Cool slightly.

2. In food processor or blender, in 2 batches, puree soup until smooth. Return soup to saucepan and cook until just heated through, about 3 minutes.

3. To serve, ladle soup evenly into 2 soup bowls; garnish with carrot curls.

MAKES 2 SERVINGS

EACH SERVING (2 CUPS) PROVIDES: 1½ Vegetables; ½ Bread; 40 Optional Calories

PER SERVING: 82 Calories, 7 g Protein, 2 g Fat, 10 g Carbohydrate, 38 mg Calcium, 162 mg Sodium, 0 mg Cholesterol, 2 g Dietary Fiber

Creamy Celery and Garlic Soup

Robert is a lifetime member who works for a major airline at its hub. His hearty soup warms the coldest Michigan winter and dishes up a dose of nature's own medicine, garlic.

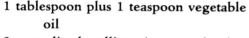

ROBERT SWEK · DETROIT, MICHIGAN

1 tablespoon plus 1 teaspoon vegetable
   oil
2 cups sliced scallions (green onions)
4 cups sliced celery
2 cups peeled garlic cloves
20 ounces pared all-purpose potatoes,
   cut into ½-inch cubes

3 packets low-sodium instant chicken
   broth mix
2 tablespoons chopped fresh parsley
¼ teaspoon salt
⅛ teaspoon fresh ground black pepper

1. In large saucepan, heat oil; add scallions. Cook over medium-high heat, stirring occasionally, until scallions are translucent, about 3 minutes. Add celery and garlic; cook, stirring occasionally, 3 minutes longer. Add remaining ingredients and 7 cups water; bring to a boil. Reduce heat to low; cover and simmer until potatoes are tender, about 30 minutes. Cool slightly.

2. In food processor, in batches, puree soup until smooth. Return mixture to saucepan; cook over high heat until heated through, about 5 minutes. Ladle evenly into 8 soup bowls.

MAKES 8 SERVINGS

EACH SERVING PROVIDES: *½ Fat; 1½ Vegetables; ½ Bread; 5 Optional Calories*

PER SERVING: *158 Calories, 5 g Protein, 3 g Fat, 31 g Carbohydrate, 121 mg Calcium, 137 mg Sodium, 0 mg Cholesterol, 3 g Dietary Fiber*

Curried Carrot Soup

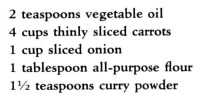 housewife, mother, and lawyer, Ellen lost 15 pounds on The At Work Program from Weight Watchers. She describes herself as "an excellent cook"—and you're sure to agree when you sample her zesty soup. Made with ham, it becomes a wonderful main meal.

ELLEN BIRNBAUM KEHR · LOS ANGELES, CALIFORNIA

2 teaspoons vegetable oil
4 cups thinly sliced carrots
1 cup sliced onion
1 tablespoon all-purpose flour
1½ teaspoons curry powder

4 cups low-sodium beef broth
1 cup low-fat (1%) milk
6 ounces diced lean cooked ham
   (optional)

1.   In large saucepan, heat oil; add carrots and onion. Cook over high heat, stirring occasionally, 5 minutes. Stir in flour and curry powder; cook 1 minute longer.

2.   Pour in broth; bring to a boil. Reduce heat to low; simmer, covered, until carrots are tender, 8 to 10 minutes. Remove from heat; cool slightly.

3.   In food processor, in 2 batches, puree carrot mixture until smooth. Return soup to saucepan; stir in milk and ham, if using. Cook over medium-high heat until heated through, about 5 minutes. Ladle evenly into 4 soup bowls.

MAKES 4 SERVINGS

EACH SERVING (1½ CUPS) PROVIDES: ¼ *Milk; ½ Fat; 2½ Vegetables; 50 Optional Calories (Add 1½ Proteins if ham is used.)*

PER SERVING: *130 Calories, 5 g Protein, 3 g Fat, 21 g Carbohydrate, 117 mg Calcium, 76 mg Sodium, 2 mg Cholesterol, 4 g Dietary Fiber*

Curried Squash Soup

Since joining Weight Watchers, Jeannine enjoys the experience of reducing calories and fats in her cooking. Her thick and creamy soup is rich in flavor but low in calories—great as a starter or satisfying snack.

JEANNINE LAHR · SANTA ROSA, CALIFORNIA

1 tablespoon vegetable oil
1 cup chopped carrot
1 cup chopped onion
2 teaspoons curry powder
6 cups mashed cooked acorn squash

2 cups low-sodium chicken broth
6 tablespoons plain low-fat yogurt
1 tablespoon pumpkin seeds for garnish (optional)

1. In medium saucepan, heat oil. Add carrot and onion; cook until tender, about 3 minutes; stir in curry powder and cook 1 minute.

2. In food processor, puree squash with chicken broth and carrot mixture in 2 batches until smooth; transfer to same saucepan.

3. Cook over medium heat until soup is heated through, 3 to 5 minutes. To serve, ladle evenly into 6 soup bowls; swirl 1 tablespoon yogurt into each. Garnish each with ½ teaspoon pumpkin seeds, if desired.

MAKES 6 SERVINGS

EACH SERVING (ABOUT 1¼ CUPS) PROVIDES: ½ Fat; ¼ Vegetable; 1 Bread; 30 Optional Calories (Add 10 calories per ½ teaspoon pumpkin seeds, if used.)

PER SERVING: 142 Calories, 4 g Protein, 3 g Fat, 27 g Carbohydrate, 103 mg Calcium, 43 mg Sodium, 1 mg Cholesterol, 1 g Dietary Fiber

Cheesy Vegetable Soup

A rib-sticking soup that's versatile enough to adapt to any vegetables you have on hand. It comes from a Colorado mother and part-time public relations coordinator.

WILMA WIERSMA · DENVER, COLORADO

4 ounces wild rice
4 cups sliced fresh mixed vegetables
    (mushrooms, carrots, celery, etc.)
2 cups frozen chopped broccoli (one 10-
    ounce package), thawed and
    drained
2 cups frozen cauliflower florets (one 10-
    ounce package), thawed and
    drained

4 packets low-sodium instant chicken
    broth mix
4 cups skim milk
1½ ounces potato flakes
5½ ounces reduced-calorie American
    cheese, cut into strips
½ teaspoon salt
½ teaspoon white pepper
Imitation bacon bits (optional)

1.   In medium saucepan, combine rice with 2 cups water; bring to a boil. Reduce heat, cover tightly, and cook until tender and water is absorbed, about 45 minutes.

2.   Meanwhile, in large saucepan, bring 2 cups water to a boil. Add vegetables; cover and cook over medium-high heat, stirring occasionally, until just tender, about 5 minutes.

3.   Add cooked rice, broth mix, and milk; cook until heated through but not boiling. Stir in potato flakes, cheese, salt, and pepper.

4.   To serve, ladle evenly into 8 soup bowls; sprinkle with bacon bits, if desired.

MAKES 8 SERVINGS

EACH SERVING PROVIDES: ½ Milk; 1 Protein; 2 Vegetables; ¾ Bread; 5 Optional Calories (Add 10 calories per 1 teaspoon bacon bits, if used.)

PER SERVING: 199 Calories, 14 g protein, 3 g Fat, 30 g Carbohydrate, 335 mg Calcium, 533 mg Sodium, 13 mg Cholesterol, 3 g Dietary Fiber

Italian Egg Drop Soup

Living on a farm keeps Virginia busy tending a bevy of dogs, cats, goats, and ducks. This active Weight Watchers member also loves running, biking, swimming, riding, and cooking.

VIRGINIA MOON · HARVEST, ALABAMA

2 teaspoons olive oil
1 large garlic clove, minced
4 packets low-sodium instant chicken broth mix
2 cups frozen chopped spinach (one 10-ounce package), thawed and drained

1 large egg, lightly beaten
1 teaspoon fresh lemon juice
¼ teaspoon freshly ground black pepper
1 tablespoon plus 1 teaspoon grated Parmesan cheese

1. In medium saucepan, heat oil; add garlic and cook over medium-high heat 30 seconds.

2. Pour in 4 cups water and chicken broth mix; stir in spinach. Bring to a boil, stirring occasionally.

3. Remove from heat; stir in beaten egg, lemon juice, and pepper. To serve, ladle evenly into 4 soup bowls; sprinkle each with 1 teaspoon Parmesan cheese.

MAKES 4 SERVINGS

PER SERVING: *77 Calories, 5 g Protein, 4 g Fat, 6 g Carbohydrate, 110 mg Calcium, 104 mg Sodium, 54 mg Cholesterol, 2 g Dietary Fiber*

EACH SERVING (1 CUP) PROVIDES: *½ Fat; ¼ Protein; 1 Vegetable; 20 Optional Calories*

Zucchini Egg Drop Soup

Every summer, squash sprouts by the bushel in Vivian's garden. Luckily, her family loves this nourishing soup, which is also delicious with egg noodles instead of rice.

VIVIAN ROBINSON · COPLEY, OHIO

½ cup chopped onion
½ cup chopped celery
1 garlic clove, minced
5 packets low-sodium instant chicken
    broth mix

4 cups shredded zucchini
2 ounces long-grain white rice
1 large egg, lightly beaten
¾ ounce grated Parmesan cheese
1 tablespoon chopped fresh parsley

1. Spray large saucepan with nonstick cooking spray; over medium-high heat, cook onion, celery, and garlic until onion is translucent, about 2 minutes.

2. Stir in chicken broth mix, zucchini, rice, and 5 cups water; bring to a boil. Reduce heat to medium; cover partially and cook until rice is tender, 15 to 20 minutes.

3. Remove from heat and whisk in remaining ingredients. Ladle evenly into 4 soup bowls.

MAKES 4 SERVINGS

EACH SERVING (ABOUT 1⅔ CUPS) PROVIDES: ½ Protein; 2½ Vegetables; ½ Bread; 15 Optional Calories

PER SERVING: *141 Calories, 8 g Protein, 4 g Fat, 21 g Carbohydrate, 115 mg Calcium, 140 mg Sodium, 57 mg Cholesterol, 1 g Dietary Fiber*

Mary's French Onion Soup

Jim and Mary Woodruff are losing weight together and find that the hardest part of dieting is accepting that "we can eat so much food that tastes so good while still following the Program."

MARY WOODRUFF · EVERGREEN, COLORADO

6 cups thinly sliced onions
2 tablespoons reduced-calorie tub
    margarine
4 packets low-sodium instant beef broth
    mix

1 tablespoon Worcestershire sauce
¼ teaspoon freshly ground black pepper
4½ ounces shredded Swiss cheese

1. In large saucepan, combine onions and margarine; cover and cook over medium-low heat, stirring occasionally, 20 minutes. Add remaining ingredients, except cheese, and 5 cups water; bring to a boil. Reduce heat; cover and simmer 15 minutes.

2. Preheat broiler.

3. To serve, ladle evenly into 6 ovenproof bowls; sprinkle ¾ ounce cheese over each. Place under broiler until cheese is melted, 2 to 3 minutes.

MAKES 6 SERVINGS

PER SERVING: *167 Calories, 9 g Protein, 8 g Fat, 16 g Carbohydrate, 237 mg Calcium, 131 mg Sodium, 20 mg Cholesterol, 3 g Dietary Fiber*

EACH SERVING PROVIDES: *½ Fat; 1 Protein; 2 Vegetables; 10 Optional Calories*

Italian Onion Soup with Prosciutto "Croutons"

A creamy version of onion soup, quite different from the French variety, topped with the tangy surprise of toasted "croutons" made of cheese-sprinkled prosciutto.

2 tablespoons plus 2 teaspoons reduced-calorie tub margarine
6 medium onions, sliced
¼ cup dry white wine
1 medium tomato, peeled, seeded, and diced
1 cup chicken broth
4 packets low-sodium instant chicken broth mix

1 tablespoon chopped fresh thyme, or 1 teaspoon dried
½ teaspoon salt
Pinch white pepper
1 ounce thinly sliced prosciutto
1 tablespoon grated Parmesan cheese

1. In heavy medium saucepan, melt margarine; add onions and cook over medium heat 20 minutes, until onions are golden brown. Add wine; cook until liquid has evaporated. Add tomato; cook 2 to 3 minutes, until soft.

2. In blender or food processor, puree 1 cup of the onion mixture with the 1 cup chicken broth. Pour back into saucepan; add 3 cups water, chicken broth mix, thyme, salt, and pepper. Simmer 1 hour.

3. To prepare "croutons," just before soup is cooked, sprinkle prosciutto slices with Parmesan cheese; arrange on foil-lined broiler pan. Broil 4 inches from heat 2 to 3 minutes, or until lightly browned. Cool slightly; cut into small squares. To serve, ladle soup evenly into 4 soup bowls; float equal amounts of "croutons" in each bowl.

MAKES 4 SERVINGS

EACH SERVING (ABOUT 1 CUP) PROVIDES: *1 Fat; ¼ Protein; ½ Vegetable; 40 Optional Calories*

PER SERVING: *134 Calories, 5 g Protein, 6 g Fat, 15 g Carbohydrate, 57 mg Calcium, 715 mg Sodium, 5 mg Cholesterol, 2 g Dietary Fiber*

Pumpkin Soup

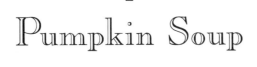

Mary writes: "My sister, who's dieting by counting calories, gave me this recipe, and I made minor changes. She can only eat half of it on her diet—I get to eat it *all* on the Weight Watchers Food Plan!"

MARY FARMER · FORT COLLINS, COLORADO

2 teaspoons reduced-calorie tub
    margarine
¼ cup chopped onion
2 tablespoons chopped green bell pepper
1 tablespoon all-purpose flour
1 cup skim milk

1 cup canned pumpkin puree
1 teaspoon low-sodium instant chicken
    broth mix
⅛ teaspoon dried thyme
Chopped parsley for garnish (optional)

1. In small saucepan, melt margarine. Add onion and pepper; cook until soft but not brown, 4 to 5 minutes.

2. Whisk in flour; stir in milk, pumpkin, 1 cup water, broth mix, and thyme. Cook over medium-high heat, stirring occasionally, until slightly thickened and just boiling. Garnish with parsley, if desired.

MAKES 1 SERVING

THIS SERVING (2 CUPS) PROVIDES: *1 Milk; 1 Fat; 2¾ Vegetables; 40 Optional Calories*

PER SERVING: *262 Calories, 13 g Protein, 5 g Fat, 44 g Carbohydrate, 379 mg Calcium, 220 mg Sodium, 5 mg Cholesterol, 5 g Dietary Fiber*

Potato-Cheese Soup

Tami feels like the hostess with the mostest when she serves this thick, cheesy soup, since guests always beg for the recipe!

TAMI KRAMER · ROSEVILLE, CALIFORNIA

10 ounces pared all-purpose potatoes,
    cut into 1-inch cubes
1 cup chopped broccoli
¾ cup chopped celery
½ cup chopped carrot
¼ cup chopped onion
1 tablespoon chopped fresh flat-leaf
    parsley

1 packet low-sodium instant chicken
    broth mix
Dash freshly ground black pepper
1½ cups low-fat (1%) milk
2 tablespoons all-purpose flour
4½ ounces pasteurized process cheese
    spread
1 ounce diced cooked ham

1. In large saucepan, combine potatoes, broccoli, celery, carrot, onion, parsley, broth mix, pepper, and 1 cup water. Bring to a boil; reduce heat to low; cover and simmer until potatoes are tender, about 20 minutes.

2. In small bowl, whisk milk and flour together; slowly pour into vegetable mixture, stirring constantly. Cook over medium-high heat, stirring occasionally, until slightly thickened, about 5 minutes. Add cheese spread and ham; cook, stirring occasionally, until cheese is melted, about 3 minutes longer. Ladle evenly into 4 soup bowls.

MAKES 4 SERVINGS

EACH SERVING (1¼ CUPS) PROVIDES: ¼ Milk; 1¾ Proteins; 1¼ Vegetables; ½ Bread; 30 Optional Calories

PER SERVING: 232 Calories, 13 g Protein, 8 g Fat, 28 g Carbohydrate, 314 mg Calcium, 651 mg Sodium, 30 mg Cholesterol, 3 g Dietary Fiber

Sherried Tomato-Shrimp Bisque

It may look and taste sinfully good, but you won't need to repent after a meal of this hearty soup.

KRISTEN HASKELL · CHARDON, OHIO

2 cups canned Italian plum tomatoes
    with juice
½ cup chopped celery
¼ cup chopped onion
¼ cup chopped carrot
1 ounce long-grain white rice
3 whole black peppercorns
2 whole cloves
1 bay leaf

1 packet low-sodium instant beef broth
    mix
1 tablespoon chopped fresh flat-leaf
    parsley
¼ teaspoon dried thyme
1 cup evaporated skimmed milk
¼ cup dry sherry
8 ounces shelled cooked shrimp (reserve
    4 shrimp with tails left on for
    garnish)

1. In large saucepan, combine all ingredients, except shrimp, with 1 cup water. Bring just to a boil; reduce heat to low and cook, stirring occasionally, 30 minutes. Cool slightly. Remove peppercorns, cloves, and bay leaf.

2. In food processor or blender, in batches, puree soup and shrimp until smooth. Return soup to pan; cook over medium-high heat, stirring occasionally, until heated through, about 5 minutes.

3. To serve, ladle evenly into 4 soup bowls; garnish each with a reserved shrimp.

MAKES 4 SERVINGS

EACH SERVING (1 CUP) PROVIDES: *½ Milk; 1 Protein; 1½ Vegetables; ¼ Bread; 15 Optional Calories*

PER SERVING: *192 Calories, 19 g Protein, 1 g Fat, 23 g Carbohydrate, 256 mg Calcium, 416 mg Sodium, 113 mg Cholesterol, 2 g Dietary Fiber*

Shrimply Delicious Buttermilk Soup

*E*asy, flavorful, elegant—this terrific soup is a winner on all counts.

DEBBIE RUSSELL · COLORADO SPRINGS, COLORADO

½ cup chopped onion
3 cups low-fat (1.5%) buttermilk
2 cups frozen chopped broccoli (one 10-
    ounce package), thawed and
    drained
4 ounces shelled cooked shrimp (reserve
    4 shrimp with tails left on
    for garnish)

1 tablespoon chopped fresh dill
Dash ground nutmeg
Dash white pepper
Dill sprigs for garnish

1. In small saucepan, combine onion and ¼ cup water. Cook over medium heat until onion is soft, about 5 minutes. Transfer to food processor.

2. Add remaining ingredients, except reserved shrimp and dill sprigs; process until pureed, about 2 minutes.

3. Pour soup into medium saucepan; cook over medium heat until just boiling. Serve hot, or refrigerate to serve chilled. To serve, ladle evenly into 4 soup bowls; garnish each with a reserved shrimp and a dill sprig.

MAKES 4 SERVINGS

EACH SERVING (1¼ CUPS) PROVIDES: *¾ Milk; ½ Protein; 1¼ Vegetables*

PER SERVING: *128 Calories, 14 g Protein, 2 g Fat, 14 g Carbohydrate, 272 mg Calcium, 274 mg Sodium, 63 mg Cholesterol, 2 g Dietary Fiber*

Corn and Crabmeat Soup

Velvety and rich, this exquisite soup is considered nursery food in China, thanks to its sweet, soothing taste and easy digestibility.

2½ cups low-sodium chicken broth
3 ounces skinless boneless chicken
    breast, cubed
1½ cups cream-style corn
1 tablespoon cornstarch

10 ounces fresh or imitation crabmeat,
    picked over and broken into
    chunks
⅛ teaspoon salt

1. In blender or food processor, combine 1 cup of the chicken broth with the chicken; process until pureed.

2. In large saucepan, bring remaining chicken broth to a boil; stir in corn. Gradually whisk in pureed chicken mixture.

3. In small cup, combine cornstarch with 2 tablespoons cold water. Slowly pour into soup, stirring constantly; cook until soup is thickened. Stir in crabmeat; season with salt. Ladle evenly into 6 soup bowls.

MAKES 6 SERVINGS

EACH SERVING (1 CUP) PROVIDES: *1 Protein; ½ Bread; 30 Optional Calories*

PER SERVING: *126 Calories, 15 g Protein, 2 g Fat, 13 g Carbohydrate, 57 mg Calcium, 781 mg Sodium, 55 mg Cholesterol, 1 g Dietary Fiber*

Cream of Broccoli-Chicken Soup

Though she originally developed this soup for turkey leftovers, Cinamon prefers it with chicken. She's the mother of a toddler and loves gardening, low-to moderate-impact aerobics, and spending time with her family.

CINAMON REED STREVA · NEW IBERIA, LOUISIANA

1 tablespoon plus 1 teaspoon reduced-calorie tub margarine
½ cup chopped onion
½ cup chopped celery
¼ cup chopped scallions (green onions)
1¾ cups sliced mushrooms
2 cups low-sodium chicken broth
2 cups skim milk
12 ounces cubed cooked chicken

4 cups frozen chopped broccoli (two 10-ounce packages), thawed and drained
4 cups cooked pasta or rice
1 tablespoon Worcestershire sauce
1 teaspoon dried basil
½ teaspoon salt
¼ teaspoon white pepper

1. In large saucepan or Dutch oven, melt margarine and add onion, celery, and scallions. Cook over medium-high heat, stirring occasionally, 3 minutes. Stir in mushrooms; cook 1 minute longer.

2. Add remaining ingredients and 2 cups water. Bring to a boil; reduce heat; cover partially and simmer 20 minutes. Ladle evenly into 8 soup bowls.

MAKES 8 SERVINGS

EACH SERVING (1½ CUPS) PROVIDES: ¼ *Milk; ¼ Fat; 1½ Proteins; 1¾ Vegetables; 1 Bread; 10 Optional Calories*

PER SERVING: *248 Calories, 21 g Protein, 5 g Fat, 29 g Carbohydrate, 139 mg Calcium, 283 mg Sodium, 39 mg Cholesterol, 3 g Dietary Fiber*

Vegetable Beef Barley Soup

Marge is a lifetime member who works with two Weight Watchers groups in her hometown. With her husband, Richard, she delights in trying flavorful, low-calorie dishes with interesting variations, like cutting carrots two ways. This satisfying soup is one of their staples during cold winter months.

MARGE AMOROSA-CONTI · KENILWORTH, NEW JERSEY

15 ounces lean beef round, cut into 1-inch cubes
½ cup chopped onion
1 cup tomato sauce
1½ cups thinly sliced carrots
1½ cups cubed carrots, cut into ½-inch pieces
2 cups chopped celery

1 cup chopped mushrooms
1 cup drained canned French-style green beans
4½ ounces pearl barley
1 tablespoon dried parsley
1 teaspoon salt
½ teaspoon freshly ground black pepper

1. Spray 5-quart saucepan with nonstick cooking spray; add beef and onion. Sauté 5 to 7 minutes, until lightly browned.

2. Add 3 quarts water and tomato sauce; cover and bring to a boil. Stir in carrots, celery, and mushrooms. Reduce heat to medium-low; cover partially and simmer 1 hour.

3. Add remaining ingredients. Cover and simmer 1 hour longer, stirring occasionally. Ladle evenly into 6 soup bowls.

Variation: For an Italian touch, sprinkle each serving with 1 to 2 teaspoons grated Parmesan cheese; add 10 Optional Calories per teaspoon.

MAKES 6 SERVINGS

———

EACH SERVING (2½ CUPS) PROVIDES: *2 Proteins; 3 Vegetables; 1 Bread*

———

PER SERVING: *229 Calories, 20 g Protein, 4 g Fat, 29 g Carbohydrate, 58 mg Calcium, 767 mg Sodium, 41 mg Cholesterol, 7 g Dietary Fiber*

Cabbage Soup

Tina's "chock full of vegetables" soup is ready in a jiffy, but tastes like you slaved all day.

TINA MILLER • LORAIN, OHIO

1 pound, 3 ounces lean beef stew meat,
    cubed, broiled 2 minutes
1 cup chopped onion
4 cups low-sodium beef broth
4 cups canned crushed tomatoes
3 cups chopped carrots
1 cup chopped celery
1 cup tomato sauce
11 cups thinly shredded cabbage
4 cups frozen mixed vegetables
¼ cup chopped fresh flat-leaf parsley
1½ teaspoons dried basil

1. Spray large saucepan or 5-quart Dutch oven with nonstick cooking spray; heat 1 minute. Add beef and onion; cook over medium-high heat, stirring occasionally, until beef is lightly browned, about 5 minutes.

2. Add broth, tomatoes, carrots, celery, and tomato sauce; add 4 cups water. Bring to a boil; reduce heat, cover partially, and simmer 1 hour. Add remaining ingredients and cook until cabbage is tender, 20 to 30 minutes longer. Ladle evenly into 10 soup bowls.

MAKES 10 SERVINGS

PER SERVING: *226 Calories, 19 g Protein, 6 g Fat, 26 g Carbohydrate, 112 mg Calcium, 408 mg Sodium, 45 mg Cholesterol, 5 g Dietary Fiber*

EACH SERVING (2 CUPS) PROVIDES: *1½ Proteins; 5 Vegetables; 15 Optional Calories*

Salads

Formerly limited to lettuce, tomato, and a few shreds of carrot for color, today's salad merits a special course of its own.

Exotic vegetables take center stage: try Kicky Kohlrabi Salad or Fragrant Fennel Salad for a new taste sensation. Go East with Zesty Oriental Cucumber Salad or Japanese Salad; either makes a perfect foil for Spicy Ginger-Garlic Chicken.

Black-Eyed Pea Salad is just the right side dish for Cajun Pork Roast; both tastes evoke the new South. Cranberry Wild Rice Salad is a healthful indulgence that not only looks spectacular but tastes divine. Serve it with Chicken in Wine for an unforgettable supper.

If you're looking for new takes on old favorites, try Macaroni Salad and No-Guilt Potato Salad. We think you'll like them better than the deli versions.

For a Continental touch, serve your salad *after* the main course, followed by rich coffee and ripe fruit in season. *Bon appétit!*

Japanese Salad

Lucille loves bowling, bingo, and volunteering at her children's school. Uncooked cellophane noodles provide the crunch in her Oriental salad.

LUCILLE CARSTAIRS · WARBURG, ALBERTA, CANADA

1 tablespoon reduced-sodium soy sauce
1 tablespoon rice wine vinegar
2 teaspoons sesame oil
¼ teaspoon freshly ground black pepper
4½ cups shredded romaine or iceberg lettuce
2½ cups fresh or drained canned bean sprouts

1 cup sliced mushrooms
¼ cup sliced scallions (green onions)
¾ ounce uncooked cellophane noodles, crumbled
½ cup chow mein noodles
½ ounce slivered almonds, toasted

1. In small bowl, combine soy sauce, vinegar, oil, pepper, and 1 tablespoon water; set aside.

2. In large bowl, combine remaining ingredients. Add dressing and toss well.

MAKES 4 SERVINGS

EACH SERVING PROVIDES: *1 Fat; ¼ Protein; 4 Vegetables; ½ Bread; 15 Optional Calories*

PER SERVING: *128 Calories, 5 g Protein, 6 g Fat, 16 g Carbohydrate, 50 mg Calcium, 186 mg Sodium, 0 mg Cholesterol, 3 g Dietary Fiber*

Kicky Kohlrabi Salad

Kohlrabi is a little-known member of the cabbage family that deserves a higher profile. Here it appears in a crunchy, zippy salad that will keep for up to two weeks in the refrigerator.

MARY FELEGY · SOUTH NYACK, NEW YORK

6 medium kohlrabi,* pared and
    julienned
¼ cup rice wine vinegar
2 tablespoons red wine vinegar
1 tablespoon vegetable oil
1½ teaspoons minced pared ginger root

½ teaspoon dried tarragon
¼ teaspoon crushed red pepper flakes
Dash salt
1 small red onion, thinly sliced and
    separated into rings
1 tablespoon toasted sesame seeds

1.   In large saucepan, bring 2 quarts water to a boil; add kohlrabi and cook until tender-crisp, about 2 minutes. Drain; rinse under cold water. Transfer to large bowl.

2.   To prepare dressing, in small bowl, combine remaining ingredients except onion and sesame seeds. Pour over kohlrabi; toss well to coat. Cover and refrigerate at least 2 hours.

3.   To serve, place kohlrabi on serving platter; arrange onion rings on top; sprinkle with sesame seeds.

MAKES 6 SERVINGS

EACH SERVING PROVIDES: ½ Fat; 1 Vegetable; 10 Optional Calories

PER SERVING: 48 Calories, 2 g Protein, 2 g Fat, 6 g Carbohydrate, 36 mg Calcium, 39 mg Sodium, 0 mg Cholesterol, 1 g Dietary Fiber

*   Kohlrabi is a light green or purple vegetable with a bulbous root end and broad green leaves. The bulb, when pared, can be eaten raw or cooked. If kohlrabi is not available, you can substitute white turnip or jicama.

Fragrant Fennel Salad

As the mother of a toddler, Roxanne relies on make-ahead meals to streamline her hectic schedule. Homegrown fennel inspired this refreshing salad, which also makes a terrific appetizer.

ROXANNE CHAN · ALBANY, CALIFORNIA

2 teaspoons fennel seeds
¾ cup plain nonfat yogurt
¼ cup chopped fresh cilantro
¼ cup chopped fresh mint leaves
1 tablespoon fresh lemon juice
¼ teaspoon ground cumin

¼ teaspoon salt
3 cups thinly sliced fennel
2 cups pared julienned jicama
4 large cherry tomatoes, halved
Cilantro sprigs for garnish (optional)

1. To prepare dressing, in small nonstick skillet, toast fennel seeds over medium heat, shaking skillet frequently, until seeds are golden, about 3 minutes. Transfer to large bowl. Stir in yogurt, cilantro, mint, lemon juice, cumin, and salt.

2. Add fennel and jicama; toss well to coat with dressing. Cover and chill at least 2 hours.

3. To serve, spoon salad evenly onto 4 plates; garnish with cherry tomatoes and cilantro sprigs, if desired.

MAKES 4 SERVINGS

EACH SERVING (1½ CUPS) PROVIDES: ¼ *Milk; 2¾ Vegetables*

PER SERVING: *72 Calories, 5 g Protein, 1 g Fat, 13 g Carbohydrate, 151 mg Calcium, 255 mg Sodium, 1 mg Cholesterol, 2 g Dietary Fiber*

Broccoli Salad

Whenever Judy is invited to a potluck supper she whips up a batch of this crunchy, nutty salad. Small wonder she gets invited to a lot of parties!

JUDY MEYERS · AURORA, COLORADO

1 cup plain nonfat yogurt
1 tablespoon plus 1 teaspoon reduced-calorie mayonnaise
1 tablespoon plus 1 teaspoon white wine vinegar
½ teaspoon celery seeds

2 cups broccoli florets, blanched
1 cup cauliflower florets, blanched
¼ cup sliced scallions (green onions)
2 tablespoons raisins
¼ ounce shelled peanuts

1.   In small bowl, combine yogurt, mayonnaise, vinegar, and celery seeds; mix well and set aside.

2.   In large bowl, combine remaining ingredients; add yogurt mixture and toss well.

MAKES 2 SERVINGS

EACH SERVING (ABOUT 1¾ CUPS) PROVIDES:
    ½ Milk; 1½ Fats; ¼ Protein; 3¼ Vegetables;
    ½ Fruit; 15 Optional Calories

PER SERVING: *197 Calories, 13 g Protein, 5 g Fat, 28 g Carbohydrate, 321 mg Calcium, 183 mg Sodium, 6 mg Cholesterol, 7 g Dietary Fiber*

Marinated Vegetable Salad

Summer means a round of family reunions and picnics, so Patricia devised this festive veggie salad to keep the clan happy and keep herself on track.

PATRICIA LASER · PLYMOUTH, OHIO

1 cup broccoli florets, blanched
1 cup cauliflower florets, blanched
1 cup sliced celery
1 cup sliced carrots
½ cup chopped green bell pepper
½ cup thinly sliced red onion
4 ounces drained cooked kidney beans

4 ounces drained cooked chick-peas
10 small green olives, pitted and sliced
10 small black olives, pitted and sliced
¾ cup reduced-calorie Italian salad
    dressing (6 calories per
    tablespoon)

In large bowl, combine all ingredients, tossing well. Refrigerate at least 3 hours or overnight to develop flavors.

MAKES 8 SERVINGS

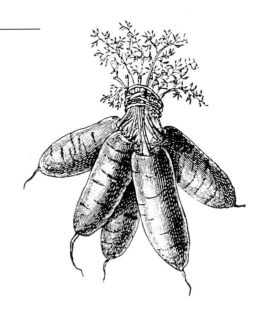

EACH SERVING (¾ CUP) PROVIDES: *¼ Fat; 1¼ Vegetables; ½ Bread; 10 Optional Calories*

PER SERVING: *65 Calories, 4 g Protein, 1 g Fat, 14 g Carbohydrate, 40 mg Calcium, 457 mg Sodium, 0 mg Cholesterol, 3 g Dietary Fiber*

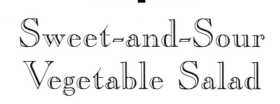

Sweet-and-Sour Vegetable Salad

Beverly, a former dean of students for a high school, lost 43 pounds. Her colorful salad dresses up any dinner. Try it with pimientos, too.

BEVERLY NICOL · MINNEAPOLIS, MINNESOTA

4½ cups broccoli florets, blanched
½ cup thinly sliced red onion
½ cup golden raisins
2 strips bacon, cooked crisp and
    crumbled

½ cup reduced-calorie mayonnaise
2 tablespoons white wine vinegar

1.   In large bowl, combine broccoli, onion, raisins, and bacon.

2.   In small bowl, combine remaining ingredients until thoroughly blended. Pour over broccoli mixture; toss well.

MAKES 8 SERVINGS

EACH SERVING (¾ CUP) PROVIDES: *1½ Fats; 1¼ Vegetables; ½ Fruit; 10 Optional Calories*

PER SERVING: *104 Calories, 4 g Protein, 5 g Fat, 13 g Carbohydrate, 39 mg Calcium, 126 mg Sodium, 6 mg Cholesterol, 3 g Dietary Fiber*

Zesty Oriental Cucumber Salad

Pamela serves this crunchy side dish with Chinese meals. It's great made with English cucumbers.

PAMELA VARGA · DENVER, COLORADO

5½ cups pared sliced cucumbers
½ teaspoon salt
½ cup grated carrot
¼ cup rice wine vinegar

2 teaspoons sesame oil
Granulated sugar substitute to equal 2 teaspoons sugar
⅛ teaspoon crushed red pepper flakes

1. In large mixing bowl, combine cucumbers and salt, tossing well to combine. Let stand at room temperature 15 minutes.

2. Rinse cucumbers with cold water and drain well. Return to mixing bowl and add carrot.

3. In small bowl, combine remaining ingredients; pour over cucumbers and carrot and toss well. Cover and refrigerate 4 hours; toss again before serving.

MAKES 4 SERVINGS

PER SERVING: *56 calories, 1 g Protein, 2 g Fat, 8 g Carbohydrate, 38 mg Calcium, 292 mg Sodium, 0 mg Cholesterol, 1 g Dietary Fiber*

EACH SERVING PROVIDES: *½ Fat; 3 Vegetables*

Cranberry Wild Rice Salad

What a showstopper! This vivid salad instantly dresses up leftover turkey or ham.

CARMELA MEELY · WALNUT CREEK, CALIFORNIA

6 ounces fresh cranberries
¼ cup low-calorie cranberry juice
    cocktail
2 tablespoons granulated sugar
6 ounces wild rice, prepared according
    to package directions

½ cup julienned carrot
¼ cup minced scallions (green onions)
1 ounce shelled walnuts, chopped
2 tablespoons apple cider vinegar
2 teaspoons peanut oil
Dash pepper

1. In medium saucepan, combine cranberries, juice, and sugar; cook over medium heat, stirring occasionally, until cranberries pop, about 5 minutes. Cool slightly.

2. Transfer cranberries and accumulated juices to large mixing bowl; add remaining ingredients and toss to combine.

3. Cover and refrigerate, or serve at room temperature.

MAKES 4 SERVINGS

PER SERVING: *274 Calories, 8 g Protein, 7 g Fat, 48 g Carbohydrate, 29 mg Calcium, 10 mg Sodium, 0 mg Cholesterol, 3 g Dietary Fiber*

EACH SERVING (ABOUT ¾ CUP) PROVIDES: *1 Fat; ¼ Protein; ¼ Vegetable; 1½ Breads; ¼ Fruit; 50 Optional Calories*

Black-Eyed Pea Salad

New Year's Day in the South is the traditional time to eat black-eyed peas for prosperity. This recipe guarantees you'll also get the year off to a healthy start.

SANDRA BRADY · ARDMORE, OKLAHOMA

6 ounces cooked black-eyed peas
1 cup grated carrots
½ cup chopped onion
½ cup chopped green bell pepper
¼ cup drained chopped pimientos

3 tablespoons white vinegar
1 tablespoon vegetable oil
Granulated sugar substitute to equal 1
    teaspoon sugar (optional)
¼ teaspoon freshly ground black pepper

In large bowl, combine all ingredients; toss well. Cover and refrigerate at least 3 hours, or overnight.

MAKES 4 SERVINGS

EACH SERVING (¾ CUP) PROVIDES: ¾ Fat; 1
    Vegetable; ¾ Bread

PER SERVING: 107 Calories, 4 g Protein, 4 g Fat, 15
    g Carbohydrate, 24 mg Calcium, 14 mg Sodium,
    0 mg Cholesterol, 6 g Dietary Fiber

Macaroni Salad

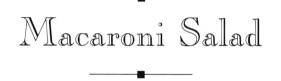

Sherry brings her salad to family gatherings but never says, "Eat this, it's good for you." She doesn't have to—it's gone in a flash!

SHERRY HUNTER · HEMINGFORD, NEBRASKA

2½ cups cooked penne or ziti
¾ cup plain nonfat yogurt
¼ cup chopped onion
¼ cup chopped celery
1 hard-cooked egg, finely chopped
1 tablespoon prepared mustard
1 tablespoon sweet pickle relish

Granulated sugar substitute to equal 2
   teaspoons sugar
½ teaspoon seasoned salt
¼ teaspoon freshly ground black pepper
Chopped freshly parsley for garnish
   (optional)

In large bowl, combine all ingredients until blended. Cover and refrigerate several hours, or overnight. Garnish with parsley, if desired.

MAKES 4 SERVINGS

EACH SERVING (1¼ CUP) PROVIDES: *¼ Milk; ¼ Protein; ¼ Vegetable; 1¼ Breads; 5 Optional Calories*

PER SERVING: *181 Calories, 9 g Protein, 2 g Fat, 31 g Carbohydrate, 107 mg Calcium, 284 mg Sodium, 54 mg Cholesterol, 2 g Dietary Fiber*

No-Guilt Potato Salad

A mother of three who enjoys needlepoint, the theater, and beach outings, Lynne has devised a party pleaser that boasts all the taste of traditional potato salad, without all the fat. Who could ask for anything more?

LYNNE SKLAR · WILMINGTON, DELAWARE

1 pound cooked unpared red potatoes,
    cubed
¼ cup chopped celery
¼ cup chopped scallions (green onions)
¼ cup reduced-calorie ranch dressing
    (25 calories per tablespoon)

3 tablespoons chopped fresh dill
Dash salt
Dash white pepper

Using rubber scraper, in medium bowl, combine all ingredients, stirring to coat vegetables with dressing.

MAKES 4 SERVINGS

EACH SERVING PROVIDES: ¼ Vegetable; 1 Bread;
    25 Optional Calories

PER SERVING: 121 Calories, 2 g Protein, 0 g Fat, 24
    g Carbohydrate, 18 mg Calcium, 190 mg So-
    dium, 0 mg Cholesterol, 2 g Dietary Fiber

Pear Salad

Oklahoma resident Shari shares her recipe for a refreshing gelatin salad.

SHARI SIRCOULOMB · OKLAHOMA CITY, OKLAHOMA

2 cups drained canned pear halves (no sugar added) plus 1 cup reserved juice
1 cup reduced-calorie cream cheese, softened
1 envelope (4 servings) sugar-free lemon-flavor gelatin mix (8 calories per serving)

1 cup reduced-calorie whipped topping (8 calories per tablespoon)
Mint sprigs for garnish (optional)

1. In medium bowl, mash pears; stir in cream cheese until blended.

2. In small saucepan, bring reserved juice to a boil; pour into separate medium bowl. Sprinkle gelatin over hot juice; pour in 1 cup cold water and stir into pear mixture. Whisk in whipped topping.

3. Spray 6-cup mold with nonstick cooking spray; pour mixture into mold. Chill until set, about 4 hours.

4. To serve, run tip of sharp knife around edge of mold; unmold onto serving plate. Garnish with mint, if desired.

MAKES 8 SERVINGS

EACH SERVING PROVIDES: *½ Fruit; 85 Optional Calories*

PER SERVING: *111 Calories, 4 g Protein, 6 g Fat, 12 g Carbohydrate, 46 mg Calcium, 192 mg Sodium, 15 mg Cholesterol, 1 g Dietary Fiber*

Island Fruit Salad

From the sunny climates of tropical islands come pineapples, bananas, and coconuts. Combined in a refreshing salad with a hint of cooling mint, this is a perfect light snack or dessert.

1 medium grapefruit, peeled and
    sectioned
¼ medium pineapple, cut into chunks
    (reserve juice)

½ medium banana, diced
¾ cup fresh or frozen blueberries
2 tablespoons chopped fresh mint leaves
2 tablespoons toasted shredded coconut

In large bowl, combine all ingredients; toss to mix well. Cover and refrigerate until well chilled.

MAKES 4 SERVINGS

EACH SERVING (ABOUT 1 CUP) PROVIDES: *1½ Fruits; 15 Optional Calories*

PER SERVING: *81 Calories, 1 g Protein, 1 g Fat, 18 g Carbohydrate, 3 mg Sodium, 0 mg Cholesterol, 1 g Dietary Fiber*

Vegetarian Entrees

Many major health organizations are joining forces with nutrition groups advocating diets richer in complex carbohydrates, grains, fruits, and vegetables that also contain less meat and dairy products. In fact, the latest USDA Food Guide Pyramid suggests that Americans should eat six to eleven servings of grains each day, three to five servings of vegetables, two to six servings of fruit and only two to three servings from both the dairy and protein groups. Fats, oils, and sweets, they tell us, should be used more sparingly.

To date, more than 10 million Americans have become vegetarians, but all of us can reap the benefits of vegetarianism—and enjoy a refreshingly new way of eating—by including a few meatless meals in our weekly meal planning.

Both Hearty Tacos and Terrific Tex-Mex Salad have a substantial, south-of-the-border appeal, while dishes like Quick Vegetarian Bean Spread and Baked Lentils with Cheese are ready and on the table in a flash. Garden Pasta Pie cleverly tops a pasta-based crust with fresh garden vegetables.

Here are forty new recipes that offer a fresh, intriguing, and, best of all, economical way of eating. Include them in your menu planning when you're looking for an interesting change of taste.

Quick Vegetarian Bean Spread

Quick, tasty nibbles are just the ticket for Tracy, a busy teacher who enjoys singing, playing guitar, walking, cooking, ballroom dancing, and gardening with her husband. She invented this sandwich filling as an alternative to meat.

TRACY DUNN · TROY, NEW YORK

4 ounces drained cooked red kidney beans

1 tablespoon plus 2 teaspoons barbecue or chili sauce

Dash hot pepper sauce

In small bowl, mash beans with fork; stir in remaining ingredients. Serve with rice cakes, crispbread, or raw vegetables.

MAKES 1 SERVING

THIS SERVING PROVIDES: *2 Proteins; 25 Optional Calories (rice cakes, crispbread, etc., not included)*

PER SERVING: *164 Calories, 10 g Protein, 1 g Fat, 29 g Carbohydrate, 37 mg Calcium, 223 mg Sodium, 0 mg Cholesterol, 4 g Dietary Fiber*

Terrific Tex-Mex Salad

Kathryn is a writer and mother. Whenever she attends church socials or potluck suppers, she brings along this colorful dish, which was adapted from her mother-in-law's recipe. It's a great make-ahead meal, but add the chips just before serving.

KATHRYN SHEEHAN · TULSA, OKLAHOMA

4 cups torn iceberg lettuce
1 pound drained cooked chick-peas
2 medium tomatoes, chopped
1 cup sliced mushrooms
20 small pitted black olives, sliced
¼ cup reduced-calorie Catalina dressing
    (18 calories per tablespoon)

1 small jalapeño pepper, diced
    (optional)
1½ ounces shredded reduced-calorie
    cheddar cheese
1 ounce corn chips

In large bowl, combine all ingredients except corn chips, tossing well to coat with dressing. Transfer to large serving tray; surround with corn chips.

MAKES 4 SERVINGS

EACH SERVING PROVIDES: *½ Fat; ½ Protein; 3½ Vegetables; 2¼ Breads; 40 Optional Calories*

PER SERVING: *315 Calories, 15 g Protein, 9 g Fat, 45 g Carbohydrate, 205 mg Calcium, 331 mg Sodium, 8 mg Cholesterol, 6 g Dietary Fiber*

Hearty Tacos

Alice loves tacos but hates the calories they carry. Fixing them one night for her family, she got jealous, then was inspired. She uses small pita breads instead of fried tortillas.

ALICE MOLTER · CLEVELAND HEIGHTS, OHIO

2 teaspoons vegetable oil
½ cup chopped onion
½ cup chopped green bell pepper
6 ounces drained cooked red kidney
    beans
1 cup tomato sauce
2 teaspoons red wine vinegar

1 teaspoon honey
¼ teaspoon Mexican seasoning
4 small (1-ounce) pita breads, cut to
    form pockets
½ cup shredded lettuce
½ cup chopped tomato
1½ ounces shredded cheddar cheese

1. In medium nonstick skillet, heat oil; stir in onion and pepper. Cook over medium heat until onion is translucent, about 2 minutes. Stir in beans, tomato sauce, vinegar, honey, and seasoning. Reduce heat; simmer, stirring occasionally, 10 minutes. Cool slightly.

2. Spoon equal amount of bean mixture into each pita; top evenly with lettuce, tomato, and cheese.

MAKES 4 SERVINGS

EACH SERVING PROVIDES: ½ Fat; 1¼ Proteins; 1½ Vegetables; 1 Bread; 5 Optional Calories

PER SERVING: 245 Calories, 10 g Protein, 7 g Fat, 38 g Carbohydrate, 113 mg Calcium, 654 mg Sodium, 11 mg Cholesterol, 4 g Dietary Fiber

Mexican Jumping Beans

Victoria, an orthodontic assistant, developed this recipe as a protein alternative to red meat. A devotee of spicy Mexican food, she heaps on the hot peppers, but you can tone it down by omitting them.

VICTORIA GRACEY · VANCOUVER, BRITISH COLUMBIA, CANADA

1 tablespoon vegetable oil
½ cup chopped onion
1 cup sliced mushrooms
½ cup chopped red bell pepper
1 small jalapeño pepper, finely chopped*

2 garlic cloves, minced
8 ounces drained cooked soybeans
½ cup tomato puree
½ teaspoon paprika
½ teaspoon freshly ground black pepper

1. In large skillet, heat oil; add onion. Cook over medium-high heat, stirring occasionally, until onion is translucent, about 2 minutes. Add mushrooms, bell pepper, jalapeño pepper, and garlic; cook, stirring occasionally, 1 minute longer.

2. Add remaining ingredients; cook, covered, over medium heat, stirring occasionally, 20 minutes.

MAKES 2 SERVINGS

* Remove seeds, wearing plastic gloves, for a milder version of this dish.

EACH SERVING PROVIDES: *1½ Fats; 2 Proteins; 3 Vegetables*

PER SERVING: *323 Calories, 22 g Protein, 17 g Fat, 26 g Carbohydrate, 147 mg Calcium, 255 mg Sodium, 0 mg Cholesterol, 3 g Dietary Fiber*

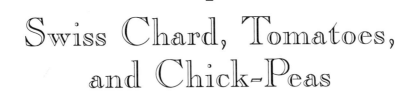

Swiss Chard, Tomatoes, and Chick-Peas

For years Martha has been reading recipes for creative inspiration. Here's one of her specialties, an unusual dish that's simple and fun to make.

MARTHA IRWIN · SOMERVILLE, MASSACHUSETTS

2 pounds Swiss chard
2 teaspoons olive oil
2 teaspoons paprika
5 whole black peppercorns, coarsely
    ground
2 teaspoons ground cumin

½ teaspoon ground turmeric
½ teaspoon garlic powder
12 ounces drained cooked chick-peas
4 medium tomatoes, quartered
3 tablespoons chopped fresh cilantro

1. Wash Swiss chard thoroughly and drain; remove and discard stems and coarsely chop leaves.

2. In 5-quart saucepan, combine Swiss chard and 2 quarts water; bring to a boil. Reduce heat to medium and cook until tender, about 5 minutes. Drain and set aside.

3. In large nonstick skillet, combine oil, paprika, pepper, cumin, turmeric, and garlic powder to make a paste. Cook over medium heat 1 minute.

4. Add Swiss chard, chick-peas, and to-matoes (with any accumulated juices), stir-ring well to combine. Bring to a boil over medium-high heat. Reduce heat and sim-mer 20 minutes, stirring occasionally, add-ing more water if necessary. Sprinkle with cilantro.

MAKES 4 SERVINGS

EACH SERVING PROVIDES: *½ Fat; 1½ Proteins; 4 Vegetables*

PER SERVING: *203 Calories, 9 g Protein, 5 g Fat, 32 g Carbohydrate, 70 mg Calcium, 50 mg Sodium, 0 mg Cholesterol, 5 g Dietary Fiber*

Baked Lentils with Cheese

Gaynel works as a coronary care nurse, so she knows it's important to set a good example by staying trim. This legume dish gives her the variety she craves while working toward her goal.

GAYNEL REYKDAL · EVERETT, WASHINGTON

12 ounces dried lentils
2 cups chopped onions
2 cups canned stewed tomatoes (no salt added)
2 cups tomato juice
1½ cups chopped carrots
1 cup chopped green bell pepper
½ cup chopped celery
2 garlic cloves, minced
1 bay leaf
1½ teaspoons salt
½ teaspoon dried thyme
½ teaspoon dried marjoram
¼ teaspoon rubbed sage
6 ounces shredded cheddar cheese
Chopped fresh parsley for garnish

1.   Preheat oven to 375°F.

2.   In 13-by-9-inch baking pan, combine all ingredients except cheese and parsley. Cover with foil; bake until carrots are tender, about 40 minutes. Sprinkle with cheese; bake until cheese is bubbly, about 5 minutes. Garnish with parsley.

MAKES 8 SERVINGS

EACH SERVING PROVIDES: *1 Protein; 2¼ Vegetables; 2 Breads*

PER SERVING: *287 Calories, 19 g Protein, 8 g Fat, 38 g Carbohydrate, 227 mg Calcium, 795 mg Sodium, 22 mg Cholesterol, 8 g Dietary Fiber*

Lentilla Salad

Shannon combined "lentil" and "tortilla" when naming her festive salad. She likes it because it brings together "a little of this and a little of that."

SHANNON CARTER · TYLER, TEXAS

1½ cups shredded lettuce
½ cup chopped tomato
2 tablespoons sliced scallions (green onions)
2 tablespoons mild salsa
2 tablespoons nonfat sour cream (10 calories per tablespoon)

2 ounces cooked lentils
¾ ounce shredded cheddar cheese
One 6-inch flour tortilla, cut into ¼-inch strips

In medium bowl, combine all ingredients, tossing well to mix.

MAKES 1 SERVING

THIS SERVING PROVIDES: *1 Protein; 4¼ Vegetables; 2 Breads; 20 Optional Calories*

PER SERVING: *287 Calories, 16 g Protein, 10 g Fat, 36 g Carbohydrate, 312 mg Calcium, 491 mg Sodium, 22 mg Cholesterol, 5 g Dietary Fiber*

Rice and Lentils Italiano

For Janet, Weight Watchers has been a "source of real understanding of healthy, nutritious eating and common sense weight management advice." Her delicious and economical creation grew out of a desire for an Italian-type legume dish.

JANET SEDGEWICK · MARTENSVILLE, SASKATCHEWAN, CANADA

1 tablespoon plus 1 teaspoon vegetable oil
8 ounces long-grain white rice
6 ounces dried lentils
4 cups low-sodium vegetable broth
1 cup chopped green bell pepper
½ cup chopped celery with leaves
½ cup chopped onion

½ cup chopped carrot
4 garlic cloves, minced
3 cups canned crushed tomatoes
1 teaspoon dried basil
½ teaspoon dried oregano
¼ teaspoon ground red pepper
½ cup thinly sliced red onion

1. In large saucepan, heat oil; add rice and lentils, stirring to coat; cook over medium heat, 3 minutes. Stir in broth; bring to a boil. Reduce heat; cover and simmer until most of liquid is absorbed, 25 to 30 minutes. Remove from heat; let stand 5 minutes.

2. Meanwhile, to prepare sauce, spray medium saucepan with nonstick cooking spray; add bell pepper, celery, onion, carrot, and garlic. Cook over medium heat, stirring occasionally, until onion is translucent, about 5 minutes. Add remaining ingredients except red onion; cook over medium-low heat, stirring occasionally, 20 minutes.

3. To serve, place rice mixture in serving bowl; top with sauce and red onion.

MAKES 4 SERVINGS

EACH SERVING PROVIDES: *1 Fat; 2 Proteins; 3 Vegetables; 2 Breads; 40 Optional Calories*

PER SERVING: *497 Calories, 20 g Protein, 6 g Fat, 93 g Carbohydrate, 123 mg Calcium, 394 mg Sodium, 0 mg Cholesterol, 8 g Dietary Fiber*

Fettuccine Alfredo

Working with cardiac care patients keeps Mary Lou vigilant about good nutrition. This adaptation of the popular classic relies on nonfat yogurt instead of heavy cream.

MARY LOU JOHNSON · DUVALL, WASHINGTON

¾ cup plain nonfat yogurt
½ cup chopped onion
2 garlic cloves, minced
½ cup evaporated skimmed milk
1 large egg, lightly beaten

2¼ ounces grated Parmesan cheese
2 cups hot cooked fettuccine
1 tablespoon chopped fresh flat-leaf
    parsley
1 tablespoon chopped fresh chives

1. To prepare yogurt cheese, set medium strainer lined with coffee filter over medium bowl. Place yogurt in lined strainer; cover and refrigerate until ½ cup yogurt cheese remains, about 5 hours. Discard drained liquid.

2. Spray medium nonstick skillet with nonstick cooking spray; add onion and garlic; cook over medium heat until softened, about 2 minutes.

3. Reduce heat to low; gradually (to keep mixture from curdling) whisk in milk, yogurt cheese, and egg. Add 2 ounces of the Parmesan cheese and the fettuccine; toss to combine. Cook over low heat until cheese is melted, about 1 minute. Transfer to serving dish; sprinkle with the remaining cheese, the parsley, and chives.

MAKES 2 SERVINGS

EACH SERVING (1 CUP) PROVIDES: *1 Milk; 2 Proteins; ½ Vegetable; 2 Breads*

PER SERVING: *496 Calories, 33 g Protein, 15 g Fat, 56 g Carbohydrate, 777 mg Calcium, 742 mg Sodium, 187 mg Cholesterol, 4 g Dietary Fiber*

Fantastic Fusilli and Feta

Time-saving recipes are essential for Valerie, a busy mother, who's also back in school. Aside from being colorful and fast, this dish is flexible—if you're not a feta fan, substitute your cheese of choice.

VALERIE BLACKMORE • EDMONTON, ALBERTA, CANADA

1½ cups broccoli florets or fresh
    asparagus, cut into 1½-inch pieces
2 teaspoons vegetable oil
¼ cup sliced red bell pepper, cut into
    1-inch pieces
¼ cup sliced green bell pepper, cut into
    1-inch pieces

¼ cup scallions (green onions), cut into
    1-inch pieces
2 cups cooked fusilli (corkscrew) pasta
1 medium tomato, cut into wedges
1 teaspoon dried dillweed
3 ounces feta cheese, crumbled

1.   In small saucepan, combine broccoli or asparagus with ⅓ cup water. Bring to a boil over medium-high heat; reduce heat to medium-low; cover and cook until tender-crisp, about 3 minutes. Drain and set aside.

2.   In large nonstick skillet, heat oil; add peppers and scallions. Sauté over medium-high heat until tender-crisp, about 2 minutes. Add pasta, tomato, dillweed, and broccoli or asparagus; cook until heated through, stirring frequently.

3.   To serve, transfer to large serving bowl. Add feta cheese; toss to combine.

MAKES 2 SERVINGS

———

EACH SERVING PROVIDES: *1 Fat; 2 Proteins; 3¼ Vegetables; 2 Breads*

———

PER SERVING: *408 Calories, 17 g Protein, 15 g Fat, 53 g Carbohydrate, 285 mg Calcium, 510 mg Sodium, 38 mg Cholesterol, 4 g Dietary Fiber*

Ricotta-Parmesan Pasta

Wendy devised this savory casserole as a healthy substitute for Fettuccine Alfredo.

WENDY OSTENDORF • NEWARK, DELAWARE

1 tablespoon reduced-calorie tub
    margarine
2 garlic cloves, crushed
1 cup part-skim ricotta cheese
1½ cups cooked angel-hair pasta
    (cappellini)

Dash freshly ground black pepper
2 tablespoons grated Parmesan cheese
Chopped fresh flat-leaf parsley for
    garnish (optional)

1. In medium nonstick skillet, melt margarine; add garlic. Cook over medium heat 1 minute.

2. Add ricotta and 2 tablespoons water; cook, stirring occasionally, until creamy, about 1 minute. Add pasta and pepper; stir to combine. Spoon evenly onto 2 serving plates; sprinkle with Parmesan and parsley.

MAKES 2 SERVINGS

EACH SERVING PROVIDES: *¾ Fat; 2 Proteins; 1½ Breads; 30 Optional Calories*

PER SERVING: *370 Calories, 21 g Protein, 15 g Fat, 37 g Carbohydrate, 416 mg Calcium, 303 mg Sodium, 42 mg Cholesterol, 2 g Dietary Fiber*

Denise's Pasta Supreme

When you're three-quarters Italian you have to love pasta—and Denise does! Here's a brightly hued dish that wins rave reviews.

DENISE GARDELLA · MIDDLESEX, NEW JERSEY

1 cup sliced mushrooms
½ cup chopped onion
½ cup chopped red bell pepper
½ cup chopped zucchini
½ cup chopped yellow squash

2 large plum tomatoes, coarsely chopped
2 cups low-sodium tomato sauce
¼ teaspoon dried red pepper flakes
4 cups hot cooked pasta shells
1 cup part-skim ricotta cheese

1.   To prepare sauce, spray medium non-stick skillet with nonstick cooking spray. Add mushrooms, onion, bell pepper, zucchini, yellow squash, and tomatoes. Cook over medium-high heat until onion is translucent, stirring occasionally, 5 minutes. Stir in tomato sauce and red pepper flakes; reduce heat to low; simmer 10 minutes.

2.   Place 1 cup pasta in each of 4 serving bowls; ladle sauce mixture evenly over each. Spoon ¼ cup ricotta in center of each serving.

MAKES 4 SERVINGS

PER SERVING: *315 Calories, 15 g Protein, 7 g Fat, 50 g Carbohydrate, 189 mg Calcium, 107 mg Sodium, 19 mg Cholesterol, 5 g Dietary Fiber*

EACH SERVING PROVIDES: *1 Protein; 3½ Vegetables; 2 Breads*

Vegetables, Macaroni, and Cheese Medley

A perfect meal for anyone in a hurry, this vegetarian dish gets a thumbs-up from every member of Alice's family.

ALICE MOLTER · CLEVELAND HEIGHTS, OHIO

1 cup low-fat (2%) cottage cheese
1 tablespoon Dijon mustard
½ teaspoon hot pepper sauce
2 cups cooked penne or ziti
2 cups cooked diced zucchini
1½ cups cooked sliced carrots

½ cup cooked broccoli florets
½ cup frozen peas, thawed and drained
1½ ounces shredded mozzarella cheese
1½ ounces shredded cheddar cheese
¾ ounce grated Romano cheese

1.   Preheat oven to 400°F.

2.   In blender, combine cottage cheese, mustard, pepper sauce, and ½ cup water until smooth.

3.   In large bowl, combine remaining ingredients; pour in cheese mixture and stir until thoroughly blended.

4.   Spray 3-quart casserole with nonstick cooking spray. Transfer pasta mixture to casserole. Cover and bake until heated through, 15 to 20 minutes.

MAKES 4 SERVINGS

EACH SERVING PROVIDES: *2 Proteins; 2 Vegetables; 1¼ Breads*

PER SERVING: *309 Calories, 20 g Protein, 10 g Fat, 36 g Carbohydrate, 272 mg Calcium, 594 mg Sodium, 29 mg Cholesterol, 6 g Dietary Fiber*

Three-Cheese Micro-Macaroni

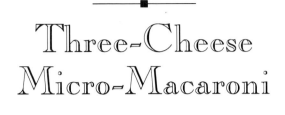

Believe it or not, Washington State resident Marlene considers herself a Southerner now—she used to live in Alaska. Marlene is busy raising a family and inventing great-tasting recipes like this ready-in-a-jiffy casserole.

MARLENE CASTOLDI · WALLA WALLA, WASHINGTON

1 tablespoon plus 1 teaspoon reduced-calorie tub margarine
1 tablespoon minced onion
1 clove elephant garlic, minced*
3 cups cooked elbow macaroni

½ cup part-skim ricotta cheese
1½ ounces shredded cheddar cheese
1 tablespoon plus 1 teaspoon grated Parmesan cheese
¼ teaspoon freshly ground black pepper

1. In 2-quart casserole, in microwave oven, melt margarine on High 30 seconds. Stir in onion and garlic; microwave on High 1 minute.

2. Stir in remaining ingredients, mixing well to combine. Cover and microwave on High 3 minutes, until heated through. Let stand 1 minute.

MAKES 4 SERVINGS

PER SERVING: *280 Calories, 14 g Protein, 10 g Fat, 34 g Carbohydrate, 205 mg Calcium, 260 mg Sodium, 26 mg Cholesterol, 2 g Dietary Fiber*

EACH SERVING PROVIDES: *1 Fat; 1 Protein; 1½ Breads; 10 Optional Calories*

* *Elephant garlic is a larger version of common garlic, which is less pungent and milder in flavor. An elephant garlic bulb is about the size of a small apple.*

Spaghetti Pancake

Marla keeps cooked pasta in her refrigerator at all times so that a tasty, hot meal is never more than minutes away.

MARLA ROYER · LAWRENCE, KANSAS

¼ cup egg substitute or 1 large egg
⅛ teaspoon dried thyme
⅛ teaspoon garlic powder
⅛ teaspoon freshly ground black pepper
1 large scallion (green onion), thinly
    sliced

½ cup drained canned mushroom stems
    and pieces
½ cup cooked spaghetti
2½ teaspoons grated Parmesan cheese

1. In small bowl or 1-cup glass measure, beat together egg substitute, thyme, garlic powder, pepper, and 1 tablespoon water; set aside.

2. Spray medium nonstick skillet with nonstick cooking spray. Sauté scallion, mushrooms, and spaghetti over medium-high heat, stirring frequently, until scallion is soft, about 1 minute. Spread mixture evenly over bottom of skillet. Reduce heat to medium-low.

3. Pour egg mixture evenly over spaghetti, tilting skillet to distribute evenly. Sprinkle cheese over top. Cover and cook until egg is set, 1 to 2 minutes.

MAKES 1 SERVING

THIS SERVING PROVIDES: *1 Protein; 1¼ Vegetables; 1 Bread; 25 Optional Calories*

PER SERVING (AS PREPARED WITH EGG SUBSTITUTE): *173 Calories, 12 g Protein, 3 g Fat, 26 g Carbohydrate, 97 mg Calcium, 472 mg Sodium, 3 mg Cholesterol, 1 g Dietary Fiber*

Garden Pasta Pie

Barbara enters so many recipe contests that her family giggles whenever she heads for the kitchen. Everyone agrees this entree's a bona fide winner.

BARBARA MEYERS · OREGON, OHIO

1 tablespoon olive oil
1 cup chopped onion
4 garlic cloves, minced
3 cups cooked linguine
¼ cup chopped fresh parsley
1 tablespoon fresh lemon juice
1½ teaspoons dried oregano
1½ teaspoons dried basil
¼ teaspoon freshly ground black pepper
1 cup part-skim ricotta cheese
¼ cup grated Parmesan cheese
1 large egg, lightly beaten
2 medium tomatoes, cored and sliced
1½ cups sliced zucchini
1½ ounces shredded part-skim
     mozzarella cheese

1.   Preheat oven to 375°F. Spray 8-inch springform pan with nonstick cooking spray; set aside.

2.   In small nonstick skillet, heat oil; add onion and garlic. Cook over medium-high heat until onion is translucent, 3 minutes.

3.   Transfer onion to medium bowl. Add linguine, parsley, lemon juice, and ½ teaspoon *each* oregano and basil. Add pepper and toss well.

4.   In small bowl, combine ricotta, 2 tablespoons of the Parmesan cheese, the egg, and remaining oregano and basil; stir into linguine mixture until blended.

5.   Place half the linguine mixture in prepared pan. Arrange half the tomato and zucchini slices on top. Add remaining linguine mixture. Top with remaining tomatoes and zucchini; sprinkle with mozzarella and remaining Parmesan. Cover with foil; place on baking sheet; bake 35 minutes. Remove foil; bake until golden, 5 minutes longer. Let stand 10 minutes before cutting.

MAKES 6 SERVINGS

EACH SERVING PROVIDES: *½ Fat; 1 Protein; 1½ Vegetables; 1 Bread; 30 Optional Calories*

PER SERVING: *254 Calories, 13 g Protein, 9 g Fat, 30 g Carbohydrate, 246 mg Calcium, 165 mg Sodium, 55 mg Cholesterol, 3 g Dietary Fiber*

Pasta with Lentil Sauce

Greta owns a bagel business and loves cooking vegetarian meals in her spare time. This family favorite is great over small pasta shells or ziti, accompanied by a leafy green salad.

GRETA WEINGAST · BENICIA, CALIFORNIA

½ cup chopped onion
½ cup chopped carrot
½ cup chopped celery
2 cups stewed tomatoes, including liquid
1 cup tomato sauce
½ cup drained canned sliced mushrooms
3 ounces dried lentils, rinsed and drained

½ teaspoon dried oregano
½ teaspoon dried basil
½ teaspoon garlic powder
¼ teaspoon crushed red pepper flakes
4 cups hot cooked pasta

1.   Spray large saucepan with nonstick cooking spray. Add onion, carrot, and celery; cook over medium-high heat until onion is translucent, about 3 minutes.

2.   Add 1⅓ cups water and remaining ingredients, except pasta. Bring to a boil, stirring occasionally. Reduce heat, cover partially, and simmer until lentils are tender, stirring occasionally, about 1 hour.

3.   Place pasta in large serving bowl. Pour lentil sauce over top and toss to combine.

MAKES 4 SERVINGS

EACH SERVING PROVIDES: *1 Protein; 2½ Vegetables; 2 Breads*

PER SERVING: *346 Calories, 16 g Protein, 2 g Fat, 70 g Carbohydrate, 93 mg Calcium, 793 mg Sodium, 0 mg Cholesterol, 7 g Dietary Fiber*

Easy Manicotti Florentine

Dana's mom taught her how to make manicotti without precooking the shells, so she saves time without scrimping on taste or nutrition.

DANA STILWELL TEMPLIN · SEAL BEACH, CALIFORNIA

1 cup frozen chopped spinach (half a 10-ounce package), thawed and drained
1 cup low-fat (1%) cottage cheese
½ cup part-skim ricotta cheese
Dash salt
¼ teaspoon freshly ground black pepper
2 cups low-sodium tomato sauce
6 ounces uncooked jumbo manicotti shells (about 8 shells)
2¼ ounces shredded part-skim mozzarella cheese

1.   Preheat oven to 375°F.

2.   In large bowl, combine spinach, cottage and ricotta cheeses, salt, and pepper until blended. Pour 1 cup of the sauce and ¼ cup water into an 11-by-7-inch baking pan; spread to make an even layer.

3.   With teaspoon, stuff each shell with an equal amount of the cheese mixture; place in baking pan. Pour remaining tomato sauce evenly over the top. Cover with foil; bake until shells are tender, about 50 minutes. Uncover; sprinkle with mozzarella cheese. Bake about 10 minutes longer, until cheese is melted and bubbly.

MAKES 4 SERVINGS

EACH SERVING (2 SHELLS) PROVIDES: *2 Proteins; 2 Vegetables; 2 Breads*

PER SERVING: *236 Calories, 18 g Protein, 7 g Fat, 25 g Carbohydrate, 244 mg Calcium, 412 mg Sodium, 24 mg Cholesterol, 3 g Dietary Fiber*

Swiss Chard, Rice, and Tofu

Libby is a busy geographer who has dropped 84 pounds. This super-healthful recipe meets her time and taste requirements by being easy, filling, and fast.

LIBBY NELSON · SAN JOSE, CALIFORNIA

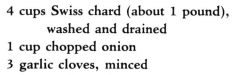

4 cups Swiss chard (about 1 pound), washed and drained
1 cup chopped onion
3 garlic cloves, minced
6 ounces firm tofu, cubed
1 cup cooked rice

1 tablespoon plus 1 teaspoon low-sodium soy sauce
⅛ teaspoon ground nutmeg
Dash ground red pepper
1½ ounces shredded cheddar cheese

1. Preheat broiler.

2. Cut stems off chard leaves; dice stems and set aside. Cut leaves into ½-inch strips; set aside.

3. Spray large nonstick skillet with nonstick cooking spray. Heat for 1 minute. Add chard stems, onion, and garlic; cook over medium-high heat, stirring occasionally, until onion is translucent, about 3 minutes. Add tofu; cook, stirring occasionally, until lightly browned, about 5 minutes. Add chard leaves and 2 tablespoons water; cook, stirring occasionally, until chard is limp, about 3 minutes. Add remaining ingredi-

ents, except cheese. Cook until rice is heated through, about 2 minutes.

4. To serve, divide mixture evenly between 2 ovenproof serving plates and sprinkle cheese evenly over top. (Or, place in an ovenproof casserole.) Place under preheated broiler for 2 minutes.

MAKES 2 SERVINGS

EACH SERVING PROVIDES: *2½ Proteins; 5 Vegetables; 1 Bread*

PER SERVING: *429 Calories, 27 g Protein, 16 g Fat, 50 g Carbohydrate, 472 mg Calcium, 993 mg Sodium, 22 mg Cholesterol, 2 g Dietary Fiber*

Tofu Tortilla Casserole

Sandy's combo is a proven hit on the potluck circuit, but doesn't cost much to fix. She works for a county social services agency and as a Weight Watchers receptionist.

SANDY CARRIGER · SACRAMENTO, CALIFORNIA

1 tablespoon plus 2 teaspoons olive oil
½ cup chopped onion
2 garlic cloves, minced
12 ounces firm tofu, crumbled
3½ cups canned crushed tomatoes
2 tablespoons chopped fresh cilantro
2 teaspoons chili powder
1½ teaspoons ground cumin

½ teaspoon salt
Nine 6-inch corn tortillas, cut into 6 wedges
2 cups low-fat (1%) cottage cheese
4½ ounces shredded cheddar cheese
½ cup sliced scallions (green onions)
10 small or 6 large black olives, thinly sliced

1. To prepare sauce, in medium saucepan, heat oil; stir in onion and garlic; cook for 1 minute. Add tofu; cook 1 minute longer. Add tomatoes, cilantro, chili powder, cumin, and salt. Bring to a boil, stirring occasionally. Reduce heat; simmer 10 minutes.

2. Preheat oven to 350°F. Spray 13-by-9-by-2-inch casserole with nonstick cooking spray.

3. Spread 1 cup sauce in bottom of casserole. Layer with half the tortillas, sauce, cheese, and scallions. Repeat layering; top with olives.

4. Bake until lightly browned and cheese is bubbly, about 30 minutes.

MAKES 6 SERVINGS

EACH SERVING PROVIDES: *1 Fat; 3 Proteins; 1½ Vegetables; 1½ Breads*

PER SERVING: *404 Calories, 29 g Protein, 19 g Fat, 33 g Carbohydrate, 438 mg Calcium, 988 mg Sodium, 25 mg Cholesterol, 4 g Dietary Fiber*

Tofu Sandwich

Jane never ate tofu before joining Weight Watchers—now she's created a winning recipe for this versatile Asian staple.

JANE ARGO ROMEO · TAMPA, FLORIDA

2 ounces firm tofu
2 teaspoons reduced-calorie mayonnaise
2 teaspoons minced onion
2 teaspoons diced green bell pepper

1 teaspoon pickle relish
2 slices reduced-calorie wheat or rye bread
¼ cup alfalfa sprouts

1. In small bowl, mash tofu with fork. Add mayonnaise, onion, bell pepper, and pickle relish; stir well to combine.

2. Spread tofu mixture on 1 slice of bread; top with sprouts and remaining slice of bread. Cut in half and serve.

MAKES 1 SERVING

THIS SERVING PROVIDES: *1 Fat; 1 Protein; 1 Vegetable; 1 Bread; 10 Optional Calories*

PER SERVING: *202 Calories, 13 g Protein, 9 g Fat, 24 g Carbohydrate, 161 mg Calcium, 289 mg Sodium, 3 mg Cholesterol, 3 g Dietary Fiber*

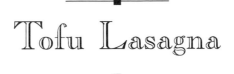

Tofu Lasagna

oni's husband loves lasagna, so she developed this version to satisfy his craving without threatening his waistline.

TONI LUSK · SAN JOSE, CALIFORNIA

1 tablespoon plus 1 teaspoon olive oil
1 cup chopped onion
1 cup sliced green bell pepper
5 garlic cloves, minced
2 cups sliced zucchini
1 cup sliced mushrooms
12 ounces firm tofu, in ½-inch cubes
2 cups canned crushed tomatoes
½ cup tomato paste

1½ teaspoons dried oregano
1½ teaspoons dried basil
½ teaspoon salt (optional)
¼ teaspoon ground red pepper
1 bay leaf
8 ounces shredded nonfat mozzarella
9 ounces lasagna noodles, cooked
    according to package directions
1 cup tomato sauce

1. In large saucepan, heat oil; add onion, green pepper, and garlic. Cook over medium-high heat until onion is translucent, 5 minutes. Add zucchini and mushrooms; cook 5 minutes longer.

2. Stir in tofu, tomatoes, tomato paste, 1 teaspoon *each* of the oregano and basil, salt if desired, red pepper, and bay leaf. Reduce heat, cover partially, and simmer 15 minutes, stirring occasionally. Remove bay leaf and cool slightly. Stir in half the mozzarella.

3. Preheat oven to 350°F. Spray 13-by-9-by-2-inch baking dish with nonstick cooking spray.

4. Spread half the tofu mixture in baking dish. Arrange half the noodles on top, overlapping slightly. Repeat with remaining tofu mixture and noodles. Top with tomato sauce, remaining herbs, and mozzarella.

5. Bake until lightly browned and bubbly, about 30 minutes. Let stand 15 minutes.

MAKES 8 SERVINGS

EACH SERVING PROVIDES: *½ Fat; 1¾ Proteins; 2¾ Vegetables; 1½ Breads*

PER SERVING: *289 Calories, 21 g Protein, 7 g Fat, 37 g Carbohydrate, 290 mg Calcium, 478 mg Sodium, 5 mg Cholesterol, 3 g Dietary Fiber*

Vegetarian Lasagna

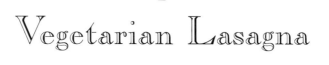

The Mansfields are going vegetarian a little at a time by converting their favorite recipes into meatless masterpieces. You won't miss the meat in this savory dish.

PHYLIS MANSFIELD • NASHVILLE, TENNESSEE

4 cups low-sodium tomato sauce
2 teaspoons garlic powder
2 teaspoons dried oregano
2 teaspoons dried basil
1 cup sliced mushrooms
2 cups frozen chopped spinach (one 10-ounce package), thawed and drained

6 ounces firm tofu, crumbled
⅔ cup low-fat (1%) cottage cheese
2 tablespoons grated Parmesan cheese
2 egg whites
3 ounces shredded mozzarella cheese
9 ounces lasagna noodles, cooked according to package directions

1.   Preheat oven to 375°F.

2.   In medium saucepan, combine tomato sauce, garlic powder, oregano, and basil. Bring to a boil over high heat; reduce heat and simmer 5 minutes. Stir in mushrooms; remove from heat.

3.   In medium bowl, combine remaining ingredients except mozzarella and lasagna noodles; mix well.

4.   Spread 1⅓ cups tomato sauce in bottom of 13-by-9-by-2-inch baking dish; arrange half the noodles on top (cut 1 in half if necessary to make an even layer). Spread spinach mixture evenly over noodles; spread 1⅓ cups sauce over the top. Top with remaining noodles and sauce; sprinkle with mozzarella.

5.   Bake until cheese is lightly browned, 30 to 40 minutes.

MAKES 6 SERVINGS

———
EACH SERVING PROVIDES: *1½ Proteins; 3⅔ Vegetables; 2 Breads; 15 Optional Calories*

———
PER SERVING: *343 Calories, 22 g Protein, 8 g Fat, 49 g Carbohydrate, 250 mg Calcium, 280 mg Sodium, 13 mg Cholesterol, 4 g Dietary Fiber*

Spinach Lasagna

Marina's Italian clan considers pasta a Sunday tradition. She converted the family recipe into vegetarian fare. Marina and her husband have another weekly date—going to Weight Watchers!

MARINA BLATTNER · TOMS RIVER, NEW JERSEY

2 cups frozen chopped spinach (one 10-ounce package), thawed and squeezed dry
2 cups nonfat ricotta cheese
1 large egg, beaten
2 tablespoons chopped fresh parsley
½ teaspoon garlic powder
4 cups low-sodium tomato sauce
7 ounces no-boil lasagna noodles* (12 noodles), *uncooked*
6 ounces part-skim mozzarella cheese, shredded
1 tablespoon plus 1 teaspoon grated Parmesan cheese

1. Preheat oven to 350°F.

2. In small bowl, combine spinach, ricotta, egg, parsley, and garlic powder.

3. Spread 1 cup tomato sauce in 13-by-9-inch baking dish. Top with 4 lasagna noodles, overlapping if necessary. (Be careful that noodles do not touch outside edges of dish.) Spread 1 cup sauce over noodles. Layer with one-third ricotta mixture; sprinkle with one-third mozzarella. Repeat layering twice with remaining ingredients. Sprinkle evenly with Parmesan cheese.

4. Cover with foil; bake 25 minutes. Remove foil and bake 5 to 10 minutes longer, until browned. Let stand 5 minutes.

MAKES 8 SERVINGS

EACH SERVING PROVIDES: *2 Proteins; 2½ Vegetables; ¾ Bread; 30 Optional Calories.*

PER SERVING: *256 Calories, 20 g Protein, 5 g Fat, 30 g Carbohydrate, 493 mg Calcium, 245 mg Sodium, 40 mg Cholesterol, 2 g Dietary Fiber*

* *No-boil lasagna noodles for microwave and conventional use should* not *be cooked before layering. They are in the pasta section of the supermarket.*

Eggplant Florentine

Brenda loves painting, knitting, sewing, and vacations that center on sight-seeing and swimming instead of eating. She created this Italian recipe to please her children and dinner guests alike.

BRENDA SCHER · BROOKLYN, NEW YORK

1 large eggplant, cut into 8 diagonal
    slices
¾ cup dried bread crumbs
1 cup chopped onion
3 garlic cloves, minced
2 cups crushed tomatoes
1 teaspoon dried basil
1 teaspoon dried oregano

¼ teaspoon dried red pepper flakes
Dash freshly ground black pepper
2 cups frozen chopped spinach (one
    10-ounce package), thawed and
    drained
1¾ cups part-skim ricotta cheese
1 large egg
1½ ounces grated Parmesan cheese

1.   Preheat oven to 350°F.

2.   On large sheet of wax paper, dredge eggplant slices in bread crumbs, coating both sides; place on 1 or 2 nonstick baking sheets. Bake 15 minutes; turn and bake 15 minutes longer, until tender. Cool slightly.

3.   Meanwhile, spray large nonstick skillet with nonstick cooking spray; add onion and garlic. Cook over medium-high heat until onion is translucent, about 3 minutes. Add tomatoes, basil, oregano, and red and black pepper. Bring to a boil; reduce heat to low, cover, and simmer 15 minutes. Set aside.

4.   In medium bowl, combine remaining ingredients until thoroughly blended.

Spread 2 heaping tablespoons of spinach mixture on each slice of eggplant and roll to enclose.

5.   Pour half the sauce into 13-by-9-inch baking pan. Arrange eggplant rolls seam side down; pour remaining sauce over top. Cover with aluminum foil and bake until heated through, about 25 minutes.

MAKES 4 SERVINGS

EACH SERVING PROVIDES: *2½ Proteins; 3¾ Vegetables; 1 Bread*

PER SERVING: *394 Calories, 27 g Protein, 15 g Fat, 42 g Carbohydrate, 667 mg Calcium, 581 mg Sodium, 96 mg Cholesterol, 7 g Dietary Fiber*

Eggplant Lasagna

A vegetarian casserole that "fills you up without filling you out." It's easy to prepare, which makes it ideal for working mothers like Robin.

ROBIN WHITMAN · MARLBOROUGH, MASSACHUSETTS

1 medium eggplant (about 8 ounces), pared and cut crosswise into ¼-inch slices
1 cup part-skim ricotta cheese
3 ounces shredded part-skim mozzarella cheese
1 large egg white
1 tablespoon chopped fresh flat-leaf parsley
¼ teaspoon garlic powder
3 ounces lasagna noodles, cooked according to package directions and cut in half crosswise
1 cup canned crushed tomatoes

1. In large skillet or saucepan, in 2 batches, steam eggplant on rack over simmering water until very tender; set aside on paper towels to drain.

2. Preheat oven to 350°F.

3. In small bowl, combine ricotta, 2 ounces of the mozzarella, the egg white, parsley, and garlic powder until well blended.

4. Spray 8-inch square baking pan with nonstick cooking spray. Arrange one-third of lasagna noodles in pan; layer with one-third of ricotta mixture, eggplant slices, and crushed tomatoes. Repeat layering twice; sprinkle remaining mozzarella on top.

5. Bake until heated through and cheese is lightly browned, 20 to 25 minutes.

MAKES 4 SERVINGS

EACH SERVING PROVIDES: *1 Protein; ¾ Vegetables; 1 Bread; 5 Optional Calories*

PER SERVING: *246 Calories, 17 g Protein, 9 g Fat, 25 g Carbohydrate, 343 mg Calcium, 291 mg Sodium, 31 mg Cholesterol, 2 g Dietary Fiber*

Asparagus Roll-Ups

Comfort food gets a twist when macaroni and cheese meet fresh asparagus in this innovative dish.

BRENDA OLIVER · NEPEAN, ONTARIO, CANADA

4½ ounces lasagna noodles (6 noodles)
12 slender asparagus spears, halved
1 tablespoon plus 1 teaspoon all-purpose flour
1 tablespoon margarine
1 teaspoon Dijon mustard

Dash Worcestershire sauce
⅔ cup skim milk
3 ounces shredded cheddar cheese
1 tablespoon chopped fresh parsley for garnish

1.   In 11-by-7-inch microwave-safe dish, combine lasagna noodles and 4 cups boiling water. Cover tightly with vented plastic wrap. Microwave on High 6 minutes, re-arranging noodles after 3 minutes. Let stand 1 minute; drain and rinse. Cover with damp paper towel; set aside.

2.   Place asparagus in same dish; sprinkle with 2 tablespoons water. Cover tightly with vented plastic wrap. Microwave on High 3 minutes. Drain and cool slightly.

3.   Cut noodles in half; roll 2 asparagus halves in each noodle half. Place seam-side down in same dish.

4.   To prepare sauce, in 2-cup glass measure, stir together remaining ingredients except parsley. Microwave on Medium-High, until thickened and cheese is melted, stirring once.

5.   Pour sauce over asparagus rolls; cover tightly with vented plastic wrap. Microwave on High 2 minutes, until heated through. Sprinkle with parsley.

MAKES 6 SERVINGS

EACH SERVING (2 ROLLS) PROVIDES: ½ Fat; ¾ Protein; 1 Bread; 30 Optional Calories

PER SERVING: 175 Calories, 8 g Protein, 7 g Fat, 20 g Carbohydrate, 146 mg Calcium, 152 mg Sodium, 15 mg Cholesterol, 1 g Dietary Fiber

Peter Piper's Pizza

Margaret is an expert on regional cuisine—her shelves are packed with more than 50 cookbooks. She assures us you don't have to pick a peck of pickled peppers to enjoy this lean alternative to restaurant pizza.

MARGARET SCHILLING · WOODLAND PARK, COLORADO

1 cup chopped onion
½ cup chopped yellow bell pepper
½ cup chopped red bell pepper
2 garlic cloves, minced
One 10-ounce refrigerated pizza crust

1 cup tomato puree
6 ounces shredded mozzarella cheese
2 tablespoons grated Parmesan cheese
1 teaspoon dried basil
½ teaspoon crushed red pepper flakes

1. Preheat oven to 425°F. Spray 12-inch pizza pan or 13-by-9-inch baking pan with nonstick cooking spray; set aside.

2. Spray large nonstick skillet with nonstick cooking spray; add onion, bell peppers, and garlic. Cook over medium-high heat, stirring occasionally, until onion is translucent, about 5 minutes.

3. Unroll pizza dough; press into prepared pan. Spread evenly with tomato puree. Spoon vegetables evenly over puree; sprinkle with remaining ingredients. Bake until cheese is bubbly and crust is golden brown, 10 to 15 minutes.

MAKES 8 SERVINGS

EACH SERVING PROVIDES: *1 Protein; 1 Vegetable; 1¼ Breads; 10 Optional Calories*

PER SERVING: *184 Calories, 9 g Protein; 6 g Fat, 23 g Carbohydrate, 142 mg Calcium, 398 mg Sodium, 18 mg Cholesterol, 1 g Dietary Fiber*

Cheese Lover's White Pizza

Holding down a job and raising a family pulled Janet in two directions, and snacking and poor eating habits became a way of life. Today she stays on track with recipes like this cheesy pizza.

JANET LEICHLITER · GREENSBURG, PENNSYLVANIA

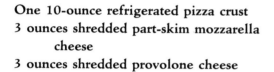

One 10-ounce refrigerated pizza crust
3 ounces shredded part-skim mozzarella
    cheese
3 ounces shredded provolone cheese

3 ounces shredded fontina cheese
1 teaspoon Italian seasoning
3 large plum tomatoes, sliced
2 tablespoons grated Parmesan cheese

1. Preheat oven to 425°F. Spray 12-inch pizza pan or 13-by-9-inch baking pan with nonstick cooking spray.

2. Unroll pizza dough; press into prepared pan. Arrange remaining ingredients over top. Bake until cheese is bubbly and golden brown, 10 to 15 minutes.

MAKES 6 SERVINGS

EACH SERVING PROVIDES: *2 Proteins; ½ Vegetable; 1½ Breads; 25 Optional Calories*

PER SERVING: *275 Calories, 16 g Protein, 13 g Fat, 24 g Carbohydrate, 308 mg Calcium, 572 mg Sodium, 36 mg Cholesterol, 0 g Dietary Fiber*

Marie's Vegetable Salad

Marie is a "semi-vegetarian" who can't get enough of chick-peas. This is one of her favorite ways to eat them.

MARIE CAREW • LEDUC, ALBERTA, CANADA

½ cup plain nonfat yogurt
¼ cup plus 2 tablespoons reduced-
    calorie mayonnaise
1 tablespoon chopped fresh parsley
Granulated sugar substitute to equal 4
    teaspoons sugar (optional)
12 ounces cooked chick-peas, rinsed and
    drained
1 cup sliced mushrooms

1 cup thinly sliced celery
½ cup thinly sliced carrot
½ cup chopped red onion
2 tablespoons plus 2 teaspoons sunflower
    seeds
2 tablespoons plus 2 teaspoons imitation
    bacon bits (optional)
3 cups thoroughly washed and drained
    spinach leaves

1. To prepare dressing, in small bowl, combine yogurt, mayonnaise, parsley, and sugar substitute, if desired, until blended; set aside.

2. In large bowl, combine remaining ingredients except spinach leaves. Add reserved dressing and toss well to combine.

3. To serve, arrange spinach leaves on large serving platter; spoon salad mixture on top.

MAKES 6 SERVINGS

EACH SERVING PROVIDES: *1½ Fats; 1 Protein; 2 Vegetables; 35 Optional Calories (Add 15 Optional Calories per serving if bacon bits are included.)*

PER SERVING: *189 Calories, 9 g Protein, 8 g Fat, 23 g Carbohydrate, 113 mg Calcium, 144 mg Sodium, 5 mg Cholesterol, 3 g Dietary Fiber*

Squash Patties

Patricia is a legal secretary who loves vegetables. Looking for a creative new use for squash, she developed this scrumptious meatless meal.

PATRICIA CLOER · TERRY, MISSISSIPPI

1 cup cooked spaghetti squash
¾ ounce shredded cheddar cheese
¼ cup chopped scallions (green onions)
1 large egg, lightly beaten

2 teaspoons all-purpose flour
Dash salt
Dash freshly ground black pepper

1.   In medium bowl, combine all ingredients. Shape mixture into 2 patties.

2.   Spray medium nonstick skillet with nonstick cooking spray. Cook patties over medium heat until lightly browned, about 3 minutes. Turn patties over; cook until other side is lightly browned, about 3 minutes longer.

MAKES 1 SERVING

THIS SERVING PROVIDES: *2 Proteins; 2½ Vegetables; 20 Optional Calories*

PER SERVING: *240 Calories, 14 g Protein, 14 g Fat, 17 g Carbohydrate, 231 mg Calcium, 359 mg Sodium, 235 mg Cholesterol, 1 g Dietary Fiber*

Baked Chile Relleno

For lovers of spicy Mexican food, this is a perfect meatless main dish with plenty of zip.

BEVERLY HIATT · BUHL, IDAHO

1 large egg, separated
1 large egg white
Dash salt
1 canned whole small green chili,
      drained

¾ ounce shredded cheddar cheese
Hot or medium salsa (optional)

1.   Preheat oven to 350°F. Spray 6-inch au gratin dish with nonstick cooking spray; set aside.

2.   In medium bowl, with electric mixer on high speed, beat egg whites and salt until stiff.

3.   In small bowl, lightly beat egg yolk; fold into egg whites. Spread half the mixture in prepared dish. Open chili and place flat on top; sprinkle with cheese. Spread remaining egg mixture on top to make an even layer.

4.   Bake until golden brown and center is set, 15 to 20 minutes. Serve with salsa, if desired.

MAKES 1 SERVING

THIS SERVING PROVIDES: *2 Proteins; ½ Vegetable; 20 Optional Calories*

PER SERVING: *188 Calories, 15 g Protein, 13 g Fat, 2 g Carbohydrate, 182 mg Calcium, 473 mg Sodium, 235 mg Cholesterol, 0 g Dietary Fiber*

Vegetarian Delight

Jeannie relies on group support to help in losing weight. She especially enjoys trading recipes, like this vegetable medley flavored with peanut butter and soy sauce.

JEANNIE COCHRAN · LAFAYETTE, INDIANA

2 tablespoons creamy peanut butter
1 tablespoon low-sodium soy sauce
1½ teaspoons honey
2 teaspoons vegetable oil
½ cup thinly sliced carrot
¼ cup chopped onion
½ cup chopped broccoli florets

½ cup chopped cauliflower florets
½ cup chopped zucchini
½ cup frozen corn kernels
¼ cup chopped red bell pepper
1 garlic clove, minced
2 cups cooked brown rice
1 ounce cashews (about 14)

1.   In small bowl, combine peanut butter, soy sauce, 1 tablespoon water, and honey until blended; set aside.

2.   In large skillet or wok, heat oil over medium-high heat. Add carrot and onion; cook, stirring frequently, until onion is translucent, about 2 minutes.

3.   Add remaining ingredients except rice and cashews; cook, stirring frequently, until vegetables are tender-crisp, about 3 minutes. Add peanut butter mixture and cook, stirring constantly, until just boiling, about 2 minutes. Stir in rice and cook until heated through, about 2 minutes. Transfer to heated serving dish and arrange cashews on top.

MAKES 4 SERVINGS

EACH SERVING (1¼ CUPS) PROVIDES: *1½ Fats; ½ Protein; 1¼ Vegetables; 1¼ Breads; 25 Optional Calories*

PER SERVING: *268 Calories, 8 g Protein, 11 g Fat, 38 g Carbohydrate, 38 mg Calcium, 206 mg Sodium, 0 mg Cholesterol, 4 g Dietary Fiber*

Vegetarian Mushroom Patties

Karen is a busy homemaker and mother who also works part-time as a health records administrator. Here's her version of a tasty veggie burger.

KAREN DOBROSKAY · SASKATOON, SASKATCHEWAN, CANADA

2½ cups chopped mushrooms
1 cup plus 2 tablespoons seasoned dried
    bread crumbs
⅔ cup low-fat (1%) cottage cheese
½ cup chopped onion
2 large eggs, lightly beaten
2¼ ounces shredded mozzarella cheese

2 ounces chopped walnuts or almonds
1 teaspoon reduced-sodium soy sauce
¼ teaspoon garlic powder
Dash salt
Dash freshly ground black pepper
2 teaspoons vegetable oil

1.   In large bowl, combine all ingredients except oil until thoroughly blended. Shape mixture into 6 patties.

2.   Preheat oven to 325°F.

3.   Spray large nonstick skillet with nonstick cooking spray; add oil and heat 1 minute. Cook patties over medium heat until lightly browned, about 3 minutes. Turn patties over; cook until other side is lightly browned, about 3 minutes longer. (Patties can be prepared to this point and frozen for later use.)

4.   Place patties in a nonstick baking pan. Bake 15 minutes.

MAKES 6 SERVINGS

EACH SERVING PROVIDES: *1 Fat; 1½ Proteins; 1 Vegetable; 1 Bread*

PER SERVING: *242 Calories, 13 g Protein, 13 g Fat, 21 g Carbohydrate, 112 mg Calcium, 783 mg Sodium, 81 mg Cholesterol, 1 g Dietary Fiber*

Zucchini Boats

Anita adapted one of her mother's recipes to create a vegetarian meal that doesn't derail her weight loss efforts. It's wonderful with Fruited Rice Pilaf.

ANITA WILSON · VANCOUVER, BRITISH COLUMBIA, CANADA

2 medium zucchini
½ cup chopped onion
½ cup diced carrot
½ cup chopped mushrooms

Dash white pepper
Dash ground red pepper
1½ ounces grated Parmesan cheese

1. Cut zucchini in half lengthwise. Remove pulp from each half, leaving ¼-inch-thick shells. Dice pulp; set aside.

2. Pour 1 cup water into Dutch oven. Place zucchini shells in steamer basket; set over water. Bring to a boil over high heat. Reduce heat, cover, and steam until shells are fork-tender, about 6 minutes.

3. Meanwhile, spray medium nonstick skillet with nonstick cooking spray; add remaining ingredients, except cheese, and cook over medium-high heat, stirring occasionally, until carrot is tender-crisp, about 3 minutes. Add reserved zucchini pulp; cook 1 minute longer.

4. Preheat broiler.

5. Place zucchini shells in nonstick broiler pan. Spoon vegetable mixture evenly into shells; sprinkle with cheese. Broil 4 inches from heat until golden brown, about 3 minutes.

MAKES 2 SERVINGS

———

EACH SERVING PROVIDES: *1 Protein; 3½ Vegetables*

———

PER SERVING: *144 Calories, 11 g Protein, 7 g Fat, 10 g Carbohydrate, 321 mg Calcium, 410 mg Sodium, 17 mg Cholesterol, 2 g Dietary Fiber*

Mock Quiche

Here's a nifty idea that tastes great and uses egg roll wrappers instead of pastry.

TRACY TRUJILLO · COLORADO SPRINGS, COLORADO

2 large eggs, lightly beaten
¼ cup finely chopped broccoli
½ ounce diced cooked lean ham
1 tablespoon grated Parmesan cheese

2 teaspoons dried onion flakes
2½ wonton skins (wrappers), 3-inch squares

1. Preheat oven to 350°F. Spray small custard cup with nonstick cooking spray; set aside.

2. In small bowl, combine all ingredients except wonton skins until blended.

3. Place 1½ wonton skins, slightly overlapping, in prepared cup. Slowly pour in egg mixture; top with remaining wonton skins, gently folding corners down side of dish; spray top lightly with nonstick cooking spray. Using tip of sharp knife, make small slit in top. Bake until golden, about 20 minutes.

MAKES 1 SERVING

THIS SERVING PROVIDES: *2½ Proteins; ½ Vegetable; ½ Bread; 30 Optional Calories*

PER SERVING: *257 Calories, 20 g Protein, 14 g Fat, 13 g Carbohydrate, 135 mg Calcium, 400 mg Sodium, 436 mg Cholesterol, 1 g Dietary Fiber*

Peppers and Eggs

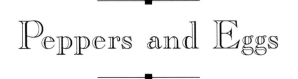

A sandwich of peppers and eggs fried in olive oil was a standard of Lisa's Italian grandmother's repertoire. Lisa's healthy update, prepared in a nonstick pan, cuts out the oil and all but one egg yolk for a wonderful, nutritious meal.

LISA MARIE SEBELLE · CORNING, NEW YORK

3 large egg whites
1 large egg
¼ teaspoon salt
⅛ teaspoon freshly ground black pepper
1 teaspoon olive oil

½ cup chopped red bell pepper
½ cup chopped green bell pepper
½ cup chopped mushrooms
2 garlic cloves, minced
4 ounces cooked cubed potato

1. In small bowl, combine egg whites, egg, salt, and pepper.

2. In medium nonstick skillet, heat oil; add red and green bell peppers, mushrooms, and garlic. Cook over medium-high heat, stirring occasionally, 2 minutes. Add potato; cook until lightly browned, about 2 minutes.

3. Pour in egg mixture; cook, stirring constantly, until eggs are just set, about 1 minute.

MAKES 1 SERVING

THIS SERVING PROVIDES: *1 Fat; 2 Proteins; 3 Vegetables; 1 Bread*

PER SERVING: *307 Calories, 21 g Protein, 10 g Fat, 35 g Carbohydrate, 66 mg Calcium, 778 mg Sodium, 213 mg Cholesterol, 4 g Dietary Fiber*

Bev's Spinach Pie

Rather than give up her favorite Greek entree, Beverly, a full-time mother, housewife, and Weight Watchers member, developed an easy phyllo recipe that would please Zorba himself.

BEVERLY SHORE · MOUNT CLEMENS, MICHIGAN

---

2 ounces phyllo dough, thawed if frozen
1 tablespoon olive oil
1 cup chopped onion
6 cups frozen chopped spinach (three 10-ounce packages), thawed and drained

4½ ounces crumbled feta cheese
1 large egg, lightly beaten
2 tablespoons fresh lemon juice
¼ teaspoon ground white pepper
⅛ teaspoon ground nutmeg

---

1.   Preheat oven to 350°F. Spray an 8-inch square glass baking dish with nonstick cooking spray; set aside. Cover phyllo dough with damp towel and plastic wrap to prevent drying.

2.   In medium skillet, heat oil; add onion. Cook over medium-high heat, stirring occasionally, until onion is translucent, about 3 minutes.

3.   Transfer onion to large bowl; add remaining ingredients, except phyllo dough, stirring well to combine.

4.   Arrange half of the phyllo sheets in prepared baking dish; spoon spinach mix-

ture on top and press gently to make smooth, even layer. Separate remaining phyllo sheets. One at a time (there will be 2 or 3 remaining), place on top of spinach mixture; spray each sheet, including the last one, with nonstick cooking spray. Bake until golden brown, about 20 to 30 minutes.

MAKES 4 SERVINGS

EACH SERVING PROVIDES: ¾ Fat; 1¾ Proteins;
     3½ Vegetables; ½ Bread

PER SERVING: 252 Calories, 14 g Protein, 13 g Fat,
     24 g Carbohydrate, 408 mg Calcium, 590 mg
     Sodium, 82 mg Cholesterol, 5 g Dietary Fiber

Cheese Blintz

Rhonda missed the taste and texture of the blintzes she grew up with, so she developed this delicious brunch entree. It's a big hit with her husband, too.

RHONDA GROH · BERKLEY, MICHIGAN

¾ cup plus 3 tablespoons all-purpose
    flour
Granulated sugar substitute to equal
    ¼ cup sugar
2½ teaspoons double-acting baking
    powder
⅛ teaspoon salt
3 large eggs
½ cup reduced-calorie tub margarine
¼ cup skim milk

2½ cups part-skim ricotta cheese
8 ounces reduced-calorie cream cheese,
    softened
2 large eggs
¼ cup granulated sugar
3 tablespoons fresh lemon juice
1 teaspoon grated lemon peel
1 teaspoon grated orange peel
Dash salt

1.   Preheat oven to 300°F. Spray 13-by-9-inch baking pan with nonstick cooking spray; set aside.

2.   To prepare batter, in large bowl, with electric mixer on medium speed, mix flour, sugar substitute, baking powder, salt, eggs, margarine, and milk until just blended. (Do not overmix.)

3.   To prepare filling, in separate large bowl, with electric mixer on low speed, mix remaining ingredients until blended.

4.   Pour half the batter into prepared pan.

Gently pour filling on top, being careful not to mix layers; pour remaining batter over cheese mixture. Bake until golden brown and set, 1½ hours. Let stand 10 minutes before cutting, or cover and refrigerate until ready to serve. (Can be served chilled or at room temperature.)

MAKES 10 SERVINGS

EACH SERVING PROVIDES: *1 Fat; 1½ Proteins; ½ Bread; 90 Optional Calories*

PER SERVING: *280 Calories, 14 g Protein, 16 g Fat, 21 g Carbohydrate, 275 mg Calcium, 493 mg Sodium, 137 mg Cholesterol, 0 g Dietary Fiber*

Veggie and Cheese Pita Melt

Frances is a nurse who works the night shift, so she needs easy, portable meals that reheat quickly. She devised this sandwich to satisfy her cravings for fresh vegetables.

FRANCES LARSON · MANCHESTER, CONNECTICUT

½ cup broccoli florets
½ cup green beans, cut into 1-inch
    pieces
2 tablespoons sliced scallions (green
    onions)
1 tablespoon rice wine vinegar

1 teaspoon low-sodium soy sauce
1 teaspoon sesame oil
¾ ounce shredded Swiss cheese
1 small (1-ounce) pita bread, cut to form
    pocket

1.   In small bowl, combine broccoli, green beans, scallion, and 2 tablespoons water. Microwave on High 1 minute. Stir in vinegar, soy sauce, and oil; set aside for 10 minutes to marinate, stirring once.

2.   Stuff vegetable mixture and cheese into pita. Wrap in paper towel; microwave on High 1 minute, or until heated through and cheese is melted.

MAKES 1 SERVING

THIS SERVING PROVIDES: *1 Fat; 1 Protein; 2¼ Vegetables; 1 Bread*

PER SERVING: *253 Calories, 12 g Protein, 11 g Fat, 29 g Carbohydrate, 268 mg Calcium, 460 mg Sodium, 20 mg Cholesterol, 4 g Dietary Fiber*

Fish and Seafood

As they become more abundant and available, there is even more reason to experiment with fish and seafood, mastering a few special recipes that will become your personal favorites.

Grilled, broiled, stir-fried, poached, or cooked in the microwave, fish responds beautifully as long as it is not overdone. Orange Roughy with Papaya Salsa combines everything that's new in fish cookery. Flounder, steamed in a packet or stuffed and cooked whole, is a treat. Red snapper stars in Chutney Baked Fish; Grilled Swordfish shares space on the barbecue with Salmon with Black Beans.

Shrimp appears here in Hot-and-Sour Shrimp, Shrimp in Peanut Butter Sauce, Shrimp Primavera, and Shrimp Vera Cruz. A seafood combination that could become your signature dish is

Julie's Spanish Paella, a stunning combination of clams, shrimp, and squid.

Sauces are the key to the scallop recipes; Scallop, Onion, and Mushroom Sauté, Scallops in Spicy Tomato Sauce, and Scallops with Green Pesto elevate this shellfish to new heights.

There's even a new take on fish cakes—Tuna Fish Patties—and an update on the Italian classic, Zuppa de Clams.

Sensational Fish

Lemon peel adds zing to the breading in this easy-to-prepare dish, devised by a mother who loves to do cross-stitch, cook, and read when she's not working as a dental assistant.

LESLIE CLERY · NEW MILFORD, CONNECTICUT

Two 5-ounce flounder or other mild white fish fillets
1 medium tomato, sliced
2 scallions (green onions), thinly sliced
2 tablespoons plain dried bread crumbs

2 teaspoons grated Parmesan cheese
2 teaspoons reduced-calorie tub margarine
1 teaspoon grated lemon peel
1 teaspoon fresh lemon juice

1.   Preheat oven to 350°F.

2.   Place fish in nonstick baking pan; divide remaining ingredients equally on top of each fillet. Bake until fish flakes easily when tested with fork, about 15 minutes.

EACH SERVING PROVIDES: ½ Fat; 2 Proteins; 1 Vegetable; 40 Optional Calories

PER SERVING: 198 Calories, 29 g Protein, 5 g Fat, 9 g Carbohydrate, 67 mg Calcium, 237 mg Sodium, 70 mg Cholesterol, 1 g Dietary Fiber

MAKES 2 SERVINGS

Fish in a Packet

Anita is a Weight Watchers lifetime member, and especially appreciates the Program's healthy approach to weight loss. She recommends this tasty fish broiled indoors or barbecued over hot coals on an outdoor grill.

ANITA BEECROFT · FORT ST. JOHN, BRITISH COLUMBIA, CANADA

5 ounces flounder fillet
¼ cup julienned celery
¼ cup julienned carrot
2 tablespoons chopped tomato
2 tablespoons diced onion

1 teaspoon dry white wine
Dash salt
Dash freshly ground black pepper
Fresh dill sprigs
Lemon wedge

1. Preheat oven to 400°F.

2. Spray 12-inch square of foil with non-stick cooking spray. Place fillet in center of foil. Arrange remaining ingredients except lemon wedge on top of fish.

3. Enclose fish in foil; fold edges to seal. Set packet on baking sheet; bake 10 minutes.

4. To serve, carefully remove packet to serving plate and pierce top to release steam. Serve immediately with lemon wedge.

MAKES 1 SERVING

THIS SERVING PROVIDES: *2 Proteins; 1½ Vegetables; 10 Optional Calories*

PER SERVING: *169 Calories, 28 g Protein, 3 g Fat, 7 g Carbohydrate, 52 mg Calcium, 285 mg Sodium, 68 mg Cholesterol, 2 g Dietary Fiber*

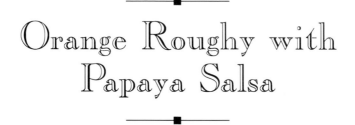

Orange Roughy with Papaya Salsa

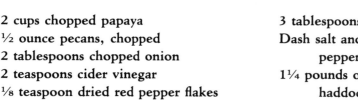

Cathy is a Weight Watchers meeting leader who also juggles homemaking, children, and numerous hobbies. She serves this taste-of-the-tropics fish whenever company comes.

CATHY YOUNGLING · MILL VALLEY, CALIFORNIA

2 cups chopped papaya
½ ounce pecans, chopped
2 tablespoons chopped onion
2 teaspoons cider vinegar
⅛ teaspoon dried red pepper flakes

3 tablespoons all-purpose flour
Dash salt and freshly ground black pepper
1¼ pounds orange roughy or cod, haddock, or flounder fillets

1.   To prepare salsa, in small bowl, combine papaya, pecans, onion, vinegar, and red pepper; set aside.

2.   On sheet of wax paper, combine flour, salt, and black pepper; coat fish on both sides with flour mixture.

3.   Spray large nonstick skillet with nonstick cooking spray; heat 1 minute. Add fish; cook over medium heat until golden brown, about 3 minutes. Carefully turn fillets over and cook until other side is browned and fish flakes easily when tested with fork, about 3 minutes longer.

4.   To serve, place a fillet on each serving plate; top evenly with salsa.

MAKES 4 SERVINGS

———

EACH SERVING PROVIDES: ½ Fat; 2 Proteins; ¼ Bread; ½ Fruit; 5 Optional Calories

———

PER SERVING: 260 Calories, 22 g Protein, 13 g Fat, 12 g Carbohydrate, 22 mg Calcium, 125 mg Sodium, 28 mg Cholesterol, 1 g Dietary Fiber

Stuffed Whole Flounder in a Blanket

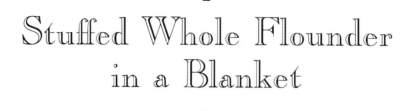

Choose the largest, most perfect sorrel or spinach leaves in the bunch for this recipe; they will enrobe the fish in a mantle of green.

2 cups large whole sorrel or spinach
    leaves, washed and drained
One 3-pound dressed flounder or other
    white fish
¼ teaspoon garlic powder

½ cup sliced leeks
½ cup sliced radishes
1 tablespoon plus 1 teaspoon unsalted
    reduced-calorie tub margarine
¼ cup dry white wine

1. Fill large bowl with boiling water; immerse sorrel leaves just to make them supple.

2. Sprinkle fish cavity evenly with garlic powder. Combine leeks and radishes; stuff into fish. Tie fish with kitchen string to enclose filling.

3. Drain sorrel leaves and pat dry. Starting at tail end, wrap leaves, overlapping each other, around fish to enclose.

4. Fit microwave baking dish with rack; place wrapped fish on rack.

5. In custard cup, microwave margarine on High 45 seconds to melt; stir in wine. Drizzle evenly over fish. Cover with vented plastic wrap. Microwave on High 6 to 10 minutes, turning dish halfway through cooking, until fish flakes easily when tested with a fork.

6. With slotted spatula, transfer fish to serving platter. Pour accumulated pan juices evenly over each serving.

MAKES 4 SERVINGS

_____

EACH SERVING PROVIDES: ½ Fat; 2 Proteins; 1½ Vegetables, 15 Optional Calories

_____

PER SERVING: 174 Calories, 28 g Protein, 4 g Fat, 3 g Carbohydrate, 40 mg Calcium, 127 mg Sodium, 77 mg Cholesterol, 0 g Dietary Fiber

Sweet Soya Fish

These days, instead of reaching for chips, Barbara sips a glass of ice water and grabs her knitting or takes her boys walking. Her healthful dinner menus feature plenty of fish, like this Orient-inspired entree.

BARBARA L. O'HALLORAN · CREEMORE, ONTARIO, CANADA

Two 5-ounce flounder fillets
2 teaspoons reduced-calorie tub
    margarine
2½ cups sliced mushrooms

½ cup diced carrot
2 teaspoons honey
¾ teaspoon low-sodium soy sauce
Dash white pepper

1.   Preheat broiler.

2.   Place fillets on nonstick baking sheet; broil 2 minutes. Carefully turn fillets over and broil until fish flakes easily when tested with fork, 2 to 3 minutes longer.

3.   Meanwhile, in medium skillet, melt margarine; add mushrooms and carrot and cook over medium-high heat, stirring occasionally, until carrot is tender-crisp, about 3 minutes. Stir in remaining ingredients.

4.   To serve, place fish on serving plates and top with equal amounts of mushroom mixture.

MAKES 2 SERVINGS

EACH SERVING PROVIDES: *1 Fat; 2 Proteins; 3 Vegetables; 20 Optional Calories*

PER SERVING: *202 Calories, 29 g Protein, 4 g Fat, 13 g Carbohydrate, 38 mg Calcium, 240 mg Sodium, 68 mg Cholesterol, 2 g Dietary Fiber*

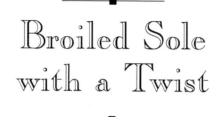

Broiled Sole with a Twist

The Buskes are committed to eating fish several times a week. They love this simple dish because it's ready in just minutes and, by adjusting the onion and garlic, adapts easily to individual tastes.

MICHELA BUSKE · WEST MILFORD, NEW JERSEY

2 tablespoons reduced-calorie
    mayonnaise
1 tablespoon plus 1 teaspoon grated
    Parmesan cheese
1 tablespoon diced onion

1 tablespoon chopped fresh flat-leaf
    parsley
2 garlic cloves, minced
Two 5-ounce sole or flounder fillets

1.   Preheat broiler.

2.   In small bowl, combine all ingredients except fillets.

3.   Place fish on nonstick broiler pan; spread mayonnaise mixture evenly over each fillet. Broil until fish flakes easily when tested with fork, 8 to 10 minutes.

MAKES 2 SERVINGS

EACH SERVING PROVIDES: *1½ Fats; 2 Proteins; 20 Optional Calories*

PER SERVING: *192 Calories, 29 g Protein, 7 g Fat, 3 g Carbohydrate, 80 mg Calcium, 259 mg Sodium, 76 mg Cholesterol, 0 g Dietary Fiber*

Grilled Swordfish

Barbara and her family think this healthful seafood dish tastes more like steak than fish when grilled outdoors.

Barbara Buckton • Cumming, Iowa

2 tablespoons balsamic vinegar
2 tablespoons fresh lemon juice
2 tablespoons fresh lime juice
1 tablespoon plus 1 teaspoon olive oil
4 garlic cloves, minced

1 tablespoon pared minced ginger root
⅛ teaspoon white pepper
Four 5-ounce swordfish, shark, or mahi-mahi fillets
Lemon and lime wedges for garnish

1. In shallow glass casserole, combine vinegar, lemon and lime juice, oil, garlic, ginger root, and pepper. Add fish; turn to coat with marinade. Cover and refrigerate at least 2 hours, turning occasionally.

2. Spray grill rack with nonstick cooking spray. Place grill rack 5 inches from coals. Prepare grill according to manufacturer's directions.

3. Drain and discard any remaining marinade. Grill fish 4 minutes on each side, until cooked through. Transfer to serving platter. Garnish with lemon and lime wedges.

Makes 4 servings

Each Serving Provides: *1 Fat; 2 Proteins*

Per Serving: *211 Calories, 28 g Protein, 9 g Fat, 2 g Carbohydrate, 11 mg Calcium, 129 mg Sodium, 55 mg Cholesterol, 0 g Dietary Fiber*

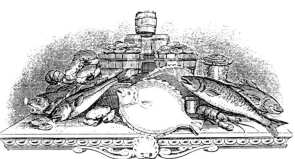

Chutney Baked Fish

Purveen drew on her Indian roots to create this pungent pleaser, which blends the best of Eastern and Western flavors.

PURVEEN CANTEENWALA · SAN JOSE, CALIFORNIA

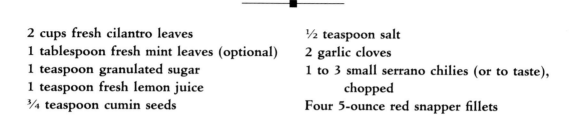

2 cups fresh cilantro leaves
1 tablespoon fresh mint leaves (optional)
1 teaspoon granulated sugar
1 teaspoon fresh lemon juice
¾ teaspoon cumin seeds

½ teaspoon salt
2 garlic cloves
1 to 3 small serrano chilies (or to taste), chopped
Four 5-ounce red snapper fillets

1. Preheat oven to 375°F.

2. To prepare chutney, in blender, combine all ingredients except fish until finely chopped.

3. Spray four 12-inch pieces of foil with nonstick cooking spray. Spread about 2 teaspoons chutney on each side of fish. Arrange 1 fillet, skin side down, in center of each piece of foil.

4. Enclose fish in foil, folding edges to seal. Set packets on baking sheet and bake 10 minutes.

5. To serve, carefully remove packets to individual serving plates and pierce top of each packet to release steam. Serve immediately.

MAKES 4 servings

EACH SERVING PROVIDES: *2 Proteins; ¼ Vegetable; 5 Optional Calories*

PER SERVING: *154 Calories, 30 g Protein, 2 g Fat, 3 g Carbohydrate, 63 mg Calcium, 368 mg Sodium, 52 mg Cholesterol, 0 g Dietary Fiber*

Julie's Spanish Paella

A high school Spanish teacher, Julie loves preparing Spanish and Mexican foods. This is a recipe she learned while living abroad, so it's authentic—right down to Spain's most popular spice, saffron.

JULIE WAGNER · LOCKPORT, NEW YORK

¼ teaspoon salt
6 ounces long-grain white rice
2 tablespoons olive oil
½ cup chopped onion
3 garlic cloves, minced
4 ounces skinless boneless chicken breast, cut into strips
1 dozen littleneck clams, soaked and scrubbed

½ cup chopped tomato
⅛ teaspoon saffron
5 ounces shelled deveined shrimp
1 cup frozen peas
4 ounces cleaned squid, cut into ⅛-inch rings

1.   In large nonstick skillet, bring 2 cups water and the salt to a boil. Stir in rice; reduce heat and simmer, covered, 5 minutes.

2.   In medium nonstick skillet, heat oil; add onion, garlic, and chicken; cook over medium heat until chicken is cooked through, about 5 minutes. Set aside.

3.   Stir clams, tomato, and saffron into rice; cover and cook over medium-low heat, 10 minutes. Add shrimp and peas; cover and cook 3 minutes. Stir in squid and reserved chicken mixture; cook, covered, un-til shrimp are opaque and firm and clams have opened, about 2 to 3 minutes. Discard any unopened clams.

MAKES 4 SERVINGS

EACH SERVING PROVIDES: *1½ Fats; 1¾ Proteins; ½ Vegetable; 2 Breads*

PER SERVING: *374 Calories, 27 g Protein, 9 g Fat, 44 g Carbohydrate, 74 mg Calcium, 280 mg Sodium, 146 mg Cholesterol, 2 g Dietary Fiber*

Salmon with Black Beans

Salmon that's bursting with exciting flavors but won't make you bust your britches. It's great with rice and stir-fried vegetables.

MELINDA BLAU · SAN FRANCISCO, CALIFORNIA

3 tablespoons canned fermented black
    beans, rinsed and drained*
2 tablespoons dry sherry
1 tablespoon plus 1 teaspoon sesame oil
1 tablespoon minced pared ginger root
1 teaspoon granulated sugar

2 garlic cloves, peeled
1 scallion (green onion), sliced
Dash white pepper
Four 4-ounce salmon fillets
Watercress for garnish

1. In blender, combine all ingredients except salmon and watercress until smooth.

2. Place salmon on nonstick baking sheet. Brush both sides of each fillet evenly with black bean mixture. Cover and refrigerate at least 2 hours.

3. Preheat broiler, or prepare outdoor grill. Broil salmon 2 minutes; turn and broil until fish is opaque and flakes easily when tested with fork, 2 to 3 minutes.

4. To serve, place on heated serving platter; garnish with watercress.

Serving suggestion: Stir-fried snow peas or broc-coli, and hot cooked rice make nice accompaniments. Add appropriate Selection Information.

MAKES 4 SERVINGS

EACH SERVING PROVIDES: *1 Fat; 2 Proteins; 10 Optional Calories.*

PER SERVING: *232 Calories, 24 g Protein, 12 g Fat, 4 g Carbohydrate, 30 mg Calcium, 378 mg Sodium, 62 mg Cholesterol, 0 g Dietary Fiber*

Note: Fermented black beans not included; information not available.

* *Fermented black beans are available in some supermarkets and in Asian markets.*

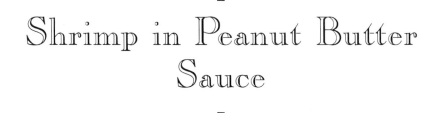

Shrimp in Peanut Butter Sauce

From lifetime member Regina comes this uniquely flavored seafood entree, which has its origins in Ecuador and is ready in under 30 minutes.

REGINA PINZON · CENTRAL ISLIP, NEW YORK

½ cup chopped tomato
½ cup cubed green bell pepper
½ cup sliced onion
½ cup sliced plantain (3 ounces)
⅓ cup plus 1 tablespoon creamy peanut butter
2 tablespoons chopped fresh flat-leaf parsley

1 package Sazon seasoning mix with cilantro and annato*
1 teaspoon granulated sugar
15 ounces shelled deveined medium shrimp

1.   In food processor or blender, combine all ingredients except shrimp with 1½ cups water; puree until smooth. Pour into medium skillet and cook over medium heat, stirring occasionally, until just boiling, about 3 minutes.

2.   Reduce heat to low and cook, stirring occasionally, 10 minutes longer. Add shrimp and cook, stirring occasionally, until shrimp turn pink, about 5 minutes.

MAKES 6 SERVINGS

EACH SERVING PROVIDES: *1 Fat; 2 Proteins; ½ Vegetable; 35 Optional Calories*

PER SERVING: *208 Calories, 20 g Protein, 10 g Fat, 11 g Carbohydrate, 49 mg Calcium, 328 mg Sodium, 108 mg Cholesterol, 1 g Dietary Fiber*

*   *Available in ethnic food sections in supermarkets.*

Shrimp Primavera

Marcelline is a nurse who's concerned about eating right. To cut the fat, she substitutes broth for oil as the base of this pasta-seafood combo.

MARCELLINE EACHUS · SEWELL, NEW JERSEY

1 tablespoon plus 1 teaspoon olive oil
1½ cups broccoli florets
½ cup thinly sliced carrot
1 cup sliced mushrooms
2 garlic cloves, minced
1 cup low-sodium chicken broth

1 tablespoon cornstarch
15 ounces shelled deveined large shrimp
2 cups hot cooked bow-tie pasta
2 tablespoons grated Parmesan cheese
2 tablespoons chopped fresh parsley
¼ teaspoon crushed red pepper flakes

1.   In large skillet, heat oil; add broccoli and carrot. Cook over medium heat, stirring frequently, until carrot is tender-crisp, about 2 minutes. Stir in mushrooms and garlic; cook 1 minute longer.

2.   Whisk in broth and cornstarch; add shrimp and cook, stirring occasionally, until shrimp begin to turn pink, about 3 minutes.

3.   Stir in remaining ingredients; toss to combine.

MAKES 4 SERVINGS

PER SERVING: *306 Calories, 29 g Protein, 8 g Fat, 29 g Carbohydrate, 125 mg Calcium, 236 mg Sodium, 164 mg Cholesterol, 4 g Dietary Fiber*

EACH SERVING PROVIDES: *1 Fat; 1½ Proteins; 1½ Vegetables; 1 Bread; 35 Optional Calories*

Shrimp Vera Cruz

Felicia says that her children are "very proud" of her weight loss of 170 pounds, and they enjoy her "new way" of cooking. She adapted this recipe from her favorite restaurant dish with great success.

FELICIA REED · WALLS, MISSISSIPPI

½ cup cooked long-grain white rice
½ cup drained sliced mushrooms
¼ cup salsa

3 ounces cooked medium shrimp
¾ ounce shredded cheddar cheese
Chopped fresh parsley for garnish

1.   In small bowl, combine all ingredients except cheese and parsley. Transfer to small microwavable dish; sprinkle with cheese.

2.   Microwave on High 1 minute, or until heated through and cheese is melted. Garnish with parsley.

MAKES 1 SERVING

THIS SERVING PROVIDES: *2½ Proteins; 1½ Vegetables; 1 Bread*

PER SERVING: *337 Calories, 27 g Protein, 8 g Fat, 37 g Carbohydrate, 202 mg Calcium, 996 mg Sodium, 188 mg Cholesterol, 0 g Dietary Fiber*

Prawn Curry

Dorothy and her two daughters are all Weight Watchers members who advocate healthy living. This entree is a hit with friends of both generations.

DOROTHY MILLIRON · BATH, NEW YORK

1 tablespoon plus 1 teaspoon vegetable
    oil
½ cup chopped onion
2 garlic cloves, minced
1 teaspoon ground cumin
1 teaspoon ground coriander
1 teaspoon chili powder
½ teaspoon ground turmeric

½ teaspoon ground cinnamon
½ teaspoon freshly ground black pepper
¼ cup tomato paste
1 teaspoon honey
4 cups thoroughly washed and drained
    spinach leaves
15 ounces shelled deveined large shrimp

1.   In large skillet, heat oil; add onion and garlic and cook over medium-high heat, stirring occasionally, until onion is translucent, about 2 minutes. Add spices and pepper; cook 1 minute longer.

2.   Add ⅓ cup water, tomato paste, and honey; cook 1 minute. Add remaining ingredients and cook, stirring occasionally, until shrimp turn pink, about 4 minutes.

MAKES 4 SERVINGS

EACH SERVING PROVIDES: *1 Fat; 1½ Proteins; 2¾ Vegetables; 5 Optional Calories*

PER SERVING: *200 Calories, 24 g Protein, 7 g Fat, 11 g Carbohydrate, 136 mg Calcium, 339 mg Sodium, 162 mg Cholesterol, 3 g Dietary Fiber*

Zuppa de Clams

Wendy reinterpreted this zesty soup, starting from a dish her parents discovered at a restaurant. Now they enjoy the flavors of Italy without leaving home.

WENDY OSTENDORF · NEWARK, DELAWARE

2 dozen medium littleneck clams
1 tablespoon extra-virgin olive oil
2 garlic cloves, minced
3 cups canned crushed tomatoes

2 tablespoons dry white wine
½ teaspoon dried basil
¼ teaspoon freshly ground black pepper

1. To clean clams, place in large bowl and cover with cold water; let soak 2 hours.

2. In large saucepan, heat oil; add garlic. Cook over medium heat 1 minute. Stir in remaining ingredients; reduce heat and simmer, stirring occasionally, 20 minutes.

3. In large colander or strainer, drain clams thoroughly; carefully add to tomato sauce. Cover and cook over high heat until clams open, 3 to 5 minutes. Discard any unopened clams.

4. To serve, divide clams and sauce evenly between 2 serving bowls; serve immediately.

Serving suggestion: Spoon over hot cooked linguine or serve with crusty Italian bread. Add appropriate Selection Information.

MAKES 2 SERVINGS

EACH SERVING PROVIDES: *1½ Fats; 1 Protein; 3 Vegetables; 15 Optional Calories*

PER SERVING: *232 Calories, 18 g Protein, 9 g Fat, 20 g Carbohydrate, 162 mg Calcium, 652 mg Sodium, 39 mg Cholesterol, 3 g Dietary Fiber*

Scallops with Green Pesto

A perfect family meal that can be made ahead, divided, and frozen for reheating. Jeanne suggests shrimp or crayfish if you can't find fresh scallops.

JEANNE DOWNS · METAIRIE, LOUISIANA

1 cup chopped scallions (green onions)
1 cup fresh flat-leaf parsley
1 cup fresh basil leaves
¼ cup grated Parmesan cheese
2 garlic cloves, peeled
1 tablespoon plus 2 teaspoons olive oil
1 pound, 2 ounces bay scallops

1 packet low-sodium instant chicken broth mix
2 ounces toasted slivered almonds
1 teaspoon grated lemon peel
¼ teaspoon salt
¼ teaspoon white pepper
4½ cups hot cooked tricolor fusilli pasta

1. To prepare pesto, in blender, combine scallions, parsley, basil, cheese, garlic, and oil until just blended; set aside.

2. In large skillet, bring 1 cup water to a boil; add scallops. Reduce heat to medium and cook, stirring occasionally, until scallops just turn opaque, about 3 minutes.

3. With slotted spoon, transfer scallops to large serving bowl; reserve poaching liquid. Add remaining ingredients, pesto, and ½ cup reserved liquid. Toss well to combine. Serve immediately.

MAKES 6 SERVINGS

EACH SERVING PROVIDES: *1½ Fats; 1½ Proteins; 1½ Breads; ½ Vegetable; 30 Optional Calories*

PER SERVING: *294 Calories, 22 g Protein, 11 g Fat, 28 g Carbohydrate, 146 mg Calcium, 306 mg Sodium, 31 mg Cholesterol, 2 g Dietary Fiber*

Scallop, Onion, and Mushroom Sauté

"I never thought I could eat so well and still lose weight," writes Patricia, a busy wife and mother. Her skillet supper is typical of the healthful fare that satisfies her entire family without leading her astray.

PATRICIA PIZAPPI · OAKLAND, NEW JERSEY

2 teaspoons reduced-calorie tub margarine
2 cups sliced mushrooms
1 cup chopped onion
1 garlic clove, minced
10 ounces bay scallops

1 tablespoon fresh lemon juice
½ teaspoon dried thyme
½ teaspoon lemon pepper
1 cup cooked long-grain white rice
Chopped parsley for garnish (optional)

1. In large nonstick skillet, melt margarine; add mushrooms, onion, and garlic. Cook over medium-high heat, stirring occasionally, until onion is translucent, about 3 minutes.

2. Stir in remaining ingredients except rice and parsley and cook, stirring occasionally, until scallops are opaque, about 3 to 4 minutes.

3. Spoon rice onto heated platter; top with scallop mixture. Garnish with parsley, if desired.

MAKES 2 SERVINGS

EACH SERVING PROVIDES: *½ Fat; 2 Proteins; 1½ Vegetables; 1 Bread*

PER SERVING: *328 Calories, 29 g Protein, 4 g Fat, 44 g Carbohydrate, 75 mg Calcium, 473 mg Sodium, 47 mg Cholesterol, 3 g Dietary Fiber*

Scallops in Spicy Tomato Sauce

A freelance specialist in public relations and an author and journalist, Vicki is also a gourmet cook specializing in Italian and other ethnic cuisines.

VICKI GREENLEAF · LOS ANGELES, CALIFORNIA

2 teaspoons olive oil
½ cup chopped onion
½ cup chopped green bell pepper
2 garlic cloves, minced
2 cups chopped tomatoes
¼ cup tomato paste

½ teaspoon dried basil
¼ teaspoon dried thyme
¼ teaspoon crushed red pepper flakes
⅛ teaspoon dried oregano
10 ounces bay scallops
2 cups cooked long-grain white rice

1. In medium skillet, heat oil; add onion, green pepper, and garlic. Cook over medium-high heat, stirring occasionally, until onion is translucent, 3 minutes.

2. Stir in remaining ingredients except scallops and rice. Reduce heat to medium-low; cook 5 minutes. Add scallops and cook, stirring occasionally, until scallops are opaque, 3 to 4 minutes.

3. To serve, place rice on heated platter; spoon scallop mixture on top.

MAKES 2 SERVINGS

EACH SERVING PROVIDES: *1 Fat; 2 Proteins; 4 Vegetables; 2 Breads*

PER SERVING: *523 Calories, 33 g Protein, 7 g Fat, 82 g Carbohydrate, 106 mg Calcium, 510 mg Sodium, 47 mg Cholesterol, 5 g Dietary Fiber*

Tuna Fish Patties

If you've run short of innovative ways to prepare tuna, try this delicious recipe—it's a knockout!

FELICIA REED · WALLS, MISSISSIPPI

1 large egg
2 ounces drained canned tuna, flaked
¼ cup diced tomato
¼ cup chopped mushroom
2 tablespoons sliced scallion (green onion)

1 tablespoon plus 1 teaspoon all-purpose flour
½ teaspoon dried parsley flakes
Dash freshly ground black pepper

1.   In medium bowl, beat egg lightly; add remaining ingredients, mixing until thoroughly combined. (Add 1 to 2 teaspoons water if mixture seems dry.) Shape into 2 patties.

2.   Spray medium nonstick skillet with nonstick cooking spray. Heat skillet over medium-high heat; add patties. Cook until golden brown, about 2 minutes. Turn and cook until other side is golden brown, about 2 minutes longer.

MAKES 1 SERVING

THIS SERVING PROVIDES: *2 Proteins; 1¼ Vegetables; 40 Optional Calories*

PER SERVING: *212 Calories, 25 g Protein, 7 g Fat, 12 g Carbohydrate, 46 mg Calcium, 272 mg Sodium, 236 mg Cholesterol, 1 g Dietary Fiber*

Maryland Crab Cakes

Fresh Maryland blue crabs are plentiful in the summer months, but you'll always find frozen or pasteurized crabmeat at the grocery store, so enjoy this dish year-round.

CAROL ANSARI · KNOXVILLE, TENNESSEE

14 ounces cooked crabmeat
12 saltine crackers, crushed
1 large egg, lightly beaten
¼ cup chopped onion
2 tablespoons plus 2 teaspoons reduced-
    calorie mayonnaise

2 tablespoons fresh lemon juice
1 tablespoon dried parsley
1 teaspoon Worcestershire sauce
½ teaspoon hot pepper sauce, or to taste
¼ cup cornmeal

1. In large bowl, combine all ingredients except cornmeal until thoroughly blended. Shape mixture into 4 patties.

2. Place cornmeal on medium plate; coat both sides of each patty with cornmeal.

3. Spray large nonstick skillet with nonstick cooking spray. Heat skillet over medium-high heat 1 minute; place cakes in skillet and cook until golden brown, about 3 minutes. Turn over and cook until other side is golden, about 3 minutes longer.

MAKES 4 SERVINGS

EACH SERVING PROVIDES: *1 Fat; 2 Proteins; 1 Bread*

PER SERVING: *130 Calories, 5 g Protein, 5 g Fat, 15 g Carbohydrate, 18 mg Calcium, 214 mg Sodium, 64 mg Cholesterol, 1 g Dietary Fiber*

Grilled Crab Sandwich

Joan and her husband love dining out, so it's no surprise that she adapted a favorite restaurant dish to fit her new lifestyle. The result deserves four stars.

JOAN KAIN · CHEHALIS, WASHINGTON

3 ounces cooked crabmeat
1 tablespoon diced celery
1 tablespoon diced onion
2 teaspoons reduced-calorie mayonnaise
1 teaspoon fresh lemon juice

¼ teaspoon hot pepper sauce
2 slices reduced-calorie whole-wheat bread
¾ ounce shredded cheddar cheese

1. Preheat broiler.

2. In small bowl, combine all ingredients except bread and cheese.

3. Spread mixture evenly on each slice of bread. Place on broiler pan; sprinkle evenly with cheese. Broil until cheese is bubbly, about 2 minutes.

MAKES 1 SERVING

THIS SERVING PROVIDES: *1 Fat; 2½ Proteins; ¼ Vegetable; 1 Bread*

PER SERVING: *286 Calories, 27 g Protein, 12 g Fat, 21 g Carbohydrate, 287 mg Calcium, 652 mg Sodium, 111 mg Cholesterol, 3 g Dietary Fiber*

Poultry

Once upon a time, chicken was Sunday dinner and turkey appeared once a year on the Thanksgiving table. Today, chicken and turkey are among nutrition-conscious diners' first choices, turning up often and in many guises.

Poultry producers are increasingly inventive in presenting their products in new forms: as sausages, as deli-style slices of "ham" and other cold cuts, and ground for recipes usually calling for beef or pork.

The most economical way to buy chicken is whole, since you provide the labor to bone and cut up the parts. Watch your supermarket for sales and stock up; package wing tips, backs, and giblets for stock; weigh and freeze drumsticks and thighs and bone breasts for cutlets. Then you'll always have the main ingredient on hand for the recipes in this chapter.

Many Chinese and Japanese favorites have been adapted using these new poultry items. You'll want to try Baked Egg Rolls,

Chicken Lo Mein, Chicken Teriyaki, and Spicy Ginger-Garlic Chicken.

The chilies and spices of the Southwest are exactly right to elevate mild poultry to sizzling temperatures. You'll find Fajitas, Hot Texas Chili Soup, and a Tex-Mex Ranch Casserole that's ideal for a crowd.

For the family, a nice midweek meal could center on Baked Buttermilk Chicken, Italian Meat Loaf, Quick and Easy Chicken "Spaghetti," Southern Hash, or Turkey Croquettes.

Chicken Lo Mein

Pat has lost 50 pounds on the Weight Watchers Program. She and her family love Chinese food, so she developed her own version of a favorite lo mein.

PATRICIA STEWART · MUSCATINE, IOWA

2 teaspoons peanut oil
2 teaspoons minced pared ginger root
1 garlic clove, minced
5 ounces boneless skinless chicken breast, cut into ½-inch strips
½ cup julienned carrot
1 cup drained bean sprouts
1 cup chopped bok choy (Chinese cabbage)
½ cup sliced mushrooms
4 medium scallions (green onions), julienned
½ cup low-sodium chicken broth
1 tablespoon low-sodium soy sauce
2 cups cooked Chinese egg noodles or thin spaghetti

1.   In large nonstick skillet, heat oil; add ginger root and garlic; cook over medium heat 1 minute. Add chicken and carrot; cook over medium-high heat, stirring occasionally, until chicken is lightly browned, about 2 minutes.

2. Add remaining ingredients except noodles; cook, stirring constantly, until carrot is tender-crisp, about 3 minutes. Stir in noodles and cook until heated through, about 1 minute.

MAKES 2 SERVINGS

EACH SERVING PROVIDES: *1 Fat; 2 Proteins; 3¼ Vegetables; 2 Breads; 10 Optional Calories*

PER SERVING: *379 Calories, 27 g Protein, 8 g Fat, 48 g Carbohydrate, 96 mg Calcium, 436 mg Sodium, 94 mg Cholesterol, 5 g Dietary Fiber*

Chicken Teriyaki

Cynthia prepares this when company's coming. Delicious with steamed vegetables and wild rice, this crowd-pleaser couldn't be easier to fix.

CYNTHIA THOMSON · BAYTOWN, TEXAS

Four 4-ounce skinless boneless chicken breasts
¼ cup low-sodium teriyaki sauce

1 tablespoon vegetable oil
4 garlic cloves, pressed
1 teaspoon minced pared ginger root

1. Place chicken in nonstick baking pan. In 1-cup glass measure, combine remaining ingredients; pour over chicken. Cover and refrigerate at least 1 hour.

2. Preheat oven to 350°F.

3. Uncover chicken; bake 15 minutes; turn and bake 10 to 15 minutes longer, until cooked through.

MAKES 4 SERVINGS

EACH SERVING PROVIDES: *¾ Fat; 3 Proteins, 20 Optional Calories*

PER SERVING: *175 Calories, 27 g Protein, 5 g Fat, 4 g Carbohydrate, 23 mg Calcium, 374 mg Sodium, 66 mg Cholesterol, 0 g Dietary Fiber*

Baked Egg Rolls

Ruth's weight has been a lifelong struggle, but today this church secretary has a new attitude and a new approach to cooking—like baking, instead of frying, this popular Chinese starter.

RUTH CAWOOD · FORT WALTON BEACH, FLORIDA

1¼ pounds ground chicken
2 cups grated carrots
1½ cups drained bean sprouts
4 ounces drained sliced water chestnuts
¼ cup chopped green bell pepper
¼ cup sliced scallions (green onions)
3 garlic cloves, crushed

1½ teaspoons reduced-sodium soy sauce
1 teaspoon sesame oil
1 teaspoon firmly packed brown sugar
1 tablespoon plus 1 teaspoon cornstarch
¼ teaspoon ground red pepper
16 wonton skins (3-inch squares)

1. In large nonstick skillet or wok, cook chicken over medium-high heat until crumbly, 5 minutes. Drain and set aside.

2. To same skillet, add carrots, bean sprouts, water chestnuts, green pepper, scallions, and garlic. Cook over medium heat, 3 minutes; return chicken to skillet.

3. In small bowl, combine 1 tablespoon water, the soy sauce, sesame oil, and brown sugar; whisk in cornstarch and pepper. Pour into chicken mixture; toss well. Remove from heat and set aside.

4. Preheat oven to 450°F.

5. Place 1 wonton skin on work surface; spoon ¼ cup chicken mixture on bottom third of wonton skin; fold both sides toward center and roll tightly. Place seam-side down on nonstick baking sheet; repeat with remaining skins and filling. (Rolls can be frozen at this point.) Bake until lightly browned, 15 minutes.

MAKES 8 SERVINGS

EACH SERVING (2 ROLLS) PROVIDES: *2 Proteins; 1 Vegetable; ¾ Bread; 60 Optional Calories*

PER SERVING: *182 Calories, 15 g Protein, 7 g Fat, 15 g Carbohydrate, 36 mg Calcium, 121 mg Sodium, 59 mg Cholesterol, 1 g Dietary Fiber*

Chinese Chicken Dinner

Like most of us, Jill hates bland diet foods. Her Oriental entree is anything but boring.

JILL HUPS · ARVADA, COLORADO

2 tablespoons cornstarch
2 tablespoons low-sodium soy sauce
1 packet low-sodium instant chicken broth mix
15 ounces skinless boneless chicken breasts, cut into ½-inch strips
1½ cups julienned carrots
1 cup sliced onion

2 cups thoroughly washed and drained spinach leaves, shredded
2 cups drained bean sprouts
1 cup sliced mushrooms
3 garlic cloves, minced
2 teaspoons minced pared ginger root
3 cups cooked long-grain white rice

1. In small bowl, combine cornstarch, soy sauce, broth mix, and 1¼ cups water until blended; set aside.

2. Spray large nonstick skillet with nonstick cooking spray; add chicken. Cook over medium-high heat, stirring frequently, until lightly browned, about 3 minutes. Add carrots and onion; cook, stirring frequently, 3 minutes longer. Add remaining ingredients except rice and cornstarch mixture; cook over high heat, stirring constantly, until onion is translucent, about 2 minutes. Pour in cornstarch mixture; cook until slightly thickened, about 1 minute.

3. To serve, place chicken mixture on large serving platter; surround with rice.

Serving suggestion: Frozen Chinese vegetables, lightly steamed, can be served alongside; add 1 Vegetable Selection for each ½ cup.

MAKES 6 SERVINGS

EACH SERVING PROVIDES: *2 Proteins; 2½ Vegetables; 1 Bread; 10 Optional Calories*

PER SERVING: *269 Calories, 22 g Protein, 2 g Fat, 41 g Carbohydrate, 59 mg Calcium, 277 mg Sodium, 41 mg Cholesterol, 3 g Dietary Fiber*

Chicken with Peanut Dipping Sauce

Having three babies in five years packed the pounds on this part-time lawyer, but she's learning how to take it off with Weight Watchers and sensible recipes like this one.

NANCY SPRITZ · BALTIMORE, MARYLAND

3 ounces boneless skinless chicken breast
3 tablespoons plain nonfat yogurt
2 teaspoons creamy peanut butter
½ teaspoon low-sodium soy sauce
½ teaspoon rice wine vinegar

⅛ teaspoon garlic powder
Dash ground red pepper
3 cherry tomatoes
¼ cup snow peas, blanched

1. Preheat broiler. Place chicken in small broiler pan and broil 4 inches from heat until lightly browned, about 3 minutes. Turn and broil until other side is lightly browned and chicken is cooked through, about 2 minutes longer; set aside to cool. Cut into ½-inch diagonal strips.

2. To prepare sauce, in small bowl, whisk together remaining ingredients, except tomatoes and snow peas, and 1 teaspoon water. Pour into small serving dish.

3. To serve, fan chicken and snow peas alternately on serving plate. Add cherry tomatoes and sauce.

MAKES 1 SERVING

THIS SERVING PROVIDES: *¼ Milk; 2 Fats; 2 Proteins; 1 Vegetable*

PER SERVING: *208 Calories, 27 g Protein, 7 g Fat, 10 g Carbohydrate, 116 mg Calcium, 243 mg Sodium, 50 mg Cholesterol, 2 g Dietary Fiber*

Sweet-and-Sour Chicken

Jane is the mother of two and a second-grade teacher. When she took this dish to school for lunch, everyone clamored for the recipe because it looks, smells, and tastes so good.

JANE POTTS · OLNEY, ILLINOIS

2 tablespoons vegetable oil
15 ounces skinless boneless chicken
    breasts, cut into 1-inch cubes
1 cup grated carrots
½ cup red bell pepper strips
½ cup green bell pepper strips
2 garlic cloves, minced
1 cup drained pineapple chunks (reserve
    ¼ cup juice)

3 tablespoons white vinegar
2 tablespoons low-sodium soy sauce
1 tablespoon firmly packed brown sugar
1 tablespoon cornstarch
1 teaspoon ground ginger
2 cups cooked long-grain white rice

1.   In large skillet, heat oil; add chicken. Cook over medium-high heat, stirring occasionally, until lightly browned, about 3 minutes. Add carrots, peppers, and garlic; cook, stirring frequently, 2 minutes longer.

2.   In small bowl, combine reserved pineapple juice, 2 tablespoons water, and remaining ingredients except rice. Pour over chicken mixture and stir in pineapple chunks. Cook until just boiling, about 2 minutes.

3.   To serve, place rice on heated serving platter; spoon chicken on top.

MAKES 4 SERVINGS

EACH SERVING PROVIDES: *1½ Fats; 3 Proteins; 1 Vegetable; 1 Bread; ½ Fruit; 25 Optional Calories*

PER SERVING: *396 Calories, 29 g Protein, 9 g Fat, 50 g Carbohydrate, 49 mg Calcium, 384 mg Sodium, 62 mg Cholesterol, 2 g Dietary Fiber*

Spicy Ginger~Garlic Chicken

Purveen happily experiments with ethnic foods and spices from around the world. She loves to cook, read, and play the piano.

PURVEEN CANTEENWALA · SAN JOSE, CALIFORNIA

1 tablespoon ketchup

1 tablespoon red wine vinegar

2 teaspoons vegetable oil

2 garlic cloves, minced

2 teaspoons minced pared ginger root

½ teaspoon ground red pepper

¼ teaspoon ground cinnamon

¼ teaspoon ground cardamom

⅛ teaspoon freshly ground black pepper

2¼ pounds chicken parts, skinned

1.   Preheat oven to 350°F.

2.   In small bowl, combine all ingredients except chicken parts. Place chicken in 11-by-7-inch baking pan; brush both sides with ketchup mixture. Bake, turning once, until tender and cooked through, 40 to 50 minutes.

MAKES 4 SERVINGS

EACH SERVING PROVIDES: *½ Fat; 3 Proteins; 5 Optional Calories*

PER SERVING: *191 Calories, 25 g Protein, 9 g Fat, 2 g Carbohydrate, 20 mg Calcium, 119 mg Sodium, 76 mg Cholesterol, 0 g Dietary Fiber*

Baked Buttermilk Chicken

A terrific make-ahead meal that's ready when you are. Martha has been using this recipe since she was in grade school.

MARTHA ANN DORRELL · PORTLAND, OREGON

1 cup low-fat (1.5%) buttermilk
½ cup chopped onion
2 teaspoons paprika
1 teaspoon dried tarragon

1 teaspoon garlic powder
½ teaspoon freshly ground black pepper
1 pound, 3 ounces chicken parts, skin removed

1.   Preheat oven to 325°F.

2.   In 13-by-9-inch glass baking dish, combine all ingredients except chicken until blended. Add chicken and turn each piece several times to coat. Bake, turning chicken twice, until cooked through, about 45 minutes.

MAKES 6 SERVINGS

EACH SERVING PROVIDES: *2½ Proteins; 20 Optional Calories*

PER SERVING: *161 Calories, 22 g Protein, 6 g Fat, 4 g Carbohydrate, 66 mg Calcium, 105 mg Sodium, 65 mg Cholesterol, 0 g Dietary Fiber*

Chicken in Wine

Joan is a quilter and homemaker who loves entertaining. This elegant, rich-tasting entree lends itself to special gatherings with good friends.

JOAN RUDMAN · PACIFIC PALISADES, CALIFORNIA

2¼ pounds chicken parts, skinned
1 cup thinly sliced onion
2 garlic cloves, minced
2 cups sliced mushrooms
2 medium tomatoes, cored and cut into 8 pieces

⅓ cup dry white wine
2 tablespoons balsamic vinegar
1 teaspoon dried thyme, crumbled
½ teaspoon salt
½ teaspoon freshly ground black pepper

1.   Spray large nonstick skillet with nonstick cooking spray; add chicken parts and cook over medium heat until chicken is browned on both sides, about 6 to 8 minutes. Transfer chicken to 13-by-9-inch baking dish; set aside.

2.   Preheat oven to 350°F.

3.   Place onion and garlic in same skillet and cook, stirring occasionally, until onion is translucent, about 2 minutes. Add mushrooms; cook 1 minute longer. Stir in remaining ingredients and cook 1 minute. Pour vegetable mixture evenly over chicken.

4.   Cover with aluminum foil and bake 25 minutes; remove foil and bake 15 minutes longer.

MAKES 4 SERVINGS

EACH SERVING PROVIDES: *3 Proteins; 1¼ Vegetables; 10 Optional Calories*

PER SERVING: *222 Calories, 27 g Protein, 7 g Fat, 10 g Carbohydrate, 41 mg Calcium, 358 mg Sodium, 76 mg Cholesterol, 2 g Dietary Fiber*

Stuffed Chicken Breast

Gladys is a lifetime member of Weight Watchers who loves this meal because it practically prepares itself!

GLADYS SUTYAK · BECKLEY, WEST VIRGINIA

½ cup thoroughly washed and drained
    spinach leaves
¼ cup minced onion
¼ cup diced mushrooms
5 ounces boneless skinless chicken
    breast, pounded thin
⅛ teaspoon garlic powder

⅛ teaspoon paprika
Dash salt
Dash freshly ground black pepper
1 tablespoon skim milk
1 tablespoon plus 1 teaspoon seasoned
    dried bread crumbs

1. Preheat oven to 350°F.

2. In small skillet, combine spinach, onion, mushrooms, and 1 teaspoon water. Cover and cook over medium heat until onion is tender, about 2 minutes.

3. Sprinkle chicken breast with garlic powder, paprika, salt, and pepper. Spread cooked vegetables over chicken; roll up tightly to enclose filling.

4. Sprinkle milk over chicken; sprinkle with bread crumbs and pat with fingers to cover. Place chicken in small nonstick baking pan. Bake until chicken is golden brown and cooked through, about 15 to 20 minutes.

5. To serve, slice chicken into 4 equal pieces; arrange 2 pieces on each serving plate.

MAKES 2 SERVINGS

EACH SERVING PROVIDES: *2 Proteins; 1 Vegetable; 25 Optional Calories*

PER SERVING: *112 Calories, 18 g Protein, 1 g Fat, 7 g Carbohydrate, 41 mg Calcium, 253 mg Sodium, 41 mg Cholesterol, 1 g Dietary Fiber*

Chicken "Ratatourie"

Eating sensibly can be tough for a newlywed juggling the demands of law school, but Jayne draws on her background in restaurant management to come up with recipes like this one.

JAYNE SHEA · HARRISBURG, PENNSYLVANIA

8 ounces skinless boneless chicken breast, cut into 1-inch pieces
½ cup chopped onion
½ cup chopped green bell pepper
½ cup chopped zucchini
½ cup sliced mushrooms

2 garlic cloves, minced
¼ teaspoon freshly ground black pepper
2 cups cooked spaghetti squash
2 cups tomato sauce
3 cups hot cooked noodles
¼ cup grated Romano cheese

1. Spray large nonstick skillet with nonstick cooking spray; add chicken. Cook, stirring occasionally, 2 minutes. Add onion and bell pepper; cook, stirring frequently, 2 minutes longer; add zucchini, mushrooms, garlic, and pepper, and cook 1 minute.

2. Add remaining ingredients, except noodles and cheese; cook over medium heat, stirring occasionally, 10 minutes.

3. To serve, place noodles on heated serving platter. Pour chicken mixture over noodles; serve immediately. Pass cheese on the side.

MAKES 4 SERVINGS

EACH SERVING PROVIDES: *1½ Proteins; 4 Vegetables; 1½ Breads; 30 Optional Calories*

PER SERVING: *320 Calories, 23 g Protein, 5 g Fat, 48 g Carbohydrate, 119 mg Calcium, 859 mg Sodium, 78 mg Cholesterol, 5 g Dietary Fiber*

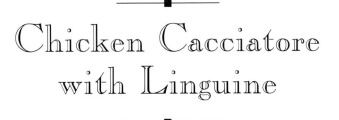

Chicken Cacciatore with Linguine

Joseph is an avid cook who takes pride in creating low-calorie gourmet meals. Here's his terrific take on an Italian classic.

JOSEPH DiCARLO · LOCKPORT, NEW YORK

2 teaspoons olive oil
5 ounces skinless boneless chicken
    breast, cut into ½-inch strips
½ cup chopped onion
1 garlic clove, minced
½ cup chopped red bell pepper

½ cup sliced mushrooms
1 tablespoon red wine vinegar
1 cup canned crushed tomatoes
Dash freshly ground black pepper
1½ cups hot cooked linguine
2 teaspoons grated Parmesan cheese

1. In large nonstick skillet, heat oil; add chicken, onion, and garlic. Cook over medium-high heat, stirring occasionally, until onion is translucent, about 3 minutes. Add bell pepper; cook 1 minute. Add mushrooms and vinegar; cook 1 minute longer. Stir in tomatoes and pepper; reduce heat to low; simmer 5 minutes.

2. To serve, place linguine on heated serving platter; spoon chicken mixture over top. Sprinkle with cheese.

MAKES 2 SERVINGS

EACH SERVING PROVIDES: *1 Fat; 2 Proteins; 2½ Vegetables; 1½ Breads; 10 Optional Calories*

PER SERVING: *322 Calories, 24 g Protein, 7 g Fat, 41 g Carbohydrate, 57 mg Calcium, 89 mg Sodium, 42 mg Cholesterol, 4 g Dietary Fiber*

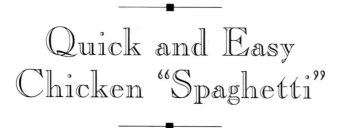

Quick and Easy Chicken "Spaghetti"

That blur in the distance is Brenda, a busy teacher (high school by day, adult computer courses by night) and active church member. She's a fan of nutritious meals that adapt to crazy scheduling. This fits the bill, and makes great use of leftovers.

BRENDA SUE DeHART · PITKIN, LOUISIANA

½ cup thinly sliced celery
¼ cup thinly sliced onion
¼ cup chopped green bell pepper
4 ounces sliced cooked chicken, cut into
    ¼-inch strips

4 cups hot cooked spaghetti squash
3 ounces shredded cheddar cheese

1.   Spray medium nonstick skillet with nonstick cooking spray; add celery, onion, and bell pepper. Cook over medium-high heat, stirring occasionally, until onion is translucent, about 2 minutes. Stir in chicken; cook until heated through, about 1 minute longer.

2.   To serve, place squash on heated serving platter. Spoon chicken mixture over top; sprinkle with cheese. Serve immediately.

MAKES 4 SERVINGS

EACH SERVING PROVIDES: *2 Proteins; 2½ Vegetables*

PER SERVING: *194 Calories, 15 g Protein, 10 g Fat, 12 g Carbohydrate, 199 mg Calcium, 198 mg Sodium, 48 mg Cholesterol, 12 g Dietary Fiber*

Fajitas

A teacher/coordinator and mother of two, Barbara is losing weight alongside her husband. Their love of ethnic cuisine led her to experiment with this Mexican standard, which is well suited to picnics and family camping trips.

BARBARA BUCKTON · CUMMING, IOWA

15 ounces skinless boneless chicken or lean pork, cut into ¼-inch strips
2 tablespoons orange juice
2 tablespoons red wine vinegar
2 garlic cloves, minced
1 teaspoon dried oregano, crumbled
¼ teaspoon ground cumin
¼ teaspoon seasoned salt
Dash hot red pepper sauce

1 tablespoon plus 1 teaspoon olive oil
1 medium onion, halved and thinly sliced
1 medium red or green bell pepper, cut into ½-inch strips
Four 6-inch flour tortillas
Diced tomatoes, sliced scallions (green onions), and shredded lettuce for garnish (optional)

1. In large bowl, combine chicken, orange juice, vinegar, garlic, oregano, cumin, seasoned salt, and pepper sauce. Let marinate for 10 minutes.

2. In large nonstick skillet, heat oil. Add onion, pepper, and chicken mixture. Cook 3 to 5 minutes, stirring frequently, until chicken is cooked through.

3. To serve, spoon equal amounts of chicken and onion-pepper mixture onto each tortilla; roll to enclose filling. Garnish with tomatoes, scallions, and lettuce, if desired.

MAKES 4 SERVINGS

EACH SERVING PROVIDES: *1 Fat; 3 Proteins; ¾ Vegetable; 1 Bread (garnishes not included)*

PER SERVING: *260 Calories, 25 g Protein, 10 g Fat, 17 g Carbohydrate, 71 mg Calcium, 378 mg Sodium, 74 mg Cholesterol, 1 g Dietary Fiber*

Dutch Favorite Chicken Salad

Six months in the Netherlands as a 4-H exchange member made Sally a fan of this simple salad. She serves it during the Kindergarten International Feast each spring in the small country school where she teaches.

SALLY PARKER · IDALIN, COLORADO

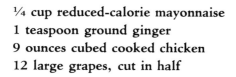

¼ cup reduced-calorie mayonnaise
1 teaspoon ground ginger
9 ounces cubed cooked chicken
12 large grapes, cut in half

1 medium banana, sliced
1 small orange, peeled and sectioned
1 ounce slivered almonds
2 cups shredded romaine lettuce

1. In small bowl, combine mayonnaise and ginger. In large bowl, combine remaining ingredients except lettuce. Add mayonnaise mixture; toss gently to combine.

2. To serve, arrange lettuce on serving platter; spoon chicken salad on top.

MAKES 4 SERVINGS

EACH SERVING PROVIDES: *2 Fats; 2½ Proteins; 1 Vegetable; 1 Fruit*

PER SERVING: *264 Calories, 21 g Protein, 13 g Fat, 17 g Carbohydrate, 56 mg Calcium, 140 mg Sodium, 62 mg Cholesterol, 3 g Dietary Fiber*

Curried Chicken Salad Sandwich

Julie and her parents have lost a whopping 160 pounds together. The Berrys serve this recipe as a salad or sandwich, and none of their friends ever suspects they're munching a low-calorie meal.

JULIE BERRY · WOODLAND HILLS, CALIFORNIA

2 tablespoons reduced-calorie
   mayonnaise
½ teaspoon curry powder
4 ounces cubed cooked chicken
½ cup drained canned crushed pineapple

2 tablespoons raisins
4 slices reduced-calorie whole-wheat
   bread
½ cup shredded iceberg or romaine
   lettuce

In medium bowl, combine mayonnaise and curry powder until blended. Add remaining ingredients except bread and lettuce; stir to combine. Layer bread evenly with chicken and lettuce, making 2 sandwiches.

MAKES 2 SERVINGS

EACH SERVING PROVIDES: *1½ Fats; 2 Proteins; ½ Vegetable; 1 Bread; 1 Fruit*

PER SERVING: *297 Calories, 21 g Protein, 9 g Fat, 37 g Carbohydrate, 74 mg Calcium, 323 mg Sodium, 55 mg Cholesterol, 4 g Dietary Fiber*

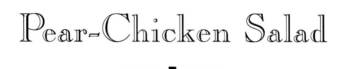

Pear-Chicken Salad

Tangy goat cheese adds a lively touch to this easy salad. For a festive summer luncheon, spoon evenly into hollowed-out yellow bell peppers or vine-ripened beefsteak tomatoes.

1 tablespoon plus 1 teaspoon reduced-
    calorie mayonnaise
1 tablespoon plus 1 teaspoon chutney
1 tablespoon Dijon mustard
1 teaspoon white wine vinegar
½ teaspoon curry powder
¼ teaspoon salt

⅛ teaspoon ground white pepper
6 ounces cubed cooked chicken
1½ ounces crumbled goat cheese
2 small pears, cored and chopped
½ cup chopped red onion
½ cup chopped celery

1.   To prepare dressing, in small bowl, combine mayonnaise, chutney, mustard, vinegar, curry powder, salt, and pepper.

2.   In medium bowl, combine chicken, goat cheese, pears, onion, and celery. Add dressing; toss to mix well.

MAKES 4 SERVINGS

EACH SERVING PROVIDES: *½ Fat; 2 Proteins; ½ Vegetable; ½ Fruit; 10 Optional Calories*

PER SERVING: *208 Calories, 15 g Protein, 8 g Fat, 19 g Carbohydrate, 392 mg Sodium, 48 mg Cholesterol, 3 g Dietary Fiber*

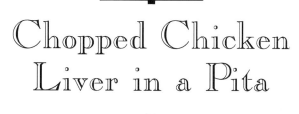

Chopped Chicken Liver in a Pita

Robin is a textile designer who loves food so much she sometimes munches things that coordinate with colors on her palette. She invented this brown-bag lunch to satisfy a yen for the rich taste of the deli classic.

ROBIN PADIAL · WALDWICK, NEW JERSEY

1 ounce broiled chicken liver
1 hard-cooked large egg
2 teaspoons reduced-calorie mayonnaise
1 teaspoon minced onion

Dash salt
Dash freshly ground black pepper
1 small pita (1 ounce), split
¼ cup torn lettuce leaves

1.   Place all ingredients except pita and lettuce in mini food processor; process until smooth, about 1 minute. Cover and refrigerate at least 1 hour or overnight to blend flavors.

2.   Spread chicken liver mixture onto bottom half of pita; top with torn lettuce and remaining pita half.

MAKES 1 SERVING

THIS SERVING PROVIDES: *1 Fat; 2 Proteins; ½ Vegetable; 1 Bread*

PER SERVING: *240 Calories, 16 g Protein, 10 g Fat, 21 g Carbohydrate, 46 mg Calcium, 445 mg Sodium, 395 mg Cholesterol, 1 g Dietary Fiber*

Turkey Schnitzel

Debby works full-time, takes low to moderate aerobics classes, and lifts weights—in addition to being a wife and mother of three. She likes this quick and easy recipe for her YMCA nights, since it's ready in a jiffy after her workout.

DEBBY GRZESIAK · ERIE, PENNSYLVANIA

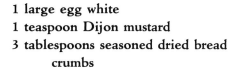

1 large egg white
1 teaspoon Dijon mustard
3 tablespoons seasoned dried bread
    crumbs

Two 3-ounce skinless boneless turkey
    breast cutlets, pounded thin
1 teaspoon vegetable oil
Lemon wedges for garnish

1. In small shallow plate, combine egg white and mustard until blended; set aside.

2. Place bread crumbs in separate small shallow plate. One at a time, dip each cutlet first into egg mixture, then into bread crumbs, coating both sides.

3. In medium nonstick skillet, heat ½ teaspoon of the oil; add cutlets. Cook over medium-high heat until golden brown, about 5 minutes. Add remaining oil; turn cutlets. Cook until golden brown, about 5 minutes longer. Garnish with lemon wedges.

MAKES 2 SERVINGS

EACH SERVING PROVIDES: ½ Fat; 2 Proteins; ½ Bread; 10 Optional Calories

PER SERVING: 166 Calories, 24 g Protein, 3 g Fat, 8 g Carbohydrate, 19 mg Calcium, 425 mg Sodium, 53 mg Cholesterol, 0 g Dietary Fiber

Turkey Enchiladas

Tracy has a full-time job and a thin husband, so fast, hearty meals are a must. Holiday leftovers prompted this revision of the Mexican classic.

TRACY BAXTER · KANSAS CITY, MISSOURI

¼ cup reduced-calorie tub margarine
1 cup chopped onion
1 cup chopped green bell pepper
9 ounces diced cooked turkey
½ cup canned green chilies, drained and diced

¼ cup all-purpose flour
2½ teaspoons low-sodium instant chicken broth mix
¾ cup plain nonfat yogurt
4½ ounces shredded cheddar cheese
Twelve 6-inch flour tortillas

---

1. Preheat oven to 350°F. Spray two 11-by-7-inch glass baking dishes with nonstick cooking spray; set aside.

2. In small saucepan, melt 2 tablespoons of the margarine; sauté onion and green pepper 3 minutes, until softened. Stir in turkey and chilies; set aside.

3. To prepare sauce, in small skillet, melt remaining 2 tablespoons margarine. Stir in flour. Add chicken broth and 2½ cups water; cook over medium heat, stirring constantly, about 5 minutes, until mixture is smooth. Reduce heat to low; cook 2 minutes longer. Whisk in yogurt and ½ cup of the cheese.

4. Pour ½ cup sauce into turkey mixture. Dip each tortilla, one at a time, into re-maining sauce; fill each with about ¼ cup turkey mixture. Roll tortilla tightly and place seam-side down in baking dish. Repeat with remaining tortillas and filling. Pour any remaining sauce over tortillas; sprinkle evenly with remaining cheese.

5. Bake until bubbly, 25 to 30 minutes.

MAKES 6 SERVINGS

EACH SERVING (2 ENCHILADAS) PROVIDES: *1 Fat; 2½ Proteins; ¾ Vegetable; 2 Breads; 50 Optional Calories*

PER SERVING: *392 Calories, 25 g Protein, 18 g Fat, 36 g Carbohydrate, 309 mg Calcium, 612 mg Sodium, 56 mg Cholesterol, 2 g Dietary Fiber*

Turkey Croquettes

Since Lorraine joined Weight Watchers, she feels good about herself, and knows she will be able to lose the weight. Here's her novel approach to "recycling" turkey.

LORRAINE HEUTHE · BAY SHORE, NEW YORK

2 tablespoons plus 2 teaspoons reduced-calorie tub margarine
½ cup chopped celery
½ cup chopped onion
3 tablespoons all-purpose flour
2 cups low-fat (1%) milk
1 pound diced cooked turkey

8 slices reduced-calorie whole-wheat bread, torn into small pieces
1½ teaspoons poultry seasoning
¼ teaspoon freshly ground black pepper
¼ cup plus 2 tablespoons seasoned dried bread crumbs

1. Preheat oven to 350°F.

2. In large nonstick skillet, heat margarine; add celery and onion. Cook, stirring occasionally, until onion is translucent, about 3 minutes. Stir in flour; cook, stirring constantly, 1 minute longer. Slowly pour in milk and cook, stirring occasionally, until slightly thickened, about 3 minutes.

3. Remove from heat; add remaining ingredients except bread crumbs, stirring well to combine. Set aside 10 minutes. Shape into 8 equal balls; roll in bread crumbs. Place balls in nonstick baking pan. Bake until golden brown, about 35 to 40 minutes.

MAKES 8 SERVINGS

EACH SERVING PROVIDES: *¼ Milk; ½ Fat; 2 Proteins; ¼ Vegetable; ¾ Bread; 10 Optional Calories*

PER SERVING: *214 Calories, 22 g Protein, 6 g Fat, 19 g Carbohydrate, 122 mg Calcium, 352 mg Sodium, 46 mg Cholesterol, 2 g Dietary Fiber*

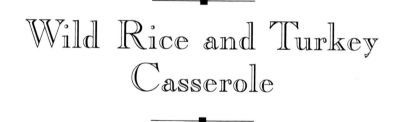

Wild Rice and Turkey Casserole

Here's a filling main dish that's a rousing success with Betty's husband, three grown children, and young granddaughter.

BETTY CONE · SASKATOON, SASKATCHEWAN, CANADA

6 ounces wild rice
1 tablespoon plus 1 teaspoon reduced-calorie tub margarine
3 cups sliced mushrooms
10 ounces diced cooked turkey
1 cup evaporated skimmed milk

2 packets low-sodium instant chicken broth mix
2 tablespoons chopped fresh chives
¼ teaspoon freshly ground black pepper
2 tablespoons grated Parmesan cheese

1. Cook rice according to package directions. Drain if necessary and set aside to cool.

2. Preheat oven to 325°F.

3. In large nonstick skillet, melt 2 teaspoons of the margarine; add mushrooms and cook over medium heat, stirring frequently, 2 minutes. Remove from heat; stir in rice, turkey, ½ cup water, and remaining ingredients, except cheese and remaining margarine.

4. Spray 9-inch square glass baking pan with nonstick cooking spray. Transfer rice mixture to prepared pan. Bake until heated through, about 40 minutes. Top evenly with cheese and remaining 2 teaspoons margarine; bake 5 minutes longer, or place under preheated broiler until lightly browned.

MAKES 4 SERVINGS

EACH SERVING PROVIDES: ½ Milk; ½ Fat; 2½ Proteins; 1½ Vegetables; 1½ Breads; 20 Optional Calories

PER SERVING: 370 Calories, 34 g Protein, 7 g Fat, 43 g Carbohydrate, 250 mg Calcium, 217 mg Sodium, 59 mg Cholesterol, 3 g Dietary Fiber

Turkey Crepes

A busy policeman's wife with two college-age kids, Mary works with mentally handicapped students and performs as a clown for local hospital patients.

MARY EDDINGTON • GARLAND, TEXAS

CREPES:
¾ cup skim milk
1 large egg
½ cup plus 1 tablespoon all-purpose flour
1 tablespoon reduced-calorie tub
    margarine, melted
Dash salt

FILLING:
11 ounces diced cooked turkey
1½ cups cooked chopped broccoli
½ cup nonfat sour cream (10 calories per
    tablespoon)
15 pitted small black olives, sliced
¼ teaspoon ground nutmeg
¼ teaspoon salt
⅛ teaspoon freshly ground black pepper

1.   To prepare crepes, in blender, combine milk, egg, flour, margarine, and salt. Blend on high speed until combined, about 1 minute. Refrigerate for 20 minutes.

2.   Spray small nonstick skillet with nonstick cooking spray; heat for 1 minute. Pour scant ¼ cup crepe batter into skillet; tilt to distribute evenly. Cook over medium-high heat until crepe is lightly browned, 1 minute. Carefully turn crepe over and cook 1 minute longer. Place on wax paper; top with second sheet of wax paper. Repeat to make 6 crepes, stacking between sheets of wax paper.

3.   In medium bowl, combine remaining ingredients. Place ⅓ cup filling on lower half of crepe; roll tightly to enclose. Repeat with remaining crepes and filling.

4.   Spray a 12-inch round microwavable plate with nonstick cooking spray. Arrange filled crepes, seam-side down, in center of plate, like spokes of a wheel. Cover loosely with plastic wrap or damp paper towel. Microwave on High 3 minutes.

MAKES 6 SERVINGS

EACH SERVING PROVIDES: *½ Fat; 2 Proteins; ½ Vegetable; ½ Bread; 25 Optional Calories*

PER SERVING: *199 Calories, 21 g Protein, 6 g Fat, 14 g Carbohydrate, 101 mg Calcium, 255 mg Sodium, 76 mg Cholesterol, 1 g Dietary Fiber*

Turkey-Artichoke Lasagna

Confronted with leftovers, AnnMarie came up with this original and very delicious meal. Since her work as a dental hygienist means late hours, she often prepares a big batch to freeze in individual portions.

ANNMARIE LUBITZ · BRICK, NEW JERSEY

2 teaspoons olive oil
½ cup chopped onion
1 garlic clove, chopped
9 ounces ground turkey
4 cups tomato sauce
1½ cups frozen artichoke hearts, thawed, drained, and chopped
2 cups part-skim ricotta cheese

6 ounces part-skim mozzarella cheese, shredded
¼ cup grated Parmesan cheese
1 large egg, lightly beaten
2 tablespoons chopped fresh parsley
7 ounces lasagna noodles, cooked according to package directions (about 9 noodles)

1.   Preheat oven to 350°F.

2.   In large skillet, heat oil; add onion and garlic and sauté until onions are translucent, stirring occasionally, 3 to 4 minutes. Add turkey and cook until lightly browned, 5 to 6 minutes, stirring frequently to break up meat. Stir in tomato sauce and artichokes; simmer 10 minutes.

3.   In medium bowl, combine cheeses, egg, and parsley.

4.   To assemble lasagna, spread one-third of the sauce mixture in 13-by-9-inch baking pan. Top with 3 lasagna noodles; spread with one-third of cheese mixture. Repeat layering with remaining ingredients.

5.   Cover with foil and bake 30 minutes; remove foil and bake 10 minutes longer. Let stand 15 minutes before cutting.

MAKES 8 SERVINGS

EACH SERVING PROVIDES: ¼ Fat; 3 Proteins; 2½ Vegetables; 1½ Breads; 15 Optional Calories

PER SERVING: 364 Calories, 25 g Protein, 14 g Fat, 34 g Carbohydrate, 360 mg Calcium, 302 mg Sodium, 83 mg Cholesterol, 4 g Dietary Fiber

Stuffed Shells

Cynthia teaches art to high schoolers near the coastal resort of Ocean City, Maryland. She loves to hunt for antiques and "to cook and eat, so Weight Watchers is a great Program for me since I can cook and enjoy real food and experiment with new recipes, and still lose weight."

CYNTHIA PILCHARD · SNOW HILL, MARYLAND

7½ ounces jumbo pasta shells (about 24 shells)
8 ounces ground turkey
1 cup finely chopped onion
2 cups frozen chopped spinach (one 10-ounce package), thawed and drained
1 cup low-fat (1%) cottage cheese

¾ ounce grated Romano or Parmesan cheese
1 teaspoon fennel seeds
1 teaspoon dried basil
1 teaspoon dried oregano
¼ teaspoon freshly ground black pepper
2 cups tomato sauce
4½ ounces shredded mozzarella cheese

1. In large pot of boiling water, cook pasta until al dente (firm), about 9 minutes. Drain, cover with damp paper towel, and set aside.

2. Preheat oven to 350°F.

3. Spray large nonstick skillet with nonstick cooking spray; add turkey and onion. Cook over medium-high heat, stirring occasionally, until turkey is crumbly and cooked, 5 to 7 minutes. Remove from heat; stir in remaining ingredients except tomato sauce and cheese; set aside to cool.

4. Fill each shell with about 2 tablespoons turkey mixture. Place shells in prepared dish. Pour tomato sauce evenly over shells; sprinkle with cheese. Bake until heated through and cheese is bubbly, about 25 minutes.

MAKES 8 SERVINGS

EACH SERVING PROVIDES: *2 Proteins; 1¾ Vegetables; 1¼ Breads*

PER SERVING: *252 Calories, 18 g Protein, 7 g Fat, 29 g Carbohydrate, 198 mg Calcium, 631 mg Sodium, 37 mg Cholesterol, 3 g Dietary Fiber*

Italian Meat Loaf

It's a good thing Joe learned to cook at his grandmother's knee—he's head chef at home, since his wife has a full-time career. Joe's hobby is horticulture —growing roses, irises, and day lilies.

JOE SAIA · HELENA, ARKANSAS

2 teaspoons vegetable oil
¼ cup chopped onion
¼ cup chopped green bell pepper
1 garlic clove, minced
7 ounces ground turkey
6 ounces cooked mashed potato

¼ cup mixed vegetable juice
1 tablespoon plus 1 teaspoon grated Parmesan cheese
1½ teaspoons fennel seeds
⅛ teaspoon freshly ground black pepper

1.   Preheat oven to 350°F.

2.   In small skillet, heat oil; add onion, green bell pepper, and garlic. Cook over medium-high heat, stirring occasionally, until onion is translucent, about 2 minutes.

3.   In medium bowl, combine cooked vegetables and remaining ingredients; stir until thoroughly blended. Shape mixture into 6-by-3-inch loaf.

4.   Spray small nonstick baking pan with nonstick cooking spray. Place loaf in pan. Bake until knife inserted in center comes out clean and warm, about 30 to 40 minutes.

MAKES 2 SERVINGS

EACH SERVING PROVIDES: *1 Fat; 2½ Proteins; ¾ Vegetable; ¾ Bread; 15 Optional Calories*

PER SERVING: *314 Calories, 21 g Protein, 17 g Fat, 20 g Carbohydrate, 110 mg Calcium, 519 mg Sodium, 77 mg Cholesterol, 2 g Dietary Fiber*

Turkey Hash

Determined to make foods the whole family could enjoy while she lost 41 pounds and achieved her goal, Sallie developed this quick hash. It's perfect for anyone on the go.

SALLIE WILHELM · OROFINO, IDAHO

12 ounces ground turkey
1 cup sliced onion
1 cup julienned green bell pepper
2 cups canned plum tomatoes with juice, coarsely chopped

2 cups tomato juice
6 ounces long-grain white rice
2 teaspoons chili powder
⅛ teaspoon freshly ground black pepper

1.   Spray ridged microwavable pan with nonstick cooking spray. Place turkey, onion, and bell pepper in pan; cover with paper towel. Microwave on High 5 minutes, stirring once during cooking to break up turkey and rearrange vegetables. Drain excess liquid.

2.   Transfer turkey mixture to shallow 3-quart casserole; stir in remaining ingredients. Cover tightly with lid or vented plastic wrap. Microwave on High 8 to 10 minutes, until just boiling. Reduce setting to Medium-High; microwave 10 minutes longer, until rice is tender. Let stand, covered, 5 minutes.

MAKES 4 SERVINGS

EACH SERVING PROVIDES: *2¼ Proteins; 3 Vegetables; 1½ Breads*

PER SERVING: *349 Calories, 21 g Protein, 8 g Fat, 50 g Carbohydrate, 79 mg Calcium, 732 mg Sodium, 62 mg Cholesterol, 3 g Dietary Fiber*

Turkey and Cabbage Patties

Like many who quit smoking, Marian gained some weight. Luckily, her new dedication to healthy living includes sensible eating and smart choices, like using ground turkey instead of beef in this longtime favorite.

MARIAN FARRELL · GREAT FALLS, MONTANA

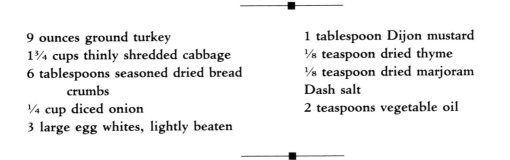

9 ounces ground turkey
1¾ cups thinly shredded cabbage
6 tablespoons seasoned dried bread
    crumbs
¼ cup diced onion
3 large egg whites, lightly beaten

1 tablespoon Dijon mustard
⅛ teaspoon dried thyme
⅛ teaspoon dried marjoram
Dash salt
2 teaspoons vegetable oil

1.   In large bowl, combine all ingredients except oil until thoroughly blended. Shape mixture into 4 equal patties.

2.   In large nonstick skillet, heat oil; add patties. Cook over medium heat until golden brown, about 5 minutes. Turn and cook until other side is golden brown, about 5 minutes longer.

MAKES 4 SERVINGS

EACH SERVING PROVIDES: *½ Fat; 2 Proteins; 1 Vegetable; ½ Bread*

PER SERVING: *179 Calories, 16 g Protein, 8 g Fat, 11 g Carbohydrate, 38 mg Calcium, 534 mg Sodium, 47 mg Cholesterol, 1 g Dietary Fiber*

Hot Texas Chili Soup

This fabulous eat-it-with-a-fork soup is a perfect do-ahead dinner. That's important to Judeth, a chemical engineer whose frenzied schedule necessitates quick, easy meals.

JUDETH CORRY · FRIENDSWOOD, TEXAS

12 ounces drained cooked red kidney
　　beans
6 ounces cooked ground turkey
3 cups canned low-sodium stewed
　　tomatoes
2 cups tomato sauce
1½ cups chopped onions
1 cup canned green chilies, rinsed,
　　drained, and chopped

1 tablespoon plus 2 teaspoons chili
　　powder
1½ teaspoons ground cumin
1 teaspoon paprika
1 teaspoon dried oregano
¼ teaspoon hot pepper sauce

In 3-quart slow-cooker, combine all ingredients and 2 cups water. Cover and cook on Low 4 hours or on High 2 hours, until onions are tender. Ladle evenly into 6 soup bowls.

MAKES 6 SERVINGS

EACH SERVING (1¼ CUPS) PROVIDES: *2 Proteins; 3 Vegetables*

PER SERVING: *230 Calories, 15 g Protein, 5 g Fat, 35 g Carbohydrate, 104 mg Calcium, 569 mg Sodium, 20 mg Cholesterol, 8 g Dietary Fiber*

Mexican Rice Cakes

A craving for nachos and taco salad sparked Teresa's pleasantly spicy invention. It's great for kids, too.

TERESA GARDNER · CANISTEO, NEW YORK

2 ounces ground turkey
⅛ teaspoon ground cumin
⅛ teaspoon garlic powder
2 rice cakes
½ cup shredded iceberg lettuce

½ medium tomato, sliced
2 tablespoons chopped onion
2 tablespoons medium salsa
2 ounces reduced-calorie American cheese

1. Preheat broiler or toaster oven.

2. Spray small nonstick skillet with nonstick cooking spray; heat over medium heat 1 minute. Add turkey, cumin, and garlic powder; cook, stirring occasionally, until turkey is cooked through, about 2 minutes.

3. Spoon turkey evenly onto rice cakes; top evenly with remaining ingredients.

4. Place in broiler or toaster oven until cheese is melted, about 2 minutes.

MAKES 2 SERVINGS

EACH SERVING PROVIDES: *1½ Proteins; 1 Vegetable; ½ Bread*

PER SERVING: *198 Calories, 19 g Protein, 7 g Fat, 16 g Carbohydrate, 418 mg Calcium, 932 mg Sodium, 31 mg Cholesterol, 1 g Dietary Fiber*

Mexican Turkey Sausage Squares

Darlie found a way to combine all her favorite foods in a scrumptious recipe. Now she enjoys sausage and cheese without guilt.

DARLIE STAHL · PLANO, TEXAS

1 cup plus 2 tablespoons buttermilk
    baking mix
1 cup skim milk
¼ cup reduced-calorie mayonnaise
12 ounces cooked crumbled turkey
    sausage

8¼ ounces shredded cheddar cheese
½ cup canned green chilies, drained and
    chopped
1 large egg, lightly beaten

1.   Preheat oven to 350°F. Spray 13-by-9-inch glass baking dish with nonstick cooking spray; set aside.

2.   In small bowl, combine baking mix, milk, and 2 tablespoons of the mayonnaise; pour into prepared dish. Sprinkle sausage evenly over top.

3.   In same small bowl, combine remaining ingredients with remaining 2 tablespoons mayonnaise until blended. Pour evenly over sausage. Bake until golden brown, 25 to 30 minutes. Cut into squares.

MAKES 12 SERVINGS

EACH SERVING PROVIDES: ½ Fat; 2 Proteins; ½ Bread; 25 Optional Calories

PER SERVING: 209 Calories, 13 g Protein, 13 g Fat, 9 g Carbohydrate, 189 mg Calcium, 513 mg Sodium, 61 mg Cholesterol, 0 g Dietary Fiber

Tex-Mex Ranch Casserole

Being retired is a boon, says Marcia, because she has time to shop and plan healthful meals. She used to make this dish with high-fat meat, eggs, cheese, and butter. Today's version is lower in fat and calories, but just as tasty.

MARCIA FRANK · KERRVILLE, TEXAS

12 ounces cooked crumbled turkey
    sausage
10 ounces cooked pinto beans
½ cup canned mild chilies, drained and
    chopped
1 teaspoon garlic powder
½ teaspoon ground cumin
½ teaspoon dried oregano
¼ teaspoon freshly ground black pepper
1 cup chopped onion
1½ cups diced yellow squash

1½ cups diced zucchini
½ cup chopped red bell pepper
2¼ ounces shredded cheddar cheese
2¼ ounces shredded part-skim
    mozzarella cheese
2 large eggs
2 egg whites
3 tablespoons seasoned dried bread
    crumbs
Chopped fresh cilantro for garnish
    (optional)

1. Preheat oven to 350°F. Spray 13-by-9-inch baking pan with nonstick cooking spray; set aside.

2. In medium bowl, combine turkey, beans, chilies, and seasonings. Coarsely mash beans; transfer to prepared pan.

3. Spray large nonstick skillet with nonstick cooking spray; add onion. Cook over medium-high heat 2 minutes. Add squash, zucchini, and bell pepper; cook 3 minutes longer. Spread vegetable mixture over turkey mixture.

4. In small bowl, whisk together remaining ingredients except bread crumbs and cilantro; pour over casserole. Sprinkle with bread crumbs. Bake until golden brown and bubbly, about 30 minutes. Garnish with cilantro, if desired.

MAKES 8 SERVINGS

———
EACH SERVING PROVIDES: 2½ Proteins; 1¼ Vegetables; ¾ Bread; 5 Optional Calories

———
PER SERVING: 243 Calories, 20 g Protein, 11 g Fat, 16 g Carbohydrate, 160 mg Calcium, 572 mg Sodium, 98 mg Cholesterol, 2 g Dietary Fiber

Single-Serving Pizzas

Though raising four kids keeps Joyce busy, she finds time for music, sewing, art, handicrafts, computer graphics, and reading.

JOYCE HERBOLD · PORT ORCHARD, WASHINGTON

½ teaspoon active dry yeast
6 tablespoons plus 2 teaspoons all-purpose flour
1 teaspoon vegetable oil
¼ teaspoon granulated sugar

¼ cup tomato sauce
3 ounces cooked crumbled turkey sausage
1½ ounces shredded part-skim mozzarella cheese

1.   Preheat oven to 425°F. Spray two 7-inch glass pie plates with nonstick cooking spray; set aside.

2.   In small bowl, dissolve yeast in 3 tablespoons warm water. Add flour, oil, and sugar, stirring to form a soft dough. Cover bowl with kitchen towel and let rest 5 minutes.

3.   Divide dough in half; press into prepared pie plates. Spread 2 tablespoons sauce over each crust; sprinkle evenly with turkey sausage and cheese. (Pizzas can be frozen at this point. Follow cooking directions, placing frozen pizzas in the oven and adding 4 to 6 minutes to baking time.) Bake until cheese is bubbly and crust is browned, about 15 minutes.

MAKES 2 SERVINGS

EACH SERVING PROVIDES: *½ Fat; 2½ Proteins; ½ Vegetable; 1 Bread; 15 Optional Calories*

PER SERVING: *276 Calories, 18 g Protein, 12 g Fat, 24 g Carbohydrate, 154 mg Calcium, 611 mg Sodium, 44 mg Cholesterol, 2 g Dietary Fiber*

Southern Hash

Dale thanks her inspirational Weight Watchers leader for providing the friendship and support that helped her lose weight and keep it off for the first time ever. Dale's hash recipe calls for smoked turkey sausage.

DALE DOMINGUE DOUCET · LAKE CHARLES, LOUISIANA

10 ounces diced pared all-purpose
    potatoes
½ cup chopped onion
5 ounces smoked turkey sausage

½ cup sliced mushrooms
½ cup tomato sauce
¼ teaspoon garlic powder

1.   Spray large nonstick skillet with nonstick cooking spray; add potatoes and onion. Cook over medium-high heat, stirring occasionally, 2 minutes. Add sausage and cook, stirring frequently, until sausage is crumbly. Add mushrooms; cook 1 minute longer.

2.   Add remaining ingredients and 1½ cups water. Reduce heat to medium-low; cook, stirring occasionally, until potatoes are tender and mixture has thickened.

MAKES 2 SERVINGS

EACH SERVING PROVIDES: *2 Proteins; 2 Vegetables; 1 Bread*

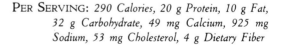

PER SERVING: *290 Calories, 20 g Protein, 10 g Fat, 32 g Carbohydrate, 49 mg Calcium, 925 mg Sodium, 53 mg Cholesterol, 4 g Dietary Fiber*

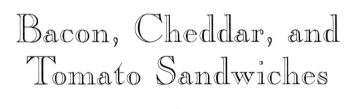

Bacon, Cheddar, and Tomato Sandwiches

These delicious sandwiches are tops with the men in Cindy's life—her husband and two sons. Best of all, the sandwiches can be assembled and refrigerated until ready to bake.

CINDY DARLING · NORMAN, OKLAHOMA

2 cups chopped tomatoes
6 ounces shredded cheddar cheese
¼ cup reduced-calorie mayonnaise
¼ cup plain nonfat yogurt

6 slices crisp cooked turkey bacon, crumbled
4 reduced-calorie hamburger buns (80 calories per bun), split

1.   Preheat oven to 350°F.

2.   In medium bowl, combine all ingredients except hamburger buns.

3.   Arrange buns cut sides up in 13-by-9-inch baking pan. Spoon equal amount of bacon-cheese mixture onto each bun half. Bake 15 minutes, until cheese is bubbling.

MAKES 4 SERVINGS

PER SERVING: *368 Calories, 21 g Protein, 23 g Fat, 20 g Carbohydrate, 401 mg Calcium, 852 mg Sodium, 64 mg Cholesterol, 5 g Dietary Fiber*

EACH SERVING (2 HALVES) PROVIDES: *1½ Fats; 2 Proteins; 1 Vegetable; 1 Bread; 50 Optional Calories*

Meat

Although the approach to meal planning has shifted over the years from a primary focus on a large portion of protein—often meat—to a larger helping of complex carbohydrates with meat as the garnish, beef, pork, and lamb still have a place in our hearts. To keep meat on the table, America's ranchers and farmers have been working on changing the nutrition profiles of beef and pork to provide cuts that are lower in fat. In addition, meat processors and your local butchers are trimming closer to offer steaks, chops, roasts, and even ground meat with much of the visible fat already removed, eliminating waste and making your purchase more economical.

Beef appears here in an Eastern mood as Beef and Broccoli Stir-Fry, Oriental Meat Bundles, and Betty's Stir-Fry; Eggplant Parmigiana with Meat Sauce and Italian-Style Swiss Steak show a European influence. The popularity of Mexican and Southwest flavors inspired Best Texas Chili, Individual Chili Pots, and Taco

Salad in Tortilla Shell. Hearty family-style meals such as Beef and Dumpling Casserole and Beef Hash are meant to be eaten at the kitchen table. They also freeze well and reheat beautifully, so you might want to stash a few portions for extra-busy days.

Beef and Broccoli Stir-Fry

An Air Force wife raising three young boys, Debbi loves experimenting with new recipes. This one presents the flavors of the Orient.

DEBBI KELLEY · ELMENDORF AFB, ARKANSAS

½ cup sliced onion
2 cups broccoli florets
½ cup sliced mushrooms
2 tablespoons plus 2 teaspoons oyster sauce
1 tablespoon chopped fresh flat-leaf parsley

12 ounces broiled lean sirloin steak, cut into thin strips
2 cups hot cooked vermicelli
Dash freshly ground black pepper

1. Spray large nonstick skillet with non-stick cooking spray; cook onion over medium heat until translucent, about 2 minutes. Add broccoli, mushrooms, oyster sauce, parsley, and 2 tablespoons water. Cover and cook over medium heat until broccoli is tender-crisp, about 5 minutes.

2. Add beef and vermicelli to vegetable mixture. Cook over medium-high heat, tossing frequently, until meat is heated through, about 1 minute. Season with pepper.

MAKES 4 SERVINGS

EACH SERVING (1¼ CUPS) PROVIDES: *3 Proteins; 1½ Vegetables; 1 Bread; 20 Optional Calories*

PER SERVING: *307 Calories, 33 g Protein, 7 g Fat, 28 g Carbohydrate, 51 mg Calcium, 550 mg Sodium, 76 Cholesterol, 4 g Dietary Fiber*

Oriental Meat Bundles

Janet loves packing these little bundles in her lunchbox when she works as a special education instructional assistant. Trouble is, her husband loves them too, so it's tough keeping them in stock!

JANET DLUGOSZ · RAPID CITY, SOUTH DAKOTA

2 cups sliced green cabbage
½ cup chopped scallions (green onions)
½ cup sliced carrot
2 teaspoons minced pared ginger root
4 ounces lean ground beef, broiled

1 large egg or ¼ cup egg substitute
2 tablespoons reduced-sodium soy sauce
¼ teaspoon freshly ground black pepper
8 refrigerated buttermilk biscuits
    (1 ounce each)

1.   Preheat oven to 450°F.

2.   Place cabbage, scallions, carrot, and ginger in food processor; process until vegetables are finely chopped, about 1 minute.

3.   Spray large nonstick skillet with nonstick cooking spray; add vegetables, beef, egg, soy sauce, and pepper. Cook over medium heat, stirring frequently, until cabbage is softened, about 5 minutes. Drain mixture in colander.

4.   Between 2 sheets of wax paper, roll each biscuit to a 6-inch round. Spoon about ⅓ cup filling in center of each biscuit. Fold bottom portion of dough up over filling, fold in sides, then fold top part of dough to enclose filling envelope-style.

5.   Spray baking sheet with nonstick cooking spray. Place bundles seam-side down on prepared sheet. Bake until golden, about 12 to 15 minutes.

MAKES 8 SERVINGS

EACH SERVING PROVIDES: *½ Protein; ¾ Vegetable; 1 Bread; 10 Optional Calories*

PER SERVING: *132 Calories, 6 g Protein, 7 g Fat, 15 g Carbohydrate, 20 mg Calcium, 472 mg Sodium, 36 mg Cholesterol, 1 g Dietary Fiber*

Betty's Fried Rice

In her endless quest for those motivation-boosters, variety and pizzazz, Betty found a terrific way to turn a Chinese side dish into a fabulous entree.

ELIZABETH SHAW · DAYTON, OHIO

2 tablespoons peanut oil
½ cup chopped onion
1½ cups cooked brown rice
2 cups shredded carrots
1½ cups shredded Napa cabbage
¾ cup canned sliced water chestnuts, rinsed and drained

2 tablespoons low-sodium soy sauce
2 large eggs, lightly beaten
½ cup frozen peas
½ cup frozen whole-kernel corn
½ cup fresh bean sprouts
12 ounces broiled lean sirloin or rib-eye steak, diced

1. In large nonstick skillet, heat oil; add onion and cook over medium heat until softened, about 2 minutes. Stir in rice, carrots, cabbage, water chestnuts, and soy sauce; cover and cook over medium-high heat 5 minutes.

2. Meanwhile, spray medium nonstick skillet with nonstick cooking spray; add eggs and scramble over medium heat, stirring frequently, until eggs are firm, about 2 minutes. Set aside.

3. Stir peas, corn, and bean sprouts into rice mixture. Cover and cook over medium-high heat 3 minutes. Stir in scrambled eggs and diced sirloin; cook, stirring occasion-ally, until meat is heated through, about 2 minutes.

MAKES 6 SERVINGS

EACH SERVING PROVIDES: *1 Fat; 2 Proteins; 1½ Vegetables; 1 Bread*

PER SERVING: *289 Calories, 23 g Protein, 11 g Fat, 25 g Carbohydrate, 52 mg Calcium, 292 mg Sodium, 121 mg Cholesterol, 3 g Dietary Fiber*

Italian-Style Swiss Steak

An avid cook who enjoys cake decorating, swimming, and reading, Gloria is a lifetime member. She inherited this recipe from her mother (also a lifetime member) and revised it for the Weight Watchers Program.

GLORIA MCELHINEY · CONCORD TOWNSHIP, OHIO

15 ounces lean boneless top round beef, cut into 4 equal pieces
1 tablespoon plus 1 teaspoon vegetable oil
2 cups sliced mushrooms
½ cup sliced onion
½ cup sliced carrot
¼ cup sliced celery

1 cup tomato sauce
¼ cup dry red wine
½ teaspoon dried oregano
½ teaspoon garlic powder
¼ teaspoon salt
¼ teaspoon freshly ground black pepper
1 cup sliced green bell pepper
10 ounces sliced all-purpose potatoes

1. Preheat broiler. Broil beef on rack 4 inches from heat 2 minutes on each side. Set aside.

2. In large nonstick skillet, heat oil; add mushrooms, onion, carrot, and celery; cook over medium heat until onions are translucent, about 2 minutes.

3. Stir in tomato sauce, wine, oregano, garlic powder, salt, pepper, and 1 cup water. Return meat to skillet. Cover and simmer over low heat 1 hour. Add green pepper and potato; simmer until meat is tender, about 35 minutes.

MAKES 4 SERVINGS

EACH SERVING PROVIDES: *1 Fat; 3 Proteins; 3 Vegetables; ½ Bread; 15 Optional Calories*

PER SERVING: *310 Calories, 31 g Protein, 9 g Fat, 24 g Carbohydrate, 39 mg Calcium, 575 mg Sodium, 71 mg Cholesterol, 4 g Dietary Fiber*

Eggplant Parmigiana with Meat Sauce

Edith makes this pleasing eggplant casserole several times a month. Her friends and family can't believe it tastes so rich, yet won't weigh them down.

Edith Lande · Scottsdale, Arizona

---

1 teaspoon salt
2 medium eggplants (1 to 1¼ pounds each), cut into ¼-inch slices
¼ cup plus 2 tablespoons seasoned bread crumbs
1 cup diced onion
9 ounces broiled lean ground beef
4 cups low-sodium tomato sauce

2 cups stewed tomatoes
½ teaspoon dried basil
½ teaspoon dried oregano
6 ounces shredded part-skim mozzarella cheese
¾ cup part-skim ricotta cheese
2 tablespoons plus 2 teaspoons grated Parmesan cheese

---

1. Preheat oven to 350°F.

2. Sprinkle salt evenly over both sides of eggplant slices. Place on large tray lined with paper towels to drain for 20 minutes.

3. Dredge eggplant slices in bread crumbs, coating both sides. Spray 2 nonstick baking sheets with nonstick cooking spray; divide eggplant slices evenly between prepared sheets and bake until golden, about 30 minutes.

4. Spray large saucepan with nonstick cooking spray; add onion and cook over medium heat until softened, about 2 minutes. Add remaining ingredients except cheese and simmer over low heat for 10 minutes.

5. In medium mixing bowl, combine cheeses.

6. In 13-by-9-inch baking dish, layer 1 cup sauce, one-third of eggplant slices, 1 cup sauce, half the cheese mixture, 1 cup sauce, one-third of eggplant slices, 1 cup sauce, remaining cheese mixture, 1 cup sauce, remaining eggplant slices, and remaining sauce.

7. Bake until bubbly and completely heated through, about 40 minutes. Let stand 10 minutes before cutting.

MAKES 8 SERVINGS

EACH SERVING PROVIDES: *2½ Proteins; 4 Vegetables; ¼ Bread; 10 Optional Calories*

PER SERVING: *300 Calories, 21 g Protein, 13 g Fat, 28 g Carbohydrate, 307 mg Calcium, 653 mg Sodium, 49 mg Cholesterol, 5 g Dietary Fiber*

Spanish Rice

Barbara's mother served this dish often when she was growing up. This adaptation blends the tastes of chilies, cumin, tomato, and onion with lean ground beef.

BARBARA SCHLAHT · GRESHAM, OREGON

8 ounces broiled lean ground beef
2 cups stewed tomatoes
¼ cup drained canned green chilies, rinsed and diced
2 tablespoons tomato paste
½ teaspoon chili powder

¼ teaspoon ground cumin
Dash salt
Dash freshly ground black pepper
3 ounces long-grain white rice
½ cup frozen whole-kernel corn
2 tablespoons chopped onion

1. Spray large nonstick skillet with non-stick cooking spray; add beef, tomatoes, chilies, tomato paste, chili powder, cumin, salt, and pepper. Bring to a boil; lower heat.

2. Stir in rice, corn, onion, and 1 cup plus 2 tablespoons water. Cover and simmer until rice is tender, about 35 minutes.

MAKES 4 SERVINGS

EACH SERVING (1 CUP) PROVIDES: *2 Proteins; 1½ Vegetables; 1 Bread*

PER SERVING: *295 Calories, 18 g Protein, 11 g Fat, 32 g Carbohydrate, 62 mg Calcium, 522 mg Sodium, 49 mg Cholesterol, 1 g Dietary Fiber*

Individual Chili Pots

"My family loves eating this hot dish in front of the television on a cold night," writes Rebecca. Whether fixed with beef or turkey, her chili is tops.

REBECCA HARTMAN-BAKER · GREENEVILLE, TENNESSEE

12 ounces broiled lean ground beef or
    cooked ground turkey
4 cups drained canned Italian plum
    tomatoes (reserve liquid), seeded
    and chopped
1½ cups chopped green bell pepper
1 cup chopped onion
1 cup chopped celery

6 ounces drained cooked kidney beans
1 garlic clove, minced
1 teaspoon dried oregano
¾ teaspoon chili powder
3 cups cooked long-grain white rice
2¼ ounces shredded cheddar cheese
18 pitted large black olives, sliced

In large saucepan, combine all ingredients except rice, cheese, and olives. Cover and simmer over low heat 25 minutes. Stir in rice; heat through. Divide chili among 6 individual serving dishes; top each with equal amounts of cheese and sliced olives.

MAKES 6 SERVINGS

EACH SERVING (1¾ CUPS) PROVIDES: ½ Fat;
    2½ Proteins; 2½ Vegetables; 1½ Breads

PER SERVING: 436 Calories, 24 g Protein, 16 g Fat,
    48 g Carbohydrate, 177 mg Calcium, 519 mg
    Sodium, 60 mg Cholesterol, 4 g Dietary Fiber

Best Texas Chili

Cheryl joined Weight Watchers to take off extra pounds following the births of her son and daughter. Cheryl's family loves chili, so she devised this recipe that cuts back on fat while adding healthy vegetables.

CHERYL PENNER · FRESNO, CALIFORNIA

1 tablespoon plus 1 teaspoon olive oil
2 cups chopped onions
1 cup finely chopped celery
3 garlic cloves, minced
1 pound broiled lean ground beef
2 cups drained canned Italian plum
    tomatoes (reserve liquid), chopped
2 cups tomato sauce
12 ounces drained cooked pinto beans
12 ounces drained cooked red kidney
    beans

2 tablespoons granulated sugar
3 bay leaves
3 whole allspice
1 tablespoon chili powder
1 teaspoon dried oregano
½ teaspoon freshly ground black pepper
¼ teaspoon ground cumin
¼ teaspoon ground red pepper

1. In medium nonstick skillet, heat oil; add onions, celery, and garlic; cook over medium heat until softened, about 2 minutes.

2. Place vegetables and remaining ingredients in slow-cooker; stir to combine. Cook on low setting 4 hours.

MAKES 8 SERVINGS

EACH SERVING PROVIDES: ½ Fat; 2 Proteins; 2¼ Vegetables; 1½ Breads; 15 Optional Calories

PER SERVING: 354 Calories, 23 g Protein, 14 g Fat, 36 g Carbohydrate, 89 mg Calcium, 536 mg Sodium, 49 mg Cholesterol, 6 g Dietary Fiber

Taco Salad in Tortilla Shell

Karen is a busy mother of two who also juggles work as a part-time bookkeeper, active volunteer, Sunday School teacher, crafts enthusiast, and full-time student. Karen's spicy salad made us say "Bravo!"

KAREN HUGO · MOUNT VERNON, ILLINOIS

1 teaspoon vegetable oil
1 cup chopped onion
1 cup chopped red bell pepper
1 cup chopped green bell pepper
7 ounces broiled lean ground beef
1 cup mild salsa
1 tablespoon minced jalapeño pepper
1 teaspoon ground cumin

1 teaspoon chili powder
Four 6-inch flour tortillas
1 cup shredded iceberg lettuce
2¼ ounces shredded reduced-calorie
    cheddar cheese
6 large or 10 small pitted black olives,
    sliced

1.   In large nonstick skillet, heat oil; add onion and bell peppers; cook over medium heat until onions are translucent, about 2 minutes. Stir in beef and break up with a fork; add ½ cup salsa, the jalapeño pepper, cumin, and chili powder; reduce heat, cover, and simmer 5 minutes.

2.   Preheat oven to 375°F. Spray 4 custard cups with nonstick cooking spray; press 1 tortilla into each cup. Bake until tortilla cups are lightly browned and crisp, about 15 minutes. Transfer to rack to cool.

3.   To serve, fill each tortilla cup with ¼ cup lettuce and equal amounts of meat mixture; top evenly with cheese, olives, and remaining ½ cup salsa.

MAKES 4 SERVINGS

EACH SERVING PROVIDES: *½ Fat; 2 Proteins; 2 Vegetables; 1 Bread*

PER SERVING: *326 Calories, 20 g Protein, 16 g Fat, 25 g Carbohydrate, 221 mg Calcium, 723 mg Sodium, 54 mg Cholesterol, 3 g Dietary Fiber*

Beef and Dumpling Casserole

Jean's weight loss inspired her husband, and together they've lost 90 pounds. The eggplant in this casserole lets Jean use less meat, so there's plenty of taste, but not a lot of fat and cholesterol.

JEAN ROBBINS · CHESAPEAKE, VIRGINIA

1 cup diced eggplant
½ cup chopped onion
½ cup chopped celery
6 ounces broiled lean ground beef

1 cup low-sodium tomato sauce
½ cup plus 1 tablespoon buttermilk
     baking mix
¼ cup low-fat (1%) milk

1.   Preheat oven to 350°F.

2.   Spray large nonstick skillet with non-stick cooking spray; add eggplant, onion, and celery; cook over medium-high heat until vegetables are softened, about 2 minutes. Add beef and tomato sauce; cook over low heat 10 minutes, stirring occasionally.

3.   Spray 1-quart casserole with nonstick cooking spray; scrape meat mixture into casserole. Set aside.

4.   In small bowl, combine baking mix and milk; stir until just combined. Drop mixture by tablespoonsful over meat mixture. Bake until golden, 30 to 35 minutes.

MAKES 2 SERVINGS

EACH SERVING PROVIDES: *3 Proteins; 4 Vegetables; 1½ Breads; 40 Optional Calories*

PER SERVING: *451 Calories, 27 g Protein, 22 g Fat, 38 g Carbohydrate, 127 mg Calcium, 528 mg Sodium, 75 mg Cholesterol, 4 g Dietary Fiber*

Beef Hash

When her daughter left for college, Grace developed a leftover problem. Now she freezes extra portions of steak until she's ready to make this hash, which relies on lean meat and doesn't add extra fat.

GRACE BERTOLONE · SETAUKET, NEW YORK

7 ounces broiled lean steak or
    roast beef, cubed
10 ounces shredded all-purpose potatoes
½ cup chopped onion

1 large egg
Dash salt
Dash freshly ground black pepper

1. Preheat broiler.

2. In food processor, process meat until coarsely chopped, about 1 minute. Transfer to medium bowl; stir in remaining ingredients. Shape mixture into 4 patties; place on nonstick baking sheet.

3. Broil patties 4 inches from heat, 6 to 8 minutes on each side, until crisp and golden.

MAKES 4 SERVINGS

_____

EACH SERVING PROVIDES: *2 Proteins; ¼ Vegetable; ½ Bread*

_____

PER SERVING: *179 Calories, 18 g Protein, 5 g Fat, 15 g Carbohydrate, 21 mg Calcium, 86 mg Sodium, 97 mg Cholesterol, 1 g Dietary Fiber*

Steak Log

Dorothy created this entree from a family standby. It helps her stick to her Food Plan while fooling her husband into thinking he's eating the old favorite.

DOROTHY SCHELER · BALTIMORE, MARYLAND

1 cup cooked long-grain white rice
½ cup diced onion
½ large egg, lightly beaten
1 tablespoon chopped fresh
    flat-leaf parsley
½ cup trimmed green beans
½ cup thinly sliced carrot
13 ounces lean flank steak, pounded
    to ¼-inch thickness

Dash salt
Dash freshly ground black pepper
1 cup tomato sauce
½ cup diced celery
2 tablespoons white vinegar
2 tablespoons firmly packed
    dark brown sugar
2 teaspoons dry mustard

1. Preheat broiler. Spray broiler rack with nonstick cooking spray.

2. In medium mixing bowl, combine rice, onion, egg, and parsley.

3. Arrange green beans and carrot in horizontal line across width of steak; top with rice mixture, salt, and pepper. Fold meat over mixture, sealing center seam and ends with toothpicks; season with salt and pepper. Broil on rack 4 inches from heat, 4 minutes on each side.

4. To prepare sauce, combine remaining ingredients and 1 cup water in large saucepan; bring to a boil. Place meat in sauce seam-side up. Reduce heat to low; cover and simmer 1 hour and 15 minutes, basting occasionally, until meat is tender.

MAKES 4 SERVINGS

EACH SERVING PROVIDES: *2¾ Proteins; 2 Vegetables; ½ Bread; 40 Optional Calories*

PER SERVING: *303 Calories, 24 g Protein, 9 g Fat, 31 g Carbohydrate, 54 mg Calcium, 499 mg Sodium, 101 mg Cholesterol, 2 g Dietary Fiber*

Skillet Pork and Sauerkraut

This economical entree was a lifesaver when Mary Anne was pinching pennies. It's still a staple of her "lean" years now that she's dropped 40 pounds.

MARY ANNE ROBINSON · DAYTON, OHIO

Four 5-ounce lean pork chops
2 teaspoons vegetable oil
1 cup sliced onion
1 garlic clove, minced
2 cups rinsed drained sauerkraut
½ cup apple juice

1 teaspoon caraway seeds
¼ teaspoon dried thyme
¼ teaspoon salt
¼ teaspoon freshly ground black pepper
1 small apple, cored and sliced

1. Preheat broiler. Broil chops on broiler rack in roasting pan 4 inches from heat source 2 minutes on each side.

2. In large nonstick skillet, heat oil; add onion and garlic and cook over medium heat until softened, about 2 minutes. Add ¼ cup water and remaining ingredients, except sliced apple; top with chops and simmer, covered, over low heat about 1 hour, or until chops are tender.

3. Stir in apple slices; cover and simmer until apple is tender-crisp, about 3 minutes.

MAKES 4 SERVINGS

EACH SERVING PROVIDES: *½ Fat; 3 Proteins; 1½ Vegetables; ½ Fruit; 5 Optional Calories*

PER SERVING: *277 Calories, 28 g Protein, 12 g Fat, 14 g Carbohydrate, 37 mg Calcium, 475 mg Sodium, 83 mg Cholesterol, 3 g Dietary Fiber*

Souvlaki

After college Dede gained weight, but she's determined to reach her goal before her 10-year reunion. One of her weapons is this great-tasting Greek dish, made with beef or pork.

DEDE DUBYNA · CALGARY, ALBERTA, CANADA

8 ounces beef sirloin tip steak or pork
    loin, cut into ½-inch cubes
½ teaspoon dried oregano
Dash freshly ground black pepper
½ cup chopped tomato
½ cup chopped cucumber
2 tablespoons finely diced
    green bell pepper

¼ cup nonfat sour cream (10 calories
    per tablespoon)
1 teaspoon red wine vinegar
1 teaspoon vegetable oil
2 large pita breads (2 ounces each),
    heated and cut into halves

1. Preheat oven to 300°F.

2. Sprinkle meat with half the oregano and the pepper. Place meat on rack in roasting pan and bake 10 to 12 minutes. (Pork should be cooked for 15 to 17 minutes and appear well done when pierced with a knife.)

3. In small bowl, combine remaining ingredients except pitas.

4. To assemble souvlaki, arrange meat evenly in pita halves. Top each with equal amounts of vegetable-sour cream mixture. Serve immediately.

MAKES 2 SERVINGS

EACH SERVING PROVIDES: *½ Fat; 3 Proteins; 1 Vegetable; 2 Breads; 50 Optional Calories*

PER SERVING: *376 Calories, 32 g Protein, 9 g Fat, 40 g Carbohydrate, 32 mg Calcium, 424 mg Sodium, 76 mg Cholesterol, 2 g Dietary Fiber*

Pork Chop Supper

66 I'm always looking for recipes using apples and pork, since I've associated applesauce with pork roast since childhood," writes Diane, who lost 52 pounds and now works as a receptionist at her local Weight Watchers meeting.

DIANE WHITE · CROFTON, MARYLAND

Four 4-ounce lean loin pork chops
1 cup chopped onion
4 ounces long-grain white rice
2 small Granny Smith apples, pared, cored, and chopped
1 tablespoon granulated brown sugar substitute

1 teaspoon low-sodium instant chicken broth mix
1 teaspoon ground cinnamon
Dash salt
Dash freshly ground black pepper

1. Preheat oven to 375°F.

2. Spray large nonstick skillet with non-stick cooking spray; add pork chops. Cook over medium-high heat until lightly browned, about 3 minutes. Turn and cook 3 minutes longer; remove from pan and set aside.

3. Add onion and rice to same skillet; cook over medium heat, stirring occasionally, until rice is golden, about 2 minutes. Transfer rice mixture to shallow 2-quart casserole or baking pan. Add remaining ingredients and 1½ cups boiling water; arrange pork chops on top. Cover and bake

until rice is tender and most of the liquid is absorbed, about 30 to 40 minutes.

MAKES 4 SERVINGS

EACH SERVING PROVIDES: *3 Proteins; ½ Vegetable; 1 Bread; ½ Fruit; 5 Optional Calories*

PER SERVING: *333 Calories, 28 g Protein, 9 g Fat, 34 g Carbohydrate, 31 mg Calcium, 112 mg Sodium, 71 mg Cholesterol, 2 g Dietary Fiber*

Easy Harvest Pork Cutlets

Here's proof that calorie-heavy favorites can be streamlined without sacrificing taste. Martha's breaded pork chops show that you can please the whole family without straying from your weight loss program.

MARTHA LAW · BEDFORD, TEXAS

2 tablespoons spicy brown mustard
2 tablespoons low-sodium soy sauce
Dash freshly ground black pepper

Four 4-ounce boneless pork loin cutlets
3 tablespoons plain dried bread crumbs
½ cup thinly sliced onion

1.   Preheat oven to 350°F.

2.   In small bowl, combine mustard, soy sauce, and pepper. Place cutlets on rack in roasting pan and spread ½ tablespoon of mustard mixture on each side.

3.   Top each cutlet with equal amounts of bread crumbs and onion. Bake until meat is cooked through, about 30 minutes.

MAKES 4 SERVINGS

EACH SERVING PROVIDES: *3 Proteins; ¼ Vegetable; ¼ Bread*

PER SERVING: *219 Calories, 27 g Protein, 9 g Fat, 6 g Carbohydrate, 17 mg Calcium, 485 mg Sodium, 72 mg Cholesterol, 1 g Dietary Fiber*

Skillet Surprise

What do you feed a meat-and-potatoes man when you're trying to slim down? Karen says the sweet-and-sour tang of this one-dish meal never fails to bring a satisfied smile to her husband's lips.

KAREN BARTLETT BASSETT · IONE, CALIFORNIA

15 ounces boneless pork tenderloin,
    cut into 1-inch cubes
Dash salt
Dash freshly ground black pepper
2 tablespoons olive oil
4 garlic cloves, minced
18 asparagus spears, sliced diagonally
    into 1-inch pieces

1½ cups sliced carrots, blanched
¾ cup drained sliced water chestnuts
¼ cup dry white wine
¼ cup low-sodium soy sauce
2 tablespoons honey
½ teaspoon crushed red pepper flakes
3 cups hot cooked brown rice

1.   Preheat broiler.

2.   Season pork with salt and pepper. Broil on rack 4 inches from heat 2 minutes, turning meat once. Set aside.

3.   In large nonstick skillet, heat oil; add garlic and cook over medium heat until softened, about 2 minutes. Add asparagus and cook, tossing frequently, 2 minutes longer.

4.   Add pork and remaining ingredients, except rice; cover and cook until asparagus is tender-crisp, about 5 minutes.

5.   To serve, spoon rice onto serving platter; top with pork mixture.

MAKES 6 SERVINGS

EACH SERVING PROVIDES: *1 Fat; 2 Proteins; 1 Vegetable; 1 Bread; 30 Optional Calories*

PER SERVING: *318 Calories, 21 g Protein, 8 g Fat, 38 g Carbohydrate, 41 mg Calcium, 479 mg Sodium, 53 mg Cholesterol, 3 g Dietary Fiber*

Rosemary Pork

Kathleen's hobbies are entertaining and cooking—which is why she joined Weight Watchers. Today she develops special recipes that don't pack on pounds, like these herb-scented chops.

KATHLEEN FIMPLE · ASTON, PENNSYLVANIA

3 garlic cloves, minced
½ cup dry white wine
1 teaspoon dried rosemary
Dash freshly ground black pepper
2 cups drained canned Italian plum
     tomatoes (reserve liquid), chopped

1 teaspoon freshly grated lemon zest
Four 4-ounce lean boneless pork chops
2 cups hot cooked long-grain white rice

1.   Preheat broiler.

2.   Spray large nonstick skillet with nonstick cooking spray; add garlic and cook over medium heat until softened, about 1 minute.

3.   Add wine, rosemary, and pepper. Cook over high heat until wine is reduced by half; stir in tomatoes, reserved liquid, and lemon zest. Simmer, uncovered, over low heat 15 minutes.

4.   Broil chops on rack 4 inches from heat 2 minutes on each side. Transfer chops to tomato sauce; simmer, covered, over low heat 5 minutes.

5.   Place rice on heated serving platter. Arrange chops on rice; pour sauce over top.

MAKES 4 SERVINGS

EACH SERVING PROVIDES: *3 Proteins; 1 Vegetable; 1 Bread; 25 Optional Calories*

PER SERVING: *379 Calories, 31 g Protein, 10 g Fat, 35 g Carbohydrate, 58 mg Calcium, 266 mg Sodium, 83 mg Cholesterol, 1 g Dietary Fiber*

Cajun Pork Roast

A cosmetologist who loves collecting cookbooks, Pat came up with a lighter rendition of a Southern staple that's traditionally loaded with butter and oil. Her new version pleases even finicky family members.

PATRICIA STEWART · MUSCATINE, IOWA

2 tablespoons reduced-calorie
    tub margarine
1 tablespoon vegetable oil
¼ cup chopped onion
¼ cup chopped celery
¼ cup choped green bell pepper
3 garlic cloves, minced

½ teaspoon freshly ground black pepper
¼ teaspoon white pepper
¼ teaspoon ground red pepper
¼ teaspoon paprika
¼ teaspoon dried thyme
⅛ teaspoon dry mustard
1 pound, 7 ounces boneless pork loin

1.   Preheat oven to 275°F.

2.   In medium nonstick skillet, heat margarine and oil; add onion, celery, bell pepper, and garlic; cook over medium heat until softened, about 2 minutes. Stir in seasonings; set aside to cool.

3.   Using sharp paring knife, make four 1-inch slits about 1½ inches deep into pork; spoon 1 tablespoon vegetable mixture into each slit.

4.   Place pork on rack in roasting pan; spoon remaining vegetable mixture over pork. Roast 1 hour. Raise oven temperature to 475°F; cook until pork is well browned and meat thermometer inserted in center reaches 160°F, about 10 minutes. Let stand 15 minutes before carving.

MAKES 6 SERVINGS

EACH SERVING (3 OUNCES) PROVIDES: *1 Fat; 3 Proteins; ¼ Vegetable*

PER SERVING: *249 Calories, 24 g Protein, 15 g Fat, 2 g Carbohydrate, 14 mg Calcium, 100 mg Sodium, 77 mg Cholesterol, 0 g Dietary Fiber*

Ham Rolls

Karen lost 117 pounds and maintains her shape with sensible fare like these easy-to-make ham rolls. They freeze well, so prepare a batch ahead of time and keep them on hand for parties and brown-bag lunches.

KAREN GRAVATT · PUEBLO, COLORADO

One 10-ounce refrigerated pizza crust
2 tablespoons plain nonfat yogurt
2 teaspoons Dijon mustard
1 teaspoon drained white horseradish

6 ounces thinly sliced boiled ham
3 ounces shredded cheddar cheese
½ cup diced onion

1.   Preheat oven to 425°F. On work surface, stretch pizza dough into 12-by-10-inch rectangle.

2.   In small bowl, whisk together yogurt, mustard, and horseradish; spread mixture evenly over dough, leaving 1½-inch border.

3.   Arrange ham over dough; sprinkle with cheese and onion. Starting from wide end, roll dough jelly-roll fashion to enclose filling; pinch seam to seal.

4.   Spray nonstick baking sheet with nonstick cooking spray. Arrange roll seam-side down on sheet. Bake 15 minutes, until golden brown. Let cool 10 minutes before cutting into 10 equal slices.

MAKES 10 SERVINGS

EACH SERVING PROVIDES: *1 Protein; 1 Bread; 2 Optional Calories*

PER SERVING: *137 Calories, 8 g Protein, 5 g Fat, 14 g Carbohydrate, 74 mg Calcium, 430 mg Sodium, 18 mg Cholesterol, 0 g Dietary Fiber*

Ham and Potato Casserole

Devah, who attended Weight Watchers At Work Program meetings at the bank where she's employed, recommends this as a terrific brunch or dinner entree for St. Patrick's Day, or anytime you feel like getting your Irish up.

DEVAH O'DOHERTY · OMAHA, NEBRASKA

1 tablespoon plus 1 teaspoon
    vegetable oil
1 cup diced mushrooms
½ cup diced onion

1 pound diced pared cooked potatoes
5 ounces diced smoked ham
3 ounces shredded cheddar cheese

In 1-quart microwavable casserole, combine oil, mushrooms, and onion. Microwave on High 1 minute. Stir in remaining ingredients. Microwave, covered, on Medium-High 5 minutes.

MAKES 4 SERVINGS

EACH SERVING PROVIDES: *1 Fat; 2¼ Proteins; ¾ Vegetable; 1 Bread*

PER SERVING: *282 Calories, 15 g Protein, 14 g Fat, 26 g Carbohydrate, 170 mg Calcium, 645 mg Sodium, 39 mg Cholesterol, 2 g Dietary Fiber*

Easy Skillet Supper

Edna is a great-grandmother who developed this recipe as an alternative to the fried potatoes and eggs her husband adores.

EDNA DAVIE · BAKERSFIELD, CALIFORNIA

2 teaspoons olive oil
½ cup chopped onion
¼ cup chopped green bell pepper
¼ cup chopped scallions (green onions)
1 pound cooked red potatoes, cubed

6 large eggs, lightly beaten
¼ cup low-fat (1%) milk
¼ teaspoon freshly ground black pepper
3 ounces shredded cheddar cheese
2 slices crisp cooked bacon, crumbled

1. In large nonstick skillet, heat oil; add onion, green bell pepper, and scallions. Cook over medium-high heat, stirring occasionally, until onion is translucent, about 2 minutes.

2. Add potatoes, eggs, milk, and pepper; cook, stirring frequently, until eggs are just set, about 3 minutes. Remove from heat and sprinkle with cheese; let stand 1 minute.

3. To serve, slide onto heated serving platter and sprinkle bacon over top. Serve immediately.

Serving Suggestion: Mild or spicy salsa is a nice accompaniment.

MAKES 4 SERVINGS

EACH SERVING PROVIDES: *½ Fat; 2½ Proteins; ½ Vegetable; 1 Bread; 25 Optional Calories*

PER SERVING: *345 Calories, 19 g Protein, 19 g Fat, 25 g Carbohydrate, 219 mg Calcium, 295 mg Sodium, 344 mg Cholesterol, 2 g Dietary Fiber*

Stuffed Spaghetti Squash

Easy meals like this one are a lifesaver for a busy office manager, Weight Watchers meeting leader, and part-time trainer who lost 87½ pounds and has learned to keep it off more than ten years.

STELLA SPIKELL · YOUNGSTOWN, OHIO

1 spaghetti squash (about 1½ pounds)
2 teaspoons olive oil
½ cup chopped onion
½ cup chopped red bell pepper
2 garlic cloves, minced
5 ounces ground veal

¼ teaspoon dried oregano
¼ teaspoon salt
⅛ teaspoon freshly ground black pepper
1½ ounces shredded part-skim
      mozzarella cheese
1 tablespoon chopped fresh parsley

1.   Pierce squash with tip of sharp knife in several places; place on paper plate and microwave on High 10 minutes, or until just softened, turning once during cooking. Let stand 5 minutes. Cut squash in half lengthwise and remove seeds. Using fork, scoop out pulp. Measure 3 cups squash into medium bowl; set aside. Reserve shells.

2.   Preheat oven to 350°F.

3.   In medium skillet, heat oil. Add onion, bell pepper, and garlic; cook over medium-high heat, stirring occasionally, until onion is translucent, about 2 minutes. Add veal; cook, stirring frequently, until veal is crumbled and cooked, about 5 minutes. Stir in squash pulp and remaining ingredients except cheese and parsley.

4.   Spoon mixture evenly into each shell; place in baking pan. Bake 20 minutes. Sprinkle with cheese; bake 3 minutes longer. Sprinkle with parsley.

MAKES 2 SERVINGS

EACH SERVING PROVIDES: *1 Fat; 3 Proteins; 3 Vegetables*

PER SERVING: *304 Calories, 21 g Protein, 14 g Fat, 24 g Carbohydrate, 227 mg Calcium, 472 mg Sodium, 70 mg Cholesterol, 1 g Dietary Fiber*

Veal Loaf Florentine

When her family pledged to adopt a healthier lifestyle, Margaret reworked her famous stuffed meatloaf recipe into this innovative dish.

MARGARET HUDAK · WELLAND, ONTARIO, CANADA

4 cups spinach leaves, thoroughly washed and drained
1 tablespoon vegetable oil
1½ cups thinly sliced onions
3 tablespoons barbecue sauce
2 slices reduced-calorie white bread
1 large egg

1 packet low-sodium instant chicken broth mix
¼ teaspoon freshly ground black pepper
¼ teaspoon dried thyme
¼ teaspoon dried marjoram
1 pound, 7 ounces ground veal
½ cup sliced mushrooms

1.   Preheat oven to 350°F. In 2-quart casserole, place spinach and 1 tablespoon water; cover and microwave on High 2 minutes. Squeeze out excess moisture.

2.   In medium nonstick skillet, heat oil; add 1 cup of the onions and cook over medium heat until softened, about 2 minutes. Stir in barbecue sauce and 1 tablespoon water. Set aside.

3.   In blender or food processor, puree the remaining onion, bread, egg, broth mix, seasonings, and 2 tablespoons water until smooth. Transfer to medium bowl; add ground veal and stir until well combined.

4.   Transfer meat mixture to wax paper and shape into 12-by-9-inch rectangle. Spread spinach over meat, leaving 1½-inch border. Top spinach with onion mixture and mushrooms.

5.   Starting from a wide end, roll meat jelly-roll fashion to enclose vegetable filling; pinch seam and ends well to seal. Discard wax paper. Arrange roll, seam-side down, on nonstick baking sheet. Bake until juices run clear, about 1 hour.

MAKES 6 SERVINGS

EACH SERVING PROVIDES: ½ Fat; 3 Proteins; 2 Vegetables; 35 Optional Calories

PER SERVING: 238 Calories, 25 g Protein, 11 g Fat, 10 g Carbohydrate, 61 mg Calcium, 409 mg Sodium, 125 mg Cholesterol, 2 g Dietary Fiber

Hearty Leek and Veal Stew

Food has been a family affair for generations of Emmy's clan: her grandfather owned a candy factory in Cairo; her parents ran a restaurant in Foster City, California. Following her heritage and her Food Plan, she contributes a zesty stew that's great over noodles.

EMMY DENTON · BELMONT, CALIFORNIA

1 tablespoon plus 1 teaspoon olive oil
2 cups thoroughly washed sliced leeks (white part and some green)
1 garlic clove, minced
15 ounces veal stew meat, cut into 1-inch cubes
2 tablespoons all-purpose flour
1 tablespoon sweet white wine

2 cups drained canned Italian plum tomatoes (reserve liquid), seeded
2 cups chopped carrots
2 cups diced celery
1½ teaspoons dried basil
1 teaspoon dried oregano
1 bay leaf

1. In large saucepan, heat oil; add leeks and garlic and cook over medium heat until softened, about 2 minutes. Add veal and cook, stirring occasionally, until meat loses its pink color, about 5 minutes.

2. Sprinkle in flour and add wine and ½ cup water, making sure flour is completely dissolved in liquid.

3. Add remaining ingredients; cook, covered, over medium-low heat until veal is tender, about 1 hour.

MAKES 4 SERVINGS

EACH SERVING PROVIDES: *1 Fat; 3 Proteins; 4 Vegetables; 20 Optional Calories*

PER SERVING: *266 Calories, 25 g Protein, 8 g Fat, 24 g Carbohydrate, 141 mg Calcium, 366 mg Sodium, 89 mg Cholesterol, 4 g Dietary Fiber*

Side Dishes

The foods that accompany the "main" dish are newly important and truly exciting. Once again in search of the complex carbohydrate, we offer pilafs that go far beyond plain rice: Barley Pilaf, Confetti Pilaf, Fruited Rice Pilaf, and Vegetable Pilau. All provide inventive, tasty ways to partner a bit of protein.

You'll find vegetables here, of course. But they're a new generation: Blanched Baby Vegetables, Frosted Cauliflower, Jicama Spinach, and Tomatoes Rockefeller elevate the vegetable to new status. Each of these could also be a spectacular first course.

There's a bit of nostalgia here as well, in the form of old favorites reinterpreted in lighter versions. French Country Potatoes, Grilled Hash Brown Potatoes, and Twice-Baked Potatoes take us back to cherished tastes—with better nutrition profiles.

We've even included some restaurant specials: Incredible French Fries are chili-dusted sweet potato sticks that provide a new twist; Oven-Fried Zucchini Spears are stand-ins for the popular fried zucchini sticks offered at casual dining places.

From the oven, some fresh home baking merits attention: Broccoli Corn-bread is a special down-home treat and Dilly Bread partners soup perfectly.

To enhance any meal or snack, we've included recipes for homemade condiments: Fresh Texas Salsa and Fruit Chutney will become standards. Obviously, the side dish has moved closer to center stage.

Asparagus with Mustard Sauce

With twin sons and a husband who loves unique meals, Leigh, a 50-pound loser, is always exercising her culinary creativity. This recipe substitutes nonfat yogurt for sour cream, with fabulous results.

LEIGH HENLINE · NORTH PLATTE, NEBRASKA

½ cup plain nonfat yogurt
1½ tablespoons prepared mustard
2 teaspoons margarine

½ teaspoon dried parsley
Dash salt
24 medium asparagus spears, cooked

1. In small saucepan, combine all ingredients except asparagus. Cook over low heat until just warm, stirring occasionally.

2. Arrange asparagus on heated serving platter, or on individual serving plates. Pour sauce over top.

MAKES 4 SERVINGS

EACH SERVING PROVIDES: ½ Fat; 1 Vegetable; 15 Optional Calories

PER SERVING: 52 Calories, 4 g Protein, 2 g Fat, 5 g Carbohydrate, 77 mg Calcium, 152 mg Sodium, 1 mg Cholesterol, 1 g Dietary Fiber

Blanched Baby Vegetables

A lively, colorful dish that adapts well to fresh seasonal vegetables throughout the year.

ELLEN HUTTO · HOUSTON, TEXAS

2 cups baby carrots, trimmed and washed
2 cups baby zucchini, trimmed and washed
2 cups baby yellow squash, trimmed and washed

2 tablespoons reduced-calorie tub margarine
¼ teaspoon salt
¼ teaspoon freshly ground black pepper
Juice of ½ lemon

1.   In large saucepan, bring 3 quarts water to a boil. Add carrots and cook until almost tender, 2 to 4 minutes. Add zucchini and squash; cook 1 to 2 minutes longer; drain.

2.   In large skillet, melt margarine over medium-high heat. Add vegetables and sauté 2 minutes, stirring occasionally. Sprinkle with salt, pepper, and lemon juice.

MAKES 4 SERVINGS

EACH SERVING (1½ CUPS) PROVIDES: ¾ Fat; 3 Vegetables

PER SERVING: 71 Calories, 2 g Protein, 3 g Fat, 10 g Carbohydrate, 41 mg Calcium, 226 mg Sodium, 0 mg Cholesterol, 3 g Dietary Fiber

Dilled Broccoli and Carrots

Here's a real bonanza when you're looking to maximize nutrition. Best of all, it cooks in no time at all in the microwave.

½ cup thinly sliced onion
½ cup thinly sliced carrot
2 cups broccoli, cut into 1-inch florets
    with thinly sliced stems

3 tablespoons chopped fresh dill
Dash salt
Dash freshly ground black pepper

1.   In 3-quart microwavable casserole, combine onion, carrot, and 2 tablespoons water. Cover tightly with lid or vented plastic wrap. Microwave on High 2 minutes, or until onion is tender.

2.   Stir in broccoli and dill. Cover and microwave on High 3 minutes, or until vegetables are tender-crisp, stirring once. Let stand, covered, 1 minute. Season with salt and pepper.

MAKES 2 SERVINGS

EACH SERVING PROVIDES: *3 Vegetables*

PER SERVING: *55 Calories, 4 g Protein, 0 g Fat, 12 g Carbohydrate, 79 mg Calcium, 103 mg Sodium, 0 mg Cholesterol, 4 g Dietary Fiber*

Frosted Cauliflower

"My husband is not a cauliflower fan, but even he takes seconds when I serve this dish," boasts Thelma, a retired assembly line worker, mother, and grandmother who enjoys gardening, crafts, and traveling.

THELMA GOETTSCH · CEDAR RAPIDS, IOWA

1 small head cauliflower (about 1
    pound), washed and trimmed
3 tablespoons reduced-calorie
    Italian dressing (6 calories per
    tablespoon)
2¼ ounces shredded cheddar cheese

¼ cup reduced-calorie mayonnaise
2 tablespoons finely chopped onion
1 teaspoon prepared mustard
Chopped parsley for garnish (optional)

1. In 2½-quart microwavable casserole, place cauliflower and ¼ cup water; sprinkle with dressing. Cover tightly with vented plastic wrap. Microwave on High 6 minutes, or until cauliflower is tender-crisp.

2. In small bowl, combine cheese, mayonnaise, onion, and mustard; spread mixture evenly over cauliflower. Microwave, uncovered, on High 2 to 3 minutes, until cheese is melted. Let stand for 1 minute. Garnish with parsley, if desired.

MAKES 4 SERVINGS

EACH SERVING PROVIDES: *1½ Fats; ¾ Protein; 1 Vegetable; 5 Optional Calories*

PER SERVING: *123 Calories, 5 g Protein, 9 g Fat, 5 g Carbohydrate, 130 mg Calcium, 360 mg Sodium, 22 mg Cholesterol, 1 g Dietary Fiber*

Oven-Fried Zucchini Spears

To get her family to eat more zucchini, Helen devised this substitute for the deep-fried restaurant appetizer. Helen loves traveling and collects American Indian crafts.

HELEN EDINBORO · WEST SUNBURY, PENNSYLVANIA

3 tablespoons seasoned dried bread
    crumbs
1 tablespoon grated Parmesan cheese
⅛ teaspoon garlic powder

⅛ teaspoon paprika
⅛ teaspoon freshly ground black pepper
2 medium zucchini (about 12 ounces)
2 teaspoons olive oil

1. Preheat oven to 475°F.

2. On shallow plate, combine all ingredients except zucchini and oil; set aside.

3. Slice off ends of zucchini. Cut each zucchini lengthwise into quarters; cut each quarter in half.

4. In large plastic bag, combine oil, zucchini, and 2 teaspoons water; close bag and shake well to moisten zucchini. Dredge zucchini in bread crumb mixture.

5. Arrange zucchini in single layer on nonstick baking sheet. Bake until golden, 10 to 12 minutes.

MAKES 2 SERVINGS

EACH SERVING PROVIDES: *1 Fat; 2 Vegetables; ½ Bread; 15 Optional Calories*

PER SERVING: *115 Calories, 5 g Protein, 6 g Fat, 13 g Carbohydrate, 70 mg Calcium, 350 mg Sodium, 3 mg Cholesterol, 1 g Dietary Fiber*

Shown with Incredible French Fries (page 238).

Jicama Spinach

Like Popeye, the Trohas love spinach. This recipe combines that iron-rich vegetable with exotic jicama, garlic, and ginger.

GIZELLA TROHA · EUCLID, OHIO

2 teaspoons olive oil
1½ teaspoons grated pared ginger root
2 garlic cloves, minced
½ cup julienned pared jicama

1¼ teaspoons low-sodium soy sauce
8 cups thoroughly washed and drained
    spinach leaves
¼ teaspoon freshly ground black pepper

1.   In large nonstick skillet or wok, heat oil; add ginger and garlic. Cook over medium heat 1 minute. Add jicama and soy sauce; cook, stirring frequently, 2 minutes.

2.   Add spinach; cook, stirring constantly, until spinach is barely limp, about 2 minutes longer. Sprinkle with pepper.

MAKES 4 SERVINGS

EACH SERVING PROVIDES: ½ Fat; 4¼ Vegetables

PER SERVING: 55 Calories, 4 g Protein, 3 g Fat, 6 g
    Carbohydrate, 117 mg Calcium, 152 mg Sodium,
    0 mg Cholesterol, 3 g Dietary Fiber

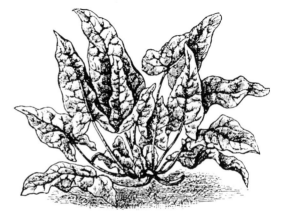

Tomatoes Rockefeller

Recapture the robust taste of the topping on Oysters Rockefeller, built on slabs of ripe beefsteak tomatoes.

2 cups frozen chopped spinach (one 10-ounce package), thawed, drained, and squeezed dry
¼ cup egg substitute
3 tablespoons plain dried bread crumbs
2 tablespoons minced scallions (green onions)
¾ ounce grated Parmesan cheese

1 tablespoon plus 1 teaspoon reduced-calorie tub margarine, melted
1 teaspoon minced garlic
¼ teaspoon dried thyme
1 medium beefsteak tomato, cut into 4 slices
¼ teaspoon garlic salt

1. Preheat oven to 350°F. In large bowl, combine spinach, egg substitute, bread crumbs, scallions, cheese, margarine, garlic, and thyme.

2. Spray 2-quart baking dish with non-stick cooking spray; arrange tomato slices in single layer. Sprinkle evenly with garlic salt.

3. Mound about ¼ cup of spinach mixture on each tomato slice; bake 15 to 20 minutes, until heated through.

MAKES 4 SERVINGS

EACH SERVING (1 SLICE) PROVIDES: ½ Fat; ½ Protein; 1½ Vegetables; ¼ Bread

PER SERVING: 96 Calories, 7 g Protein, 4 g Fat, 9 g Carbohydrate, 169 mg Calcium, 362 mg Sodium, 4 mg Cholesterol, 2 g Dietary Fiber

French Country Potatoes

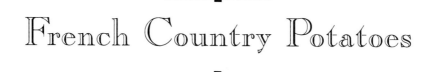

A former Weight Watchers leader, Virginia loves developing new recipes, and this one is a particular favorite. It's easily doubled, but use shallow casseroles so that the broth covers the potatoes.

VIRGINIA MOON · HARVEST, ALABAMA

2 teaspoons reduced-calorie tub
    margarine
¼ cup chopped onion
¼ cup sliced mushrooms
10 ounces thinly sliced pared all-purpose
    potatoes

⅛ teaspoon dried rosemary, crushed
⅛ teaspoon freshly ground black pepper
1 packet low-sodium instant chicken
    broth mix
¾ ounce Gruyère or Swiss cheese,
    shredded

1. Preheat oven to 425°F. Spray 1-quart casserole with nonstick cooking spray.

2. In medium nonstick skillet, melt margarine over medium heat; add onion and mushrooms; cook over medium heat until onion is translucent, about 2 minutes. Stir in potatoes, rosemary, and pepper; transfer to prepared casserole.

3. In 1-cup measure, stir together chicken broth mix and ⅓ cup water; pour over potatoes; top evenly with cheese.

4. Bake, uncovered, until potatoes are fork-tender, about 30 to 35 minutes.

MAKES 2 SERVINGS

EACH SERVING PROVIDES: *½ Fat; ½ Protein; ½ Vegetable; 1 Bread; 5 Optional Calories*

PER SERVING: *190 Calories, 7 g Protein, 6 g Fat, 28 g Carbohydrate, 123 mg Calcium, 577 mg Sodium, 12 mg Cholesterol, 3 g Dietary Fiber*

#
Grilled Hash Brown Potatoes

arsha is a Weight Watchers weigher and receptionist who's lost 30 pounds. Whether grilled or baked in a 350° oven, her delicious side dish can be doubled or tripled to feed a hungry crowd.

MARSHA HOLZHAUER · NASHVILLE, ILLINOIS

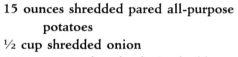

15 ounces shredded pared all-purpose
    potatoes
½ cup shredded onion
1½ ounces reduced-calorie cheddar or
    Swiss cheese, shredded

½ teaspoon salt
¼ cup low-fat (1%) milk
1 tablespoon plus 1 teaspoon reduced-
    calorie tub margarine

1.   Place grill rack 5 inches from coals. Prepare grill according to manufacturer's directions. Tear off two 18-inch pieces of aluminum foil.

2.   In medium bowl, combine potatoes, onion, cheese, and salt. Spoon potato mixture onto 1 piece of foil; shape into 12-inch log. Pour milk over potatoes; dot with margarine.

3.   Wrap foil around mixture, making sure seams are tightly sealed. Wrap foil package in second length of foil; place on grill and cook 1 hour, turning every 5 minutes to ensure even cooking and prevent burning. Carefully unwrap foil layers; cut into slices.

MAKES 2 SERVINGS

EACH SERVING PROVIDES: *1 Fat; 1 Protein; ½ Vegetable; 1½ Breads; 10 Optional Calories*

PER SERVING: *297 Calories, 12 g Protein, 8 g Fat, 44 g Carbohydrate, 251 mg Calcium, 799 mg Sodium, 16 mg Cholesterol, 4 g Dietary Fiber*

Potatoes Diablo

Sylvia's guests never guess they're dining "lite" when the fare is this good and hearty. She's a social service worker and cares for a household of cats.

SYLVIA JONES · SAN PABLO, CALIFORNIA

2 teaspoons vegetable oil
10 ounces red potatoes, cut into ¼-inch
    slices

½ cup mild salsa
1½ ounces shredded cheddar cheese
6 pitted large black olives, sliced

1. Preheat broiler.

2. In large nonstick skillet, heat oil; add potatoes in a single layer. Cook over medium-high heat until undersides are browned, about 4 minutes. Turn potatoes and cook until browned, about 4 minutes longer.

3. Transfer potatoes to ovenproof platter. Pour salsa evenly over top; sprinkle with cheese.

4. Broil until cheese is melted, about 2 minutes. Arrange olives over top; serve immediately.

MAKES 2 SERVINGS

EACH SERVING PROVIDES: *1½ Fats; 1 Protein; 1 Bread*

PER SERVING: *275 Calories, 8 g Protein, 13 g Fat, 31 g Carbohydrate, 166 mg Calcium, 671 mg Sodium, 22 mg Cholesterol, 3 g Dietary Fiber*

Potatoes in Mustard Sauce

Judy adapted this recipe from one of her mother's standards. It's great served with ham.

JUDY BALCOM · AUSTIN, TEXAS

1 tablespoon plus 1 teaspoon reduced-calorie tub margarine
½ cup chopped onion
1 tablespoon plus 1 teaspoon all-purpose flour
1 teaspoon low-sodium instant chicken broth mix

1 tablespoon prepared mustard
¼ teaspoon freshly ground black pepper
16 ounces cooked potatoes, cut into ½-inch cubes
1 tablespoon plain dried bread crumbs
1 tablespoon grated Parmesan cheese

1.   Preheat oven to 400°F.

2.   In small saucepan, melt margarine; add onion. Cook over medium heat until onion is translucent, about 2 minutes. Whisk in flour, chicken broth mix, and ¾ cup water. Add mustard and pepper; cook, stirring constantly, until mixture thickens, about 2 minutes.

3.   Spray shallow baking dish with non-stick cooking spray. Spread potatoes in dish; pour sauce evenly over top. Sprinkle evenly with bread crumbs and cheese. Bake until lightly browned, about 20 minutes.

MAKES 4 SERVINGS

EACH SERVING PROVIDES: ½ Fat; ¼ Vegetable; 1 Bread; 30 Optional Calories

PER SERVING: 151 Calories, 4 g Protein, 3 g Fat, 28 g Carbohydrate, 36 mg Calcium, 128 mg Sodium, 1 mg Cholesterol, 2 g Dietary Fiber

Twice-Baked Potatoes

When Dionne, a 32-pound loser, isn't designing jewelry and leading Weight Watchers meetings, she likes traveling, so she's no stranger to restaurant fare. Here's her reduced-calorie version of a popular side dish.

DIONNE STEVENS · LUTZ, FLORIDA

Two 4-ounce baked potatoes, halved
    lengthwise
⅓ cup low-fat (1%) cottage cheese
1 tablespoon minced onion

Dash hot sauce
2 teaspoons imitation bacon bits
2 tablespoons sliced scallions (green
    onions)

1. Preheat oven to 350°F. Scoop out pulp from potato halves into medium bowl, leaving ¼-inch shells. Mash pulp; reserve shells.

2. Place cottage cheese, onion, hot sauce, and 1 teaspoon water in blender; process until completely pureed, about 1 minute. Add cottage cheese mixture and bacon bits to potato pulp; stir to combine.

3. Spoon potato mixture evenly into reserved shells; place on baking sheet and bake until heated through, about 15 minutes. Sprinkle evenly with sliced scallions.

MAKES 2 SERVINGS

EACH SERVING PROVIDES: *½ Protein; 1 Bread; 10 Optional Calories*

PER SERVING: *128 Calories, 8 g Protein, 2 g Fat, 21 g Carbohydrate, 43 mg Calcium, 202 mg Sodium, 4 mg Cholesterol, 2 g Dietary Fiber*

Incredible French Fries

They're baked, not fried, but the great taste of America's favorite spud comes shining through in this simple recipe.

MARY WADDEN • WEST YARMOUTH, MASSACHUSETTS

1 large egg white
2 teaspoons chili powder
½ teaspoon salt
¼ teaspoon garlic powder

¼ teaspoon onion powder
16 ounces pared sweet potatoes, cut into
    ½-inch strips

1.   Preheat oven to 450°F.

2.   In large bowl, whisk together egg white, chili powder, salt, and garlic and onion powder until frothy. Add potatoes; toss to coat well.

3.   Using slotted spoon, transfer potatoes to nonstick baking sheet; spread to make single layer. Bake until golden brown and crisp, about 20 minutes, stirring once during baking.

MAKES 4 SERVINGS

EACH SERVING PROVIDES: *1 Bread; 5 Optional Calories*

PER SERVING: *128 Calories, 3 g Protein, 1 g Fat, 29 g Carbohydrate, 31 mg Calcium, 315 mg Sodium, 0 mg Cholesterol, 4 g Dietary Fiber*

Shown with Oven-Fried Zucchini Spears on page 229.

Stuffed Sweet Potatoes

From a Weight Watchers leader in the South comes this rendition of sweet potatoes that combines the sweetness of raisins with the tartness of pineapple chunks.

EVERETT PULLIAM, JR. · RICHMOND, VIRGINIA

Two 6-ounce baked sweet potatoes, halved lengthwise
½ cup drained crushed pineapple
¼ cup raisins

1 tablespoon plus 1 teaspoon reduced-calorie tub margarine
½ teaspoon pumpkin pie spice
Dash salt

1. Preheat oven to 400°F. Scoop out pulp from potato halves into mixing bowl, leaving ¼-inch shells. Mash pulp; reserve shells.

2. Add remaining ingredients to potato pulp; stir to combine. Spoon potato mixture evenly into reserved shells; place on baking sheet and bake until heated through, about 10 minutes.

MAKES 4 SERVINGS

EACH SERVING PROVIDES: *½ Fat; 1 Bread; ¾ Fruit* ·

PER SERVING: *128 Calories, 1 g Protein, 2 g Fat, 27 g Carbohydrate, 24 mg Calcium, 79 mg Sodium, 0 mg Cholesterol, 3 g Dietary Fiber*

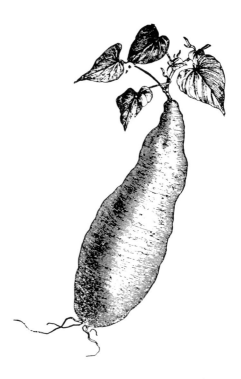

Fruited Sweet Potatoes

A talented musician who plays harpsichord, organ, and piano, Erika also finds time to attend exercise class almost daily. She adapted this recipe from one invented by her aerobics teacher.

ERIKA-MARIA MATTHES · SAN FRANCISCO, CALIFORNIA

16 ounces pared sweet potatoes, cut into
    1-inch pieces
12 dried apricot halves, chopped
1 small Granny Smith apple, pared,
    cored, and chopped
2 tablespoons raisins

¼ cup orange juice
1 ounce orange-flavored liqueur
1 teaspoon ground cinnamon
¼ teaspoon ground nutmeg
Dash salt

1. In 2-quart microwavable casserole, combine potatoes and 2 tablespoons water. Cover and microwave on High 10 minutes, or until potatoes are tender, stirring once.

2. Add remaining ingredients; stir well to combine. Cover and microwave on High 3 minutes, or until apple is tender-crisp.

MAKES 4 SERVINGS

EACH SERVING PROVIDES: *1 Bread; 1 Fruit; 30 Optional Calories*

PER SERVING: *202 Calories, 3 g Protein, 1 g Fat, 46 g Carbohydrate, 42 mg Calcium, 50 mg Sodium, 0 mg Cholesterol, 5 g Dietary Fiber*

Butternut Squash Casserole

A bountiful summer harvest of butternut squash inspired Gail to concoct a sweet casserole that's equally at home as a hot side dish or a cold dessert.

GAIL GILBERT · BOLINGBROKE, GEORGIA

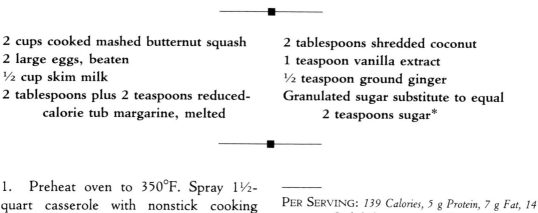

2 cups cooked mashed butternut squash
2 large eggs, beaten
½ cup skim milk
2 tablespoons plus 2 teaspoons reduced-calorie tub margarine, melted

2 tablespoons shredded coconut
1 teaspoon vanilla extract
½ teaspoon ground ginger
Granulated sugar substitute to equal 2 teaspoons sugar*

1. Preheat oven to 350°F. Spray 1½-quart casserole with nonstick cooking spray; set aside.

2. In large bowl, combine all ingredients until thoroughly blended. Pour into prepared casserole.

3. Bake until set, 50 to 60 minutes. (Or microwave on Medium 12 minutes, then on High 3 minutes. Let stand 2 minutes.)

MAKES 4 SERVINGS

PER SERVING: *139 Calories, 5 g Protein, 7 g Fat, 14 g Carbohydrate, 92 mg Calcium, 138 mg Sodium, 107 mg Cholesterol, 0 g Dietary Fiber*

EACH SERVING (½ CUP) PROVIDES: *1 Fat; ½ Protein; ½ Bread; 20 Optional Calories*

* *Do not use low-calorie sweetener with aspartame in this recipe; it may lose sweetness during baking.*

Barley Pilaf

An easy-to-prepare side dish that's also very filling, from a cook who counts entertaining and painting among her best-loved hobbies.

LANCENE DAVIS · GLADSTONE, OREGON

2 tablespoons reduced-calorie tub margarine
¼ cup chopped onion
¼ cup diced carrot
4½ ounces quick-cooking barley

1½ cups low-sodium chicken broth
1 cup drained canned sliced mushrooms
2 tablespoons parsley flakes
¼ teaspoon freshly ground black pepper

1. Preheat oven to 350°F.

2. In medium nonstick skillet, melt margarine; add onion and carrot. Cook over medium heat 2 minutes, until onion is translucent. Add barley, stirring to coat.

3. Transfer barley mixture to 2-quart casserole; stir in remaining ingredients. Cover and bake until liquid is absorbed, about 15 minutes. Let stand 2 minutes. Fluff with fork and serve.

MAKES 4 SERVINGS

EACH SERVING (1¼ CUPS) PROVIDES: *1½ Fats; ¾ Vegetable; 1½ Breads*

PER SERVING: *167 Calories, 5 g Protein, 4 g Fat, 28 g Carbohydrate, 14 mg Calcium, 234 mg Sodium, 0 mg Cholesterol, 4 g Dietary Fiber*

Confetti Pilaf

Martha eliminated the butter but not the great flavor that makes this pretty pilaf a winner with family and friends.

Martha Law · Bedford, Texas

1 tablespoon plus 1 teaspoon margarine
½ cup chopped red, green, or yellow
    bell pepper
½ cup chopped onion
½ cup drained canned sliced mushrooms
4 ounces long-grain white rice

1 teaspoon low-sodium instant chicken
    broth mix
1 teaspoon Worcestershire sauce
¼ teaspoon garlic powder
⅛ teaspoon freshly ground black pepper

1.   Preheat oven to 350°F.

2.   In small nonstick skillet, heat margarine. Add bell pepper, onion, and mushrooms; sauté until vegetables soften, about 2 minutes.

3.   In 1½-quart casserole, combine remaining ingredients and 1 cup plus 2 tablespoons water; stir in vegetables. Cover and bake 35 to 40 minutes, until liquid is absorbed.

4.   Fluff with fork and serve.

Note: This recipe can be prepared in advance. Cool and refrigerate, covered, until ready to serve. Reheat in a conventional oven, or microwave on High 4 minutes.

MAKES 4 servings

Each Serving Provides: *1 Fat; ¾ Vegetable; 1 Bread; 5 Optional Calories*

Per Serving: *156 Calories, 3 g Protein, 4 g Fat, 27 g Carbohydrate, 16 mg Calcium, 379 mg Sodium, 0 mg Cholesterol, 1 g Dietary Fiber*

Fruited Rice Pilaf

Cooking, quilt-making, and music are Ellen's frequent pleasures. Her hearty whole-grain side dish is perfect with simply prepared meats.

ELLEN BIRNBAUM KEHR • LOS ANGELES, CALIFORNIA

1 tablespoon vegetable oil
½ cup chopped onion
¼ cup chopped celery
7 ounces bulgur (cracked wheat)
5 ounces long-grain white rice
¼ cup golden raisins
6 dried apricot halves, chopped

4 packets low-sodium instant chicken broth mix
1 teaspoon dried rosemary
1 teaspoon curry powder
Chopped fresh parsley for garnish (optional)

1. In large saucepan, heat oil; stir in onion and celery. Cook over medium-high heat until onion is translucent, about 3 minutes.

2. Stir in remaining ingredients and 4 cups water. Cook until mixture comes to a boil. Reduce heat, cover, and simmer until liquid is absorbed, 20 to 30 minutes.

3. Let stand 5 minutes. Fluff with fork. Place in serving dish; garnish with parsley, if desired.

MAKES 6 SERVINGS

EACH SERVING (1 CUP) PROVIDES: *½ Fat; ¼ Vegetable; 2 Breads; ½ Fruit; 10 Optional Calories*

PER SERVING: *262 Calories, 7 g Protein, 3 g Fat, 54 g Carbohydrate, 32 mg Calcium, 16 mg Sodium, 0 mg Cholesterol, 7 g Dietary Fiber*

Vegetable Pilau

With its richly satisfying aroma and flavor, this is an excellent companion for roasted or broiled meats, or its natural Indian partner, tandoori chicken. Linda and her husband love ethnic foods and find that the Weight Watchers Program makes it easy to adapt or create new versions of their favorite dishes.

LINDA GALE · MARIETTA, GEORGIA

1½ cups cauliflower florets
1½ cups broccoli florets
1 cup thinly sliced carrots
½ cup thawed frozen peas
½ cup sliced onion
2 tablespoons vegetable oil
2 teaspoons cumin seeds
½ teaspoon ground cardamom

½ teaspoon ground coriander
½ teaspoon chili powder
½ teaspoon ground cinnamon
¼ teaspoon ground cloves
¼ teaspoon freshly ground black pepper
6 ounces brown Basmati rice, rinsed
1¼ cups low-sodium chicken broth

1. In 2-quart microwavable casserole, combine cauliflower, broccoli, carrots, peas, and 2 tablespoons water. Cover and microwave on High 3 minutes, or until tender-crisp; set aside.

2. In 3-quart microwavable casserole, combine onion and oil; microwave on High 1 minute. Stir in spices and microwave on High 1 minute longer. Add rice, chicken broth, and 1¼ cups hot water; cover and microwave on High 6 minutes. Reduce setting to Medium and cook 20 minutes; stir. Continue to cook, covered, until most of the liquid is absorbed, about 20 minutes. Let stand 5 minutes. Fluff with fork and add reserved vegetables; toss to combine. Microwave, covered, on High 2 minutes, or until heated through.

MAKES 6 SERVINGS

EACH SERVING PROVIDES: *1 Fat; 1½ Vegetables; 1 Bread; 20 Optional Calories*

PER SERVING: *194 Calories, 5 g Protein, 6 g Fat, 31 g Carbohydrate, 49 mg Calcium, 48 mg Sodium, 0 mg Cholesterol, 4 g Dietary Fiber*

Garlic Parmesan Risotto

Marlene loves adapting recipes to make them more healthful for her family. Here she puts a new spin on traditional Italian risotto.

MARLENE CASTOLDI · WALLA WALLA, WASHINGTON

2 teaspoons reduced-calorie tub
    margarine
½ cup sliced mushrooms
¼ cup chopped onion
¼ cup chopped red bell pepper

¼ cup chopped green bell pepper
2 garlic cloves, minced
1 cup cooked long-grain white rice
2 teaspoons grated Parmesan cheese
Chopped parsley for garnish (optional)

1.   In medium saucepan, melt margarine; add mushrooms, onion, peppers, and garlic. Cook over medium-high heat, stirring frequently, until onions are translucent, about 2 minutes.

2.   Add rice and cheese; combine thoroughly. Garnish with parsley, if desired.

MAKES 2 SERVINGS

EACH SERVING (¾ CUP) PROVIDES: ½ Fat; 1
    Vegetable; 1 Bread; 10 Optional Calories

PER SERVING: 180 Calories, 4 g Protein, 3 g Fat, 34
    g Carbohydrate, 47 mg Calcium, 72 mg Sodium,
    1 mg Cholesterol, 1 g Dietary Fiber

Mardi Gras Rice Mold

Nancy has become an expert on international cuisine since studying in Copenhagen and Mallorca. Here's her take on a Southern specialty that's as healthful as it is pretty.

NANCY MYERS · CALIFON, NEW JERSEY

6 ounces brown rice
2 packets low-sodium instant beef
    broth mix
½ cup chopped red bell pepper
½ cup chopped green bell pepper
½ cup chopped celery

½ cup sliced mushrooms
½ cup sliced scallions (green onions)
½ cup grated carrot
Dash white pepper
Parsley sprigs for garnish (optional)

1. In medium saucepan, combine rice, broth mix, and 2¼ cups water; cover and bring to a boil over high heat. Reduce heat and simmer until liquid is almost absorbed, about 50 minutes. Let stand 5 minutes.

2. Spray large nonstick skillet with non-stick cooking spray. Add remaining ingredients except parsley and cook over medium-high heat, stirring occasionally, until celery is tender-crisp, about 3 minutes. Stir vegetables into rice.

3. Spray 6-cup decorative mold with non-stick cooking spray. Press rice mixture firmly into mold. Place flat serving dish over mold; invert and lift mold. Garnish with parsley sprigs, if desired.

Serving suggestion: For an attractive holiday presentation, omit carrot from rice mixture and use cherry tomatoes as garnish with parsley. Adjust Vegetable Selection Information.

MAKES 6 SERVINGS

———

EACH SERVING (¾ CUP) PROVIDES: *1 Vegetable; 1 Bread; 5 Optional Calories*

———

PER SERVING: *125 Calories, 3 g Protein, 1 g Fat, 26 g Carbohydrate, 21 mg Calcium, 19 mg Sodium, 0 mg Cholesterol, 2 g Dietary Fiber*

Rice Dressing

This "company's coming" side dish was invented by Ruth's grandmother. Now that Ruth herself is a "young, sexy-looking grandmother" and a Weight Watchers leader, she maintains her 40-pound loss with sensible substitutions like turkey sausage for pork.

RUTH ANN POOLE · JARRETTSVILLE, MARYLAND

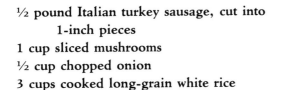

½ pound Italian turkey sausage, cut into 1-inch pieces
1 cup sliced mushrooms
½ cup chopped onion
3 cups cooked long-grain white rice

1½ cups diced celery and celery leaves
¼ teaspoon dried thyme
Dash salt
Dash freshly ground black pepper

1.   Preheat oven to 350°F. Spray 2-quart casserole with nonstick cooking spray.

2.   Spray medium nonstick skillet with nonstick cooking spray; add sausage, mushrooms, and onion; cook over medium heat until sausage is cooked through, about 5 minutes.

3.   Stir in remaining ingredients; transfer to prepared casserole. Bake, uncovered, 45 minutes.

MAKES 6 SERVINGS

EACH SERVING PROVIDES: *1 Protein; 1 Vegetable; 1 Bread*

PER SERVING: *210 Calories, 10 g Protein, 5 g Fat, 32 g Carbohydrate, 28 mg Calcium, 314 mg Sodium, 27 mg Cholesterol, 1 g Dietary Fiber*

Moroccan Couscous

Gayle is a working mother with two young boys. Her version of this North African standard tastes great alongside baked, grilled, or barbecued chicken and steamed vegetables.

GAYLE WERNER · PLYMOUTH, MINNESOTA

6 ounces couscous
1 tablespoon honey
2 teaspoons margarine
¼ cup raisins
1 ounce chopped walnuts
½ teaspoon ground cumin

½ teaspoon ground ginger
½ teaspoon salt
¼ teaspoon ground cinnamon
⅛ teaspoon ground cloves
⅛ teaspoon ground turmeric

In a 2-quart casserole, combine all ingredients with 1½ cups boiling water. Cover and set aside 5 minutes. Fluff with fork and serve. (Can be made in advance. To reheat, microwave on High 5 minutes, or until heated through.)

MAKES 4 SERVINGS

EACH SERVING (¾ CUP) PROVIDES: *1 Fat; ¼ Protein; 1½ Breads; ½ Fruit; 15 Optional Calories*

PER SERVING: *268 Calories, 7 g Protein, 7 g Fat, 46 g Carbohydrate, 29 mg Calcium, 303 mg Sodium, 0 mg Cholesterol, 1 g Dietary Fiber*

Baking Powder Biscuits

Lyn is a 78-pound loser who rides horses and cooks in her free time. After much trial and error, she captured the great taste of restaurant biscuits without all the fat and calories.

LYN ELKIN • BLOOMINGTON, ILLINOIS

2¼ cups all-purpose flour (reserve 2 teaspoons)
1 tablespoon granulated sugar
2 teaspoons double-acting baking powder

½ teaspoon salt
½ teaspoon cream of tartar
½ cup reduced-calorie tub margarine, well chilled
¾ cup low-fat (1.5%) buttermilk

1.   Preheat oven to 425°F. Spray nonstick baking sheet with nonstick cooking spray; set aside.

2.   In medium bowl, combine flour, sugar, baking powder, salt, and cream of tartar.

3.   Using pastry blender or 2 knives, cut in margarine until mixture resembles coarse crumbs; using fork, stir in buttermilk until just combined.

4.   Sprinkle reserved 2 teaspoons flour on work surface; roll out dough to ½-inch thickness. Using 3-inch round biscuit cutter, cut out 12 biscuits, gathering up scraps and rerolling dough as necessary.

5.   Place biscuits on prepared baking sheet; bake until golden, 15 to 20 minutes.

MAKES 12 SERVINGS

EACH SERVING (1 BISCUIT) PROVIDES: *1 Fat; 1 Bread; 10 Optional Calories*

PER SERVING: *132 Calories, 3 g Protein, 5 g Fat, 20 g Carbohydrate, 42 mg Calcium, 252 mg Sodium, 1 mg Cholesterol, 1 g Dietary Fiber*

Broccoli Cornbread

Pat adapted this family favorite to fit the Weight Watchers Program. This colorful bread looks as great as it tastes.

PATRICIA GRAHAM · KINGSPORT, TENNESSEE

2 cups frozen chopped broccoli (one 10-ounce package), thawed and well drained
⅔ cup nonfat cottage cheese
½ cup chopped onion

½ cup egg substitute
2 tablespoons plus 2 teaspoons margarine, softened
¼ teaspoon salt
6 ounces self-rising white cornmeal

1. Preheat oven to 350°F. Spray a 9-inch glass pie plate with nonstick cooking spray; set aside.

2. In large mixing bowl, combine broccoli, cottage cheese, onion, egg substitute, margarine, and salt until blended; stir in cornmeal.

3. Scrape mixture into prepared pie plate; smooth to make even layer. Bake 30 minutes, until golden. Let stand 10 minutes before serving.

MAKES 8 SERVINGS

EACH SERVING PROVIDES: *1 Fat; ½ Protein; ½ Vegetable; 1 Bread; 5 Optional Calories*

PER SERVING: *142 Calories, 6 g Protein, 4 g Fat, 20 g Carbohydrate, 121 mg Calcium, 494 mg Sodium, 2 mg Cholesterol, 2 g Dietary Fiber*

Dilly Bread

LuElla has worked for Weight Watchers since 1976 and says the best part of her job is meeting new members. This wonderfully textured bread is a longtime family favorite.

LuELLA HANSON · YAKIMA, WASHINGTON

1 tablespoon plus 1 teaspoon active dry yeast*
2 cups low-fat (1%) cottage cheese, heated to lukewarm
¼ cup sugar
2 tablespoons margarine, melted

2 tablespoons minced onion
2 large eggs
1 tablespoons plus 1 teaspoon dill seeds
2 teaspoons salt
½ teaspoon baking soda
4½ cups all-purpose flour

1.   In large bowl, dissolve yeast in ½ cup lukewarm water. Stir in remaining ingredients except flour.

2.   Add 4¼ cups of the flour, 1 cup at a time, stirring with wooden spoon after each addition, until soft dough forms.

3.   Sprinkle work surface with 2 tablespoons of remaining flour. Turn dough out onto floured surface; knead until dough is smooth and elastic, about 5 minutes.

4.   Spray medium bowl with nonstick cooking spray. Shape dough into ball and place in prepared bowl. Cover with damp cloth and let rise in warm place about 1 hour, until dough has doubled in size.

5.   Sprinkle work surface with remaining 2 tablespoons flour. Punch dough down and turn out onto floured surface; knead 2 to 3 minutes. Transfer back to mixing bowl (spray with nonstick cooking spray again if necessary); cover and let rise in warm place 45 minutes.

6.   Preheat oven to 350°F.

7.   Divide dough in half, shape into loaves, and place in two 9-by-5-inch loaf pans. Cover and let rise in warm place 20 minutes.

8.   Bake 40 minutes. Cool in pans on rack 10 minutes; remove from pans and cool on rack before wrapping to store.

MAKES 24 SERVINGS, 2 LOAVES OF 12 SLICES
EACH

EACH SERVING (1 SLICE) PROVIDES: ¼ *Fat; ¼*
Protein; 1 Bread; 10 Optional Calories

PER SERVING: *126 Calories, 6 g Protein, 2 g Fat, 21
g Carbohydrate, 25 mg Calcium, 294 mg Sodium, 18 mg Cholesterol, 1 g Dietary Fiber*

* *Quick-rise yeast can also be used. Reduce rising times
according to package directions.*

Fresh Texas Salsa

Melinda writes: "Since I started making my own fat-free salsa, it's become a staple at home and neighbors beg for the recipe. We use it as a dip, a sauce for almost everything, a salad dressing, even as a cold soup."

MELINDA JOHNSON · FLOWER MOUND, TEXAS

10 medium tomatoes, quartered
½ cup chopped onion
½ cup sliced scallions (green onions)
1 large jalapeño pepper, quartered and
    seeded

2 tablespoons chopped fresh cilantro
1 tablespoon granulated sugar
1 teaspoon freshly ground black pepper
Juice of ½ lime
Salt to taste

1. In food processor, combine tomatoes, onion, scallions, jalapeño pepper, and cilantro; process until sauce is just chunky.

2. Pour into large mixing bowl; stir in remaining ingredients. Cover and store in refrigerator up to 2 weeks. Serve as an appetizer dip or a sauce for fish, chicken, beef, or pork.

MAKES 12 SERVINGS

EACH SERVING (½ CUP) PROVIDES: *2 Vegetables;
5 Optional Calories*

PER SERVING: *36 Calories, 1 g Protein, 0 g Fat, 8 g
Carbohydrate, 12 mg Calcium, 13 mg Sodium,
0 mg Cholesterol, 2 g Dietary Fiber*

Spicy Peanut Sauce

Barbara loves Thai food with peanut sauces, but regrets that they are "loaded" with coconut milk and oil. Her own version offers the same taste of the food she loves while helping her maintain her 32-pound weight loss. Try it over raw vegetables, salads, cole slaw, or as a marinade for grilled meats.

BARBARA MIGLANI • DANVILLE, CALIFORNIA

¼ cup peanut butter
3 tablespoons rice wine vinegar
2 tablespoons lime juice
1 tablespoon low-sodium soy sauce
1 tablespoon firmly packed dark brown sugar
1 tablespoon dehydrated minced onion
1 tablespoon dehydrated minced green pepper
1 teaspoon dehydrated minced garlic
1 teaspoon ground ginger
¼ teaspoon crushed red pepper flakes
¼ teaspoon coconut extract

1.   In medium saucepan, combine all ingredients. Stir in 1 cup water; bring just to a boil, stirring.

2.   Reduce heat and simmer, stirring occasionally, 5 minutes. Cool, or refrigerate until ready to use.

MAKES 4 SERVINGS

EACH SERVING (¼ CUP) PROVIDES: *1 Fat; 1 Protein; 15 Optional Calories*

PER SERVING: *121 Calories, 5 g Protein, 8 g Fat, 9 g Carbohydrate, 14 mg Calcium, 229 mg Sodium, 0 mg Cholesterol, 1 g Dietary Fiber*

Sally's Mustard

In Big Sky country, they love this spicy condiment Kim learned from her mother, Sally, with steak, poultry, game, ham, even hot dogs. Try brushing it on meat or fish before grilling.

KIM ASHWELL · FRENCHTOWN, MONTANA

¼ cup whole mustard seeds
1 tablespoon dry mustard
⅓ cup cider vinegar
1 tablespoon light corn syrup or honey
2 teaspoons firmly packed dark brown
    sugar

¼ teaspoon salt
¼ teaspoon onion powder
⅛ teaspoon garlic powder
⅛ teaspoon ground cinnamon
⅛ teaspoon ground allspice
Dash ground cloves

1.   In electric spice grinder or mini food processor, grind mustard seeds to texture of coarse meal.

2.   In small bowl, combine ground seeds, mustard powder, and ½ cup boiling water; set aside at least 2 hours.

3.   In small nonmetallic saucepan, combine remaining ingredients; bring to a boil. Reduce heat to low; simmer 5 minutes. Cool slightly.

4.   In blender, combine reserved mustard mixture with vinegar mixture on high speed until smooth; add additional water if mustard is too thick. Pour into small storage container; cover and refrigerate overnight or several days to allow flavors to develop.

5.   To serve, brush on fish, meat, or poultry before grilling; use as a condiment with wild game, ham, or chilled salads.

MAKES 6 SERVINGS

———

EACH SERVING (2 TABLESPOONS) PROVIDES:
    15 Optional Calories

———

PER SERVING: *58 Calories, 2 g Protein, 2 g Fat, 8 g Carbohydrate, 45 mg Calcium, 96 mg Sodium, 0 mg Cholesterol, 0 g Dietary Fiber*

Tofu Mayonnaise

For Marilyn, a registered nurse, feeling good, looking sharp, and living a healthy lifestyle are top priorities. She uses this condiment whenever regular mayonnaise is called for.

MARILYN BROWN · SAN LEANDRO, CALIFORNIA

15 ounces soft tofu
6 tablespoons plain nonfat yogurt
3 tablespoons vinegar
2 teaspoons Dijon mustard
1 garlic clove

Granulated sugar substitute to equal
    1 teaspoon sugar (optional)
½ teaspoon salt
2 tablespoons vegetable oil

1. In food processor, combine all ingredients except oil until smooth.

2. With motor running, slowly drizzle oil through feed tube until mixture is creamy.

3. Refrigerate in covered container. (Mixture thickens when chilled.)

MAKES 2 CUPS

EACH SERVING (1 TABLESPOON) PROVIDES: *20 Optional Calories*

PER SERVING: *17 Calories, 1 g Protein, 1 g Fat, 1 g Carbohydrate, 9 mg Calcium, 46 mg Sodium, 0 mg Cholesterol, 0 g Dietary Fiber*

Desserts, Snacks, and Beverages

At the end of a meal, with a cup of tea, or for that planned midafternoon or evening snack, this collection of recipes should surprise and delight you.

Fruits are treated in intriguing and wonderful ways. Baked Alaska Berry Boats could be the star of a dinner party; Bananas Baked with Rum will transport you to New Orleans; and Ginger Pears have a subtle, mysterious flavor with a counterpoint of creamy sauce. Even puddings get their turn. Pumpkin Pudding and Southern Banana Pudding are perfect midweek desserts.

Knowing how much you love ice cream, we present a recipe for Homemade Ice Cream as well as one for Lime Sherbet and even one for a Tin Roof Sundae.

Sweet treats from the oven include Fresh Banana Cake, Dreamy Cheese-cake, and Strawberry Cheesecake Squares. Little bites like Chocolate Raspberry Squares and Peanut Butter Fluffs are great for snacks. Our three sweet breads, Carrot and Currant Pan Bread, Country Bread, and Swedish Coffee Bread, would be just right to serve with coffee after the movies. Keep a loaf or two on hand in your freezer.

Hot Banana Glory

This simple, low-fat snack was devised by a choral singer and portrait artist from Long Island who is also active in a consumer advocacy group.

FRAN FISHBANE • PLAINVIEW, NEW YORK

1 medium banana
⅛ teaspoon ground cinnamon

1 tablespoon reduced-calorie whipped topping (8 calories per tablespoon)

1. Preheat oven to 350°F.

2. Wrap unpeeled banana in aluminum foil and bake 30 minutes.

3. Carefully unwrap and peel banana; transfer to serving plate. Sprinkle with cinnamon; top with whipped topping.

MAKES 1 SERVING

THIS SERVING PROVIDES: *2 Fruits; 8 Optional Calories*

PER SERVING: *110 Calories, 1 g Protein, 1 g Fat, 27 g Carbohydrate, 10 mg Calcium, 1 mg Sodium, 0 mg Cholesterol, 2 g Dietary Fiber*

Bananas Baked with Rum

Charleen reached her goal just in time to celebrate her 50th birthday in 1988. She maintains her goal weight by making healthy substitutions in her favorite recipes—like evaporated skimmed milk for heavy cream in this people-pleaser.

CHARLEEN FOOTE · ELMHURST, NEW YORK

1 cup evaporated skimmed milk
2 tablespoons firmly packed dark brown
    sugar
2½ teaspoons dark rum
1 teaspoon butter, melted

⅛ teaspoon ground cinnamon
⅛ teaspoon ground ginger
⅛ teaspoon ground nutmeg
2 medium bananas, cut into 8 pieces

1. Preheat oven to 350°F.

2. In 2-cup measure, combine milk, sugar, rum, butter, cinnamon, ginger, and nutmeg.

3. Place four 8-ounce baking dishes on cookie sheet; place 2 banana pieces in each. Pour milk mixture evenly into each dish.

4. Bake 15 minutes, or until bananas are soft when pierced with fork. Sprinkle with additional cinnamon or nutmeg, if desired. Serve immediately.

MAKES 4 SERVINGS

————

EACH SERVING PROVIDES: *½ Milk; 1 Fruit; 40 Optional Calories*

————

PER SERVING: *142 Calories, 5 g Protein, 1 g Fat, 27 g Carbohydrate, 196 mg Calcium, 86 mg Sodium, 5 mg Cholesterol, 1 g Dietary Fiber*

Baked Alaska Berry Boats

Pretty as a picture and bursting with rich flavor, this is the perfect cap to a dinner party with special friends who would never suspect a low-fat dessert could be so luscious.

TANYA FROMAN • CLEARWATER, FLORIDA

2¼ cups fresh blueberries or raspberries
2 medium papayas, halved and seeded
2 large egg whites, at room temperature
⅛ teaspoon salt

2 tablespoons granulated sugar
2 tablespoons shredded coconut
½ teaspoon vanilla extract

1.   Preheat oven to 450°F.

2.   Reserve ½ cup berries for garnish; place remaining berries evenly in papaya halves.

3.   In large bowl, with electric mixer on high speed, beat egg whites and salt to form soft peaks. Beat in sugar, a few teaspoonfuls at a time, beating until whites are glossy and firm. Fold in coconut and vanilla.

4.   Spread meringue mixture evenly over papayas (or place egg white mixture in pastry bag and pipe decoratively on top).

5.   Place filled papayas on baking sheet.

Bake until meringue is lightly browned, 5 to 7 minutes. To serve, garnish with reserved berries.

MAKES 4 SERVINGS

EACH SERVING PROVIDES: *1¾ Fruits; 50 Optional Calories*

PER SERVING: *150 Calories, 3 g Protein, 1 g Fat, 34 g Carbohydrate, 43 mg Calcium, 112 mg Sodium, 0 mg Cholesterol, 3 g Dietary Fiber*

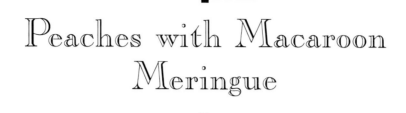

Peaches with Macaroon Meringue

Here's a light dessert with the good looks and delicious taste of gourmet fare. Mary adapted it to fit the Weight Watchers Program after she lost 15 pounds and became a lifetime member.

MARY RIES · MARQUETTE, MICHIGAN

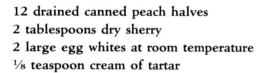

12 drained canned peach halves
2 tablespoons dry sherry
2 large egg whites at room temperature
⅛ teaspoon cream of tartar

2 tablespoons granulated sugar
1 ounce Amaretti cookies, crumbled
¼ teaspoon almond extract

1.   Preheat oven to 375°F.

2.   In 13-by-9-inch baking pan, arrange peaches cut-side up; pour ½ teaspoon sherry into each; set aside.

3.   In medium bowl, with electric mixer on high speed, beat egg whites and cream of tartar to soft peaks. Gradually add sugar; beat until stiff. Fold in Amaretti crumbs and almond extract.

4.   Spread about 2 tablespoons meringue mixture over each peach half. Bake until meringue is lightly browned, 6 to 8 minutes.

MAKES 6 SERVINGS

EACH SERVING PROVIDES: *1 Fruit; 55 Optional Calories*

PER SERVING: *103 Calories, 2 g Protein, 0 g Fat, 24 g Carbohydrate, 9 mg Calcium, 24 mg Sodium, 0 mg Cholesterol, 1 g Dietary Fiber*

Apricot Cream

Lois cans and freezes her own fruits and vegetables and loves cooking with them. For a change, try this light dessert with pears instead of apricots. Either way, it tastes like a heavenly mousse.

LOIS NORTHOUSE · SPRING VALLEY, MINNESOTA

2 teaspoons (1 packet) unflavored gelatin
1 cup drained canned apricot halves
        (reserve ¼ cup liquid)
½ cup part-skim ricotta cheese

¼ cup whipped cream cheese
2 tablespoons honey
Mint sprigs for garnish

1.   Place gelatin and ¼ cup water in blender; let stand 2 minutes to soften.

2.   Meanwhile, in small saucepan, bring reserved liquid plus enough water to equal 1 cup to a boil. Pour into blender; add apricots, cheese, and honey. Process on low speed until just blended.

3.   Pour mixture evenly into four 8-ounce dessert dishes. Cover and refrigerate until set, about 2 hours. Garnish with mint.

MAKES 4 SERVINGS

EACH SERVING PROVIDES: ½ Protein; ½ Fruit; 60 Optional Calories

PER SERVING: *142 Calories, 6 g Protein, 6 g Fat, 18 g Carbohydrate, 98 mg Calcium, 78 mg Sodium, 19 mg Cholesterol, 0 g Dietary Fiber*

Blueberry Salad

Cynthia is a single mother raising an adopted son while attending nursing school. An avid reader, cook, and cross-stitcher, she serves this gelatin salad at family dinners and sends leftovers home with her father.

CYNTHIA SKELTON · MURFREESBORO, TENNESSEE

2 envelopes (eight ½-cup servings) sugar-free triple-berry-flavored gelatin mix (8 calories per serving)
2 cups drained canned crushed pineapple
1½ cups fresh or frozen blueberries
6 tablespoons light cream cheese, softened

¼ cup nonfat sour cream (10 calories per tablespoon)
¼ cup plain nonfat yogurt
2 tablespoons plus 2 teaspoons granulated sugar
½ teaspoon vanilla extract
½ ounce shelled pecans, chopped

1. In medium bowl or 4-cup decorative mold, combine gelatin and 2 cups boiling water. Stir until gelatin is completely dissolved; add pineapple, blueberries, and 1 cup cold water. Chill until set, about 4 hours.

2. In blender, combine remaining ingredients except pecans; blend until smooth.

3. Unmold gelatin onto serving plate; pour cream cheese mixture over top; sprinkle with pecans.

MAKES 8 SERVINGS

EACH SERVING PROVIDES: ¼ Fat; ¾ Fruit; 60 Optional Calories

PER SERVING: 121 Calories, 4 g Protein, 3 g Fat, 20 g Carbohydrate, 50 mg Calcium, 133 mg Sodium, 6 mg Cholesterol, 1 g Dietary Fiber

Fruit Parfait

When her taste buds are bored, Wendy wakes them up with this tangy dessert. She's a Weight Watchers leader who also raises show dogs and works full-time.

WENDY GREBER · RED DEER, ALBERTA, CANADA

¾ cup plain nonfat yogurt
¼ cup part-skim ricotta cheese
1 tablespoon frozen orange juice
    concentrate, thawed
½ teaspoon vanilla extract
1 cup reduced-calorie whipped topping
    (8 calories per tablespoon)

1 medium peach, peeled and diced
¼ cup drained canned crushed
    pineapple
1 teaspoon shredded coconut
1 maraschino cherry, cut in half

1. In small bowl, combine yogurt, ricotta, juice, and vanilla until blended; fold in whipped topping.

2. Spoon one-third cheese mixture into 2 tall parfait glasses; add about 2 teaspoons peach and pineapple to each. Repeat layering twice; top with coconut and cherry half. Cover and chill 1 hour.

MAKES 2 SERVINGS

EACH SERVING PROVIDES: ½ Milk; ½ Protein; 1 Fruit; 35 Optional Calories

PER SERVING: 224 Calories, 9 g Protein, 7 g Fat, 33 g Carbohydrate, 264 mg Calcium, 106 mg Sodium, 11 mg Cholesterol, 1 g Dietary Fiber

Pumpkin Pudding

Phyllis is a Weight Watchers leader who's maintained a 90-pound loss for over a decade. She loves her 50+ group because the members are so vibrant and excited about the Program.

PHYLLIS WEBER · PHOENIX, ARIZONA

1 cup reduced-calorie nonfat vanilla
    yogurt
½ cup canned pumpkin puree
Granulated sugar substitute to equal
    1 teaspoon sugar

⅛ teaspoon pumpkin pie spice
2 tablespoons reduced-calorie whipped
    topping (8 calories per
    tablespoon)
Ground cinnamon for garnish

1. In small bowl, combine all ingredients, except whipped topping and cinnamon, until blended. Spoon into 2 dessert dishes. Cover and refrigerate, or serve immediately.

2. To serve, place 1 tablespoon whipped topping on each pudding. Garnish with cinnamon.

MAKES 2 SERVINGS

EACH SERVING PROVIDES: ½ Milk; ½ Vegetable;
    10 Optional Calories

PER SERVING: 80 Calories, 5 g Protein, 1 g Fat, 15
    g Carbohydrate, 167 mg Calcium, 76 mg So-
    dium, 2 mg Cholesterol, 1 g Dietary Fiber

Southern Banana Pudding

A yummy dessert from the kitchen of a nurse-practitioner in women's health care who loves to cross-stitch, read, and collect recipes. Janie is mother to a twelve-year-old daughter and two dogs.

JANIE TRIMBLE · EDMOND, OKLAHOMA

12 graham crackers (2½-inch squares), made into crumbs
1 tablespoon plus 1 teaspoon margarine, melted
1 envelope (four ½-cup servings) reduced-calorie vanilla pudding mix

2 cups low-fat (1%) milk
½ teaspoon vanilla extract
1 medium banana, sliced
2 large egg whites
2 tablespoons granulated sugar

1. Preheat oven to 350°F. Spray a 1½-quart casserole with nonstick cooking spray; set aside.

2. In medium bowl, combine graham cracker crumbs and margarine. Press half the crumb mixture into bottom of casserole. Bake until firm, 3 to 5 minutes. Set aside and increase oven temperature to 425°F.

3. Prepare vanilla pudding with low-fat milk according to package directions. Stir in vanilla.

4. Layer half the banana slices over crust; top with half the pudding. Repeat layering with remaining graham cracker crumbs, banana, and pudding.

5. In medium bowl, with electric mixer on high speed, beat egg whites 1 minute, until foamy. Gradually add sugar; continue beating on high speed until egg whites are stiff but not dry. Spoon meringue mixture on top of pudding; smooth meringue with a rubber spatula. Bake until golden brown, about 5 minutes.

MAKES 4 SERVINGS

EACH SERVING PROVIDES: ½ Milk; 1 Fat; 1 Bread; ½ Fruit; 65 Optional Calories

PER SERVING: 252 Calories, 8 g Protein, 7 g Fat, 41 g Carbohydrate, 163 mg Calcium, 596 mg Sodium, 5 mg Cholesterol, 1 g Dietary Fiber

Ginger Pears

An easy, delicious dish that's terrific hot or cold. Carmela makes this year-round, experimenting with different seasonal pears for endless variations of this special treat.

CARMELA MEELY · WALNUT CREEK, CALIFORNIA

6 firm small pears
3 tablespoons honey
½ teaspoon grated lemon peel
2 tablespoons fresh lemon juice
One 1-inch piece peeled ginger root, cut into 6 thin slices

¾ cup reduced-calorie nonfat vanilla yogurt
Ground nutmeg for garnish (optional)

1.   Cut a thin slice from the bottom of each pear so that pears will stand upright. Pare about 1 inch of peel from the top of each pear. Using small paring knife, gently remove stems, leaving small cavity.

2.   In small saucepan, heat honey, lemon peel, and juice over medium heat, stirring until blended. (Or place in small glass dish and microwave on High 30 seconds.)

3.   Pour equal amount of the liquid into each pear cavity; place slice of ginger in the center of each.

4.   Pour 1 inch of water into large Dutch oven; place vegetable steamer or rack in bottom. Place pears upright on rack; cover and bring to a boil. Reduce heat and steam, covered, 15 to 20 minutes, or until pears are tender. Let cool slightly. Serve pears with equal amounts of yogurt; sprinkle with nutmeg, if desired.

MAKES 6 SERVINGS

EACH SERVING PROVIDES: *1 Fruit; 45 Optional Calories*

PER SERVING: *152 Calories, 2 g Protein, 1 g Fat, 38 g Carbohydrate, 60 mg Calcium, 21 mg Sodium, 1 mg Cholesterol, 4 g Dietary Fiber*

Homemade Ice Cream

Linda's clever adaptation not only helps her lose weight, but it's a sweet treat her diabetic father can enjoy, too.

LINDA JENNINGS · GRAY, GEORGIA

1½ cups evaporated skimmed milk
1 large egg or ¼ cup egg substitute
4 medium bananas, mashed
1½ teaspoons vanilla extract

Sugar substitute to equal ½ cup sugar
    (12 packets)
½ cup low-fat (1%) milk

In 5-cup ice cream maker, combine all ingredients except milk. Add milk to bring mixture up to fill line. (Add more milk if necessary.) Freeze according to manufacturer's directions.

MAKES 8 SERVINGS

EACH SERVING (½ CUP) PROVIDES: *¼ Milk; 1 Fruit; 55 Optional Calories (Add appropriate Milk Selections if more milk is used.)*

PER SERVING (AS PREPARED WITH EGG): *112 Calories, 5 g Protein, 1 g Fat, 21 g Carbohydrate, 164 mg Calcium, 76 mg Sodium, 29 mg Cholesterol, 1 g Dietary Fiber*

Lime Sherbet

Darlene is a beautician, wife, and mother who loves walking, bowling, sewing, and crafts. She also loves ice cream—but not its fat and calories, so she developed this deliciously light sherbet to satisfy her urge for something sweet and cool.

DARLENE SNYDER · SALEM, OHIO

2½ teaspoons lemon-lime sugar-free drink mix (4 calories per 8-ounce prepared serving)
4 cups low-fat (1.5%) buttermilk

2 cups diet lemon-lime soda
1 tablespoon plus 1 teaspoon unflavored gelatin (2 packets)
1 tablespoon fresh lemon juice

1. In large bowl, stir lemon-lime drink mix into buttermilk.

2. In 2-quart saucepan, bring soda to a boil; let cool to lukewarm. Sprinkle gelatin over soda and reheat over medium-low heat, stirring constantly, until gelatin is completely dissolved. Stir gelatin mixture and lemon juice into flavored buttermilk.

3. Pour mixture into 2-quart plastic resealable container; place in freezer until mixture resembles set gelatin, 4 to 6 hours. In 2 batches, process briefly in food processor fitted with steel blade. Return mixture to resealable container; place in freezer overnight.

4. To serve, let stand at room temperature 5 minutes; spoon into dessert dishes.

MAKES 4 SERVINGS

EACH SERVING (1½ CUPS) PROVIDES: *1 Milk; 10 Optional Calories*

PER SERVING: *140 Calories, 10 g Protein, 4 g Fat, 14 g Carbohydrate, 33˙ mg Calcium, 290 mg Sodium, 15 mg Cholesterol, 0 g Dietary Fiber*

Tin Roof Sundae

Craving something sweet, Dana devised this totally decadent treat. Try it, you'll like it!

DANA FRANCIS · CLOVIS, CALIFORNIA

½ cup frozen low-fat vanilla dairy
  dessert
½ ounce shelled peanuts, chopped

1 packet reduced-calorie chocolate dairy
  shake mix

1. Scoop frozen dessert into small dessert dish; sprinkle peanuts over the top.

2. In small bowl, combine shake mix and about 2 teaspoons hot water to make thick syrup. Pour over dessert and serve immediately.

MAKES 1 SERVING

THIS SERVING PROVIDES: *1 Milk; 1 Fat; ½ Protein; 80 Optional Calories*

PER SERVING: *233 Calories, 11 g Protein, 7 g Fat, 35 g Carbohydrate, 258 mg Calcium, 266 mg Sodium, 5 mg Cholesterol, 1 g Dietary Fiber*

Fresh Banana Cake

"I wanted to celebrate special family occasions with a delicious cake that didn't taste like a diet dessert," writes Christine. The result is so terrific it vanishes faster than you can say "Monkeyshines!"

CHRISTINE BARTLEY · SAN FRANCISCO, CALIFORNIA

¼ cup margarine, at room temperature
¾ cup granulated sugar
3 large eggs, at room temperature
1½ teaspoons vanilla extract
3 very ripe medium bananas, mashed
1½ cups low-fat (1.5%) buttermilk, at
    room temperature

2¼ cups all-purpose flour
2 teaspoons baking soda
1 teaspoon salt
Confectioners' sugar for garnish

1. Preheat oven to 350°F. Spray a 12-cup Bundt pan with nonstick cooking spray; set aside.

2. In large bowl, with electric mixer at medium speed, beat margarine and granulated sugar until light and fluffy; beat in eggs, one at a time. Stir in 1 teaspoon of the vanilla, the bananas, and buttermilk until well combined.

3. In medium bowl, combine flour, baking soda, and salt; add to banana mixture, stirring until just combined.

4. Pour batter into prepared pan; bake 40 to 45 minutes, until top springs back when lightly touched. Cool cake in pan on rack 30 minutes before turning out of pan to cool completely. Sprinkle with confectioners' sugar.

MAKES 12 SERVINGS

EACH SERVING PROVIDES: *1 Fat; ¼ Protein; 1 Bread; ½ Fruit; 65 Optional Calories*

PER SERVING: *230 Calories, 5 g Protein, 6 g Fat, 39 g Carbohydrate, 18 mg Calcium, 414 mg Sodium, 55 mg Cholesterol, 1 g Dietary Fiber*

Raisin Spice Cake

Katherine lost weight so she'd look great at her grandson's wedding. Her favorite recipe dates back to the Depression, when eggs and sugar were hard to come by.

KATHERINE LUCILLE COOMBES · SAND SPRINGS, OKLAHOMA

½ cup raisins
2 tablespoons plus 2 teaspoons reduced-calorie tub margarine
2 tablespoons granulated sugar
1 large egg, lightly beaten
½ cup all-purpose flour
½ teaspoon ground cinnamon
½ teaspoon ground nutmeg
½ teaspoon baking soda
½ teaspoon double-acting baking powder
⅛ teaspoon ground cloves
⅛ teaspoon ground allspice
Dash salt

1.   Preheat oven to 350°F. Spray a 6½-inch square baking dish with nonstick cooking spray; set aside.

2.   In medium saucepan, combine raisins, margarine, sugar, and ½ cup water; bring to a boil. Remove from heat and set aside to cool. Stir in beaten egg.

3.   In medium bowl, stir together remaining ingredients; add raisin mixture, stirring until just combined.

4.   Pour batter into prepared baking dish; bake until toothpick inserted in center comes out clean, about 15 minutes.

MAKES 4 SERVINGS

EACH SERVING PROVIDES: *1 Fat; ¼ Protein; ½ Bread; 1 Fruit; 45 Optional Calories*

PER SERVING: *192 Calories, 4 g Protein, 6 g Fat, 33 g Carbohydrate, 49 mg Calcium, 280 mg Sodium, 53 mg Cholesterol, 1 g Dietary Fiber*

Dreamy Cheesecake

Alison turned to Weight Watchers for help losing post-pregnancy pounds after delivering two boys 18 months apart. Her cheesecake recipe has a wonderfully light texture and tastes glorious.

ALISON MOLVIG · GLASGOW, MONTANA

2 cups part-skim ricotta cheese
16 ounces light cream cheese, softened
Granulated sugar substitute to equal
    8 tablespoons sugar*
1 cup egg substitute
¼ cup reduced-calorie tub margarine,
    melted
3 tablespoons all-purpose flour

3 tablespoons cornstarch
1 teaspoon vanilla extract
1 teaspoon almond extract
Juice of ½ lemon
2 cups nonfat sour cream
    (10 calories per tablespoon)
1½ cups fresh raspberries or blueberries
    (optional)**

1. In large bowl, with electric mixer on low speed, combine ricotta, cream cheese, and sugar substitute until blended.

2. Slowly pour in egg substitute; continue to beat on low speed until no yellow streaks remain. Add remaining ingredients except sour cream and berries; mix until just combined. Fold in sour cream.

3. Pour mixture into ungreased 10-inch springform pan. Place pan in cold oven.

4. Turn oven to 325°F. Bake 1 hour. Turn oven off; leave cake in oven 2 hours. Do not open door during baking or cooling.

5. Remove cake from oven; refrigerate until ready to serve. Remove side of pan. Garnish cake with fruit, if desired**, and cut into 16 wedges.

MAKES 16 SERVINGS

EACH SERVING PROVIDES: ¾ Protein; 60 Optional Calories (Add 10 Optional Calories if fresh fruit garnish is used.)

PER SERVING: 157 Calories, 10 g Protein, 9 g Fat, 9 g Carbohydrate, 167 mg Calcium, 289 mg Sodium, 25 mg Cholesterol, 0 g Dietary Fiber

* Do not use low-calorie sweetener with aspartame in this recipe; it may lose sweetness during baking.

** One cup preserves can also be used in place of fruit. Add 50 Optional Calories per serving.

Ricotta-Lemon Cheesecake

An easy-to-follow recipe from a busy Weight Watchers leader who also works full-time as a teacher's aide, attends aerobics classes, and runs a household.

VICKI BOVEE · CARSON CITY, NEVADA

9 graham crackers (2½-inch squares), made into crumbs
1 cup low-fat (1%) cottage cheese
¾ cup part-skim ricotta cheese
1 cup instant nonfat dry milk powder
¾ cup egg substitute

¼ cup granulated sugar
3 tablespoons fresh lemon juice
Granulated sugar substitute to equal ¾ cup sugar*
2 teaspoons vanilla extract

1.   Preheat oven to 300°F.

2.   Spray a 9-inch glass pie plate with nonstick cooking spray; sprinkle graham cracker crumbs over bottom of pie plate; set aside.

3.   In blender or food processor, puree remaining ingredients until smooth, about 1 minute; pour mixture into prepared pie plate.

4.   Bake 50 to 60 minutes, or until knife inserted in center comes out clean. Cool completely on rack. Cover and refrigerate until ready to serve.

MAKES 6 SERVINGS

EACH SERVING PROVIDES: ½ Milk; 1½ Proteins; ½ Bread; 40 Optional Calories

PER SERVING: 216 Calories, 16 g Protein, 4 g Fat, 29 g Carbohydrate, 261 mg Calcium, 455 mg Sodium, 13 mg Cholesterol, 0 g Dietary Fiber

*   Do not use low-calorie sweetener with aspartame in this recipe; it may lose sweetness during baking.

Strawberry Cheesecake Squares

Since her 62-pound loss, Carol has been leading Weight Watchers meetings for 18 years. Her luscious dessert is perfect at Christmas or Valentine's Day.

CAROL AVERITT · TULSA, OKLAHOMA

24 graham crackers (2½-inch squares), made into crumbs
½ cup reduced-calorie tub margarine, melted
1 envelope (four ½-cup servings) reduced-calorie instant vanilla pudding mix
¾ cup light cream cheese
⅔ cup instant nonfat dry milk powder
¼ cup plus 1 tablespoon granulated sugar
1 teaspoon vanilla extract

2 cups drained canned crushed pineapple (reserve juice)
2 tablespoons cornstarch
1 envelope (four ½-cup servings) reduced-calorie strawberry-flavored gelatin mix
1 medium banana, sliced
2 cups strawberries, sliced
1½ cups reduced-calorie whipped topping (8 calories per tablespoon)

1. Preheat oven to 350°F.

2. In 13-by-9-inch baking pan, combine graham cracker crumbs and margarine; press into bottom and up sides of pan. Bake 10 minutes; set aside.

3. In medium bowl, with electric mixer on medium speed, beat pudding mix, cheese, dry milk, sugar, vanilla, and 1½ cups water until blended; pour over crust.

4. In medium saucepan, combine pineapple, reserved juice, and cornstarch; cook over medium heat, stirring constantly, until thickened, about 2 minutes. Stir in gelatin mix and banana; remove from heat and cool slightly. Spread evenly over cheese layer.

5. Arrange berries attractively over top. Refrigerate 1 hour, or until ready to serve. Using a pastry bag fitted with a star tip, pipe whipped topping on cake.

MAKES 16 SERVINGS

EACH SERVING PROVIDES: ¾ Fat; ½ Bread; ½ Fruit; 75 Optional Calories

PER SERVING: 169 Calories, 4 g Protein, 7 g Fat, 26 g Carbohydrate, 62 mg Calcium, 298 mg Sodium, 6 mg Cholesterol, 1 g Dietary Fiber

Chocolate Cream Pie

A sweet tooth prompts this grandmother to devise clever desserts. When she's not cooking, Linda is often "heel-and-toeing it" down the road—so she doesn't mind being called a "streetwalker" by good-natured neighbors!

LINDA DAVIS · LINCOLN, ILLINOIS

¼ cup smooth peanut butter
1 tablespoon plus 1 teaspoon honey
2¼ ounces toasted rice cereal
1 envelope (four ½-cup servings) reduced-calorie chocolate pudding mix

2 cups low-fat (1%) milk
¼ cup reduced-calorie whipped topping (8 calories per tablespoon)

1. In medium bowl, combine peanut butter and honey; stir in rice cereal, coating cereal evenly with peanut butter.

2. Spray 9-inch pie plate with nonstick cooking spray. With back of spoon, press cereal mixture into bottom and up sides of pie plate. Freeze, uncovered, ½ hour.

3. Prepare chocolate pudding with milk, following package directions. Pour into crust; refrigerate, uncovered, 1 hour.

4. With pastry bag fitted with star tip, decoratively pipe whipped topping onto pie.

MAKES 6 SERVINGS

EACH SERVING PROVIDES: ¾ Fat; ¾ Protein; ½ Bread; 70 Optional Calories

PER SERVING: 190 Calories, 7 g Protein, 7 g Fat, 27 g Carbohydrate, 107 mg Calcium, 219 mg Sodium, 3 mg Cholesterol, 1 g Dietary Fiber

Crustless Honey-Cinnamon Pumpkin Pies

You won't miss the crust when you bite into Emily's delicious pumpkin pie.

EMILY DORIS RENNER • WAYNESBURGH, PENNSYLVANIA

3 cups canned pumpkin puree
3 large eggs
2 cups low-fat (1%) milk
½ cup plus 2 tablespoons honey
¼ cup margarine, melted
2 tablespoons vanilla extract
4 slices reduced-calorie white bread,
    diced

3 tablespoons all-purpose flour
2 teaspoons ground cinnamon
¾ cup reduced-calorie whipped topping
    (8 calories per tablespoon) for
    garnish (optional)

1.   Preheat oven to 350°F. Spray two 9-inch deep-dish pie plates with nonstick cooking spray; set aside.

2.   In food processor, combine pumpkin, eggs, milk, honey, margarine, and vanilla; puree until blended. Add remaining ingredients; process 1 minute, stopping once to scrape sides of bowl.

3.   Pour into prepared pie plates. Bake until knife inserted 1 inch from center comes out clean, 40 to 50 minutes.

4.   Cool pies on wire rack. Refrigerate until ready to serve.

5.   To serve, cut chilled pies into wedges. Garnish each serving with 1 tablespoon whipped topping, if desired.

MAKES 2 PIES, 6 SERVINGS EACH

EACH SERVING PROVIDES: *1 Fat; ¼ Protein; ½ Vegetable; ¼ Bread; 65 Optional Calories (Add 8 Optional Calories per tablespoon if whipped topping is used.)*

PER SERVING: *173 Calories, 5 g Protein, 6 g Fat, 27 g Carbohydrate, 86 mg Calcium, 116 mg Sodium, 55 mg Cholesterol, 1 g Dietary Fiber*

Strawberry Pie

An avid reader, cross-stitcher, and crocheter, Jane reinvented this sweet treat when she was a Weight Watchers leader in the late 1980s.

JANE McCORMICK • NORTH CANTON, OHIO

¾ cup all-purpose flour
¼ teaspoon salt
2 tablespoons plus 2 teaspoons
    margarine, well chilled
¼ cup plain nonfat yogurt

4 cups strawberries, halved
¼ cup plus 2 tablespoons granulated
    sugar
3 tablespoons cornstarch
½ cup whipped topping

1.   To prepare crust, in medium bowl, stir together flour and salt; using pastry blender or 2 knives, cut in margarine until mixture resembles coarse meal. Quickly stir in yogurt and 1 tablespoon water. Form dough into a ball, cover with plastic wrap, and refrigerate 1 hour.

2.   Preheat oven to 400°F.

3.   Roll pastry between 2 sheets of wax paper into 9-inch circle. Fit into 9-inch pie plate; prick with fork. Line crust with aluminum foil; fill with dried beans or pie weights. Bake 15 to 18 minutes, until golden brown. Remove foil and beans; cool on rack.

4.   To prepare filling, place 1 cup strawberries and ⅔ cup water in 2-quart saucepan; cook over medium heat for 2 minutes. In small bowl, combine sugar, cornstarch, and ⅓ cup water; add to strawberry mixture and cook until mixture boils and thickens, about 1 minute.

5.   Reserve 8 strawberry halves for garnish. Place remaining berries in cooled pie crust; pour cooked strawberry mixture over top. Refrigerate, uncovered, until filling is completely cool, about 1 hour.

6.   Using pastry bag fitted with star tip, decoratively pipe whipped topping onto pie. Garnish with reserved strawberry halves.

MAKES 8 SERVINGS

EACH SERVING PROVIDES: *1 Fat; ½ Bread; ½ Fruit; 75 Optional Calories*

PER SERVING: *164 Calories, 2 g Protein, 5 g Fat, 28 g Carbohydrate, 29 mg Calcium, 120 mg Sodium, 0 mg Cholesterol, 2 g Dietary Fiber*

Chocolate Raspberry Squares

The Ashwoods are dedicated to baking with whole grains and fruit juice instead of sugar. When she's not looking after her two kids or working as a designer and illustrator, Elizabeth is a musician and a Weight Watchers weigher and receptionist.

ELIZABETH ASHWOOD · ROSEVILLE, MINNESOTA

¾ cup thawed frozen apple-raspberry juice concentrate
3 large egg whites or ¼ cup egg substitute
2 tablespoons plus 2 teaspoons reduced-calorie tub margarine, melted
2 teaspoons vanilla extract

½ cup all-purpose flour
¼ cup whole-wheat flour
¼ cup unsweetened cocoa powder
½ teaspoon double-acting baking powder
3 tablespoons whipped cream cheese

1. Preheat oven to 350°F. Spray an 8-inch square baking pan with nonstick cooking spray; set aside.

2. In small bowl, whisk together juice, egg, margarine, and vanilla; set aside.

3. In medium bowl, whisk together white and whole-wheat flour, cocoa, and baking powder. Whisk in juice mixture. Pour into prepared pan. Bake until cake tester inserted in center comes out almost clean, about 15 minutes. Cool in pan on rack.

4. Using long spatula, remove from pan; place on cutting board. Spread cream cheese evenly over top; cut into 16 squares.

MAKES 8 SERVINGS

EACH SERVING (2 SQUARES) PROVIDES: ½ *Fat;* ¾ *Fruit;* ½ *Bread; 20 Optional Calories*

PER SERVING: *123 Calories, 3 g Protein, 3 g Fat, 22 g Carbohydrate, 27 mg Calcium, 86 mg Sodium, 4 mg Cholesterol, 1 g Dietary Fiber*

Shown with Fruity Yogurt Milkshake (page 296).

Chocolate Almond Cookies

As a registerd nurse, Shirley understands the pitfalls of overeating—but that doesn't stop her sweet tooth from nagging her occasionally. She indulges herself with these delicious cookies.

SHIRLEY JONES · EASLY, SOUTH CAROLINA

2 large egg whites, room temperature
⅛ teaspoon cream of tartar
1 envelope (four ½-cup servings) reduced-calorie chocolate mousse mix

1 tablespoon confectioners' sugar
½ teaspoon almond extract

1. Preheat oven to 250°F. Line baking sheet with parchment paper; set aside.

2. In large bowl, with electric mixer on high speed, beat egg whites and cream of tartar to form soft peaks. Gradually add mousse mix, 1 tablespoon at a time, and sugar, beating until incorporated and batter is thick and fluffy. Fold in extract.

3. Drop batter by rounded teaspoons 1½ inches apart onto prepared baking sheet, to make 24 cookies. Bake 35 to 40 minutes, or until crisp. Cool completely. Store in airtight container. (Note: These are thin, flat cookies.)

MAKES 12 SERVINGS

EACH SERVING (2 COOKIES) PROVIDES: *25 Optional Calories*

PER SERVING: *25 Calories, 1 g Protein, 1 g Fat, 2 g Carbohydrate, 34 mg Calcium, 29 mg Sodium, 0 mg Cholesterol, 0 g Dietary Fiber*

Meringue Kisses

Gail is a Weight Watchers leader who also teaches CPR, so she's attentive to creating healthy meals. When she's not whipping up batches of kisses, Gail may be cross-country skiing, doing moderate-impact aerobics, or mountain biking with her husband.

GAIL GUTTERUD · POST FALLS, IDAHO

2 egg whites, at room temperature
¼ teaspoon cream of tartar
Pinch salt

½ cup granulated sugar
½ teaspoon vanilla extract
4 ounces semisweet chocolate chips

1. Preheat oven to 375°F. Line baking sheet with parchment paper; set aside.

2. In medium bowl, with electric mixer on medium speed, beat egg whites until frothy; add cream of tartar and salt. Beat on high speed until stiff; beat in sugar 1 tablespoon at a time. Add vanilla; fold in chocolate chips.

3. Drop batter by heaping teaspoonfuls onto prepared baking sheet. Place in oven. Turn oven off; leave cookies in oven 5 hours.

Variation: Add food coloring for festive holiday touch: green for Christmas; pink and yellow for Easter, etc.

MAKES 12 SERVINGS

EACH SERVING (2 COOKIES) PROVIDES: *80 Optional Calories*

PER SERVING: *80 Calories, 1 g Protein, 3 g Fat, 15 g Carbohydrate, 3 mg Calcium, 20 mg Sodium, 0 mg Cholesterol, 0 g Dietary Fiber*

Peanut Butter Fluffs

With five children and three grandchildren, Beverly cooks a lot. This simple dessert pleases both her husband (who dislikes super-sweet dishes) and the kids. Best of all, it freezes well, so it's ready anytime.

BEVERLY LEMOINE · COLFAX, LOUISIANA

9 graham crackers (2½-inch squares), made into crumbs

2 tablespoons reduced-calorie tub margarine, melted

2 cups reduced-calorie whipped topping (8 calories per tablespoon)

1 cup low-fat (1%) milk

½ cup plus 1 tablespoon creamy peanut butter

1 envelope (four ½-cup servings) reduced-calorie vanilla pudding mix

2 tablespoons reduced-calorie strawberry spread (8 calories per teaspoon)

1. Line twelve 2½-inch muffin cups with paper liners; set aside.

2. In small bowl, combine crumbs and margarine; press about 1 tablespoon mixture into each cup. Top each with about 2 teaspoons whipped topping.

3. In a large bowl, with an electric mixer on low speed, mix milk and peanut butter together until smooth.

4. Add pudding mix; beat until blended, about 1 minute. Fold in remaining whipped topping.

5. Distribute evenly among cups; top with ½ teaspoon strawberry spread. Freeze several hours, or overnight.

6. To serve, remove fluffs from muffin cups, peel off paper liners, and let stand at room temperature to soften slightly, about 5 minutes.

MAKES 12 SERVINGS

EACH SERVING PROVIDES: *1 Fat; ¾ Protein; ¼ Bread; 40 Optional Calories*

PER SERVING: *142 Calories, 5 g Protein, 9 g Fat, 12 g Carbohydrate, 31 mg Calcium, 228 mg Sodium, 1 mg Cholesterol, 1 g Dietary Fiber*

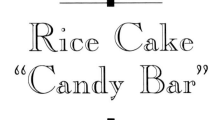

Rice Cake "Candy Bar"

Dina likes "a good and gooey snack that fits into the Food Plan without requiring me to give up too many Optional Calories." Her creation helps her to enjoy the great taste of "honest-to-goodness peanut butter and chocolate" anytime.

DINA PROJANSKY · MOUNT VERNON, NEW YORK

1 tablespoon creamy peanut butter
2 rice cakes
2 teaspoons chocolate syrup

2 tablespoons raisins
Ground cinnamon

Spread peanut butter evenly on rice cakes. Drizzle 1 teaspoon chocolate syrup on top of each; sprinkle evenly with raisins and cinnamon.

MAKES 2 SERVINGS

EACH SERVING PROVIDES: ½ Fat; ½ Protein; ½ Bread; ½ Fruit; 20 Optional Calories

PER SERVING: 123 Calories, 4 g Protein, 4 g Fat, 20 g Carbohydrate, 8 mg Calcium, 55 mg Sodium, 0 mg Cholesterol, 1 g Dietary Fiber

Carrot and Currant Pan Bread

A homey whole-grain dessert that's not overly sweet, from the files of a busy artist who loves nature, animals, photography, boating, fishing, and exercise.

BARBARA VALE · PORT TOWNSEND, WASHINGTON

1 cup shredded carrots
1 cup low-fat (1.5%) buttermilk
3 ounces rolled oats
½ cup thawed frozen apple juice concentrate
½ cup dried currants
1 large egg
2 tablespoons plus 2 teaspoons vegetable oil

¾ cup whole-wheat flour
3 tablespoons wheat germ
1 teaspoon double-acting baking powder
½ teaspoon baking soda
½ teaspoon salt
½ teaspoon ground cinnamon
½ teaspoon ground cloves

1.   In medium bowl, combine carrots, buttermilk, and oats; set aside 1 hour.

2.   Meanwhile, in small saucepan, combine juice concentrate and currants; bring to a boil. Remove from heat and set aside.

3.   Preheat oven to 375°F. Spray an 8-inch square pan with nonstick cooking spray; set aside.

4.   In small bowl, beat egg and oil; pour into oat mixture. Add remaining ingredients and currants with juice; stir well.

5.   Pour into prepared pan; spread to make even layer. Bake until lightly browned and cracked on top, 25 to 30 minutes. Cool in pan on rack. Cut into squares.

MAKES 8 SERVINGS

EACH SERVING PROVIDES: *1 Fat; ¼ Vegetable; 1 Bread; 1 Fruit; 30 Optional Calories*

PER SERVING: *213 Calories, 6 g Protein, 7 g Fat, 34 g Carbohydrate, 94 mg Calcium, 293 mg Sodium, 28 mg Cholesterol, 4 g Dietary Fiber*

Country Bread

Every summer the Littles go camping, and they always pack this homey recipe. With whipped topping it makes a great, wholesome dessert.

DIANE LITTLE · TUSCOLA, ILLINOIS

8 slices reduced-calorie whole-wheat bread, torn into pieces
1⅓ cups instant nonfat dry milk powder
½ cup firmly packed dark brown sugar
¼ cup whole-wheat flour
2½ teaspoons double-acting baking powder
2 cups canned pumpkin puree

2 cups drained canned crushed pineapple (reserve ½ cup juice)
2 large eggs, lightly beaten
2 tablespoons vegetable oil
1½ teaspoons pumpkin pie spice
1 teaspoon vanilla extract
½ teaspoon ground cinnamon
Dash salt

1. Preheat oven to 350°F. Spray 13-by-9-inch baking pan with nonstick cooking spray; set aside.

2. In large bowl, combine bread, milk powder, sugar, flour, and baking powder.

3. In medium bowl, combine remaining ingredients until well blended. Pour into bread mixture; stir until thoroughly combined.

4. Pour mixture into prepared pan. Bake until golden brown and knife inserted in center comes out clean, about 40 minutes. Cool in pan on rack.

MAKES 8 SERVINGS

EACH SERVING PROVIDES: ½ Milk; ¾ Fat; ¼ Protein; ½ Vegetable; ½ Bread; ½ Fruit; 75 Optional Calories

PER SERVING: 257 Calories, 9 g Protein, 6 g Fat, 46 g Carbohydrate, 273 mg Calcium, 331 mg Sodium, 55 mg Cholesterol, 4 g Dietary Fiber

Swedish Coffee Bread

A nurse and mother of five, Debbie adapted this recipe as a tribute to her Swedish grandmother's irresistible sweet rolls. It's perfect with a piping-hot beverage when the hungries hit.

DEBBIE KIEDA · ENFIELD, CONNECTICUT

2 packages active dry yeast
2¼ cups all-purpose flour
⅓ cup granulated sugar
1 teaspoon salt

1 teaspoon ground cardamom
¼ cup vegetable oil
1 large egg, lightly beaten
¾ cup raisins

1. In small bowl, sprinkle yeast over 1 cup very warm water (105° to 115°F); let stand until foamy, about 5 minutes.

2. Meanwhile, in large bowl, whisk together flour, sugar, salt, and cardamom. Pour yeast mixture into flour mixture; add vegetable oil and egg; stir until thoroughly combined. Stir in raisins.

3. Cover bowl with plastic wrap and let stand in warm, draft-free place until doubled in volume, 45 to 60 minutes.

4. Preheat oven to 375°F. Spray 9-by-5-inch loaf pan with nonstick cooking spray.

5. Scrape dough into prepared pan. Bake until golden brown, about 30 minutes. Cool in pan on rack.

Variation: Mix ¼ cup sugar with 1 tablespoon cinnamon. Spoon half the batter into pan; sprinkle half sugar mixture over batter, spoon remaining batter on top, and sprinkle remaining sugar over bread. (Add 20 Optional Calories per serving.)

MAKES 12 SERVINGS

EACH SERVING PROVIDES: *1 Fat; 1 Bread; ½ Fruit; 30 Optional Calories*

PER SERVING: *184 Calories, 4 g Protein, 5 g Fat, 31 g Carbohydrate, 12 mg Calcium, 191 mg Sodium, 18 mg Cholesterol, 1 g Dietary Fiber*

Cranberry Cooler

Having lost weight energizes Sylvia, who now walks or rides her bike every day.

SYLVIA WILHIDE · DENTON, MARYLAND

⅓ cup cranberry-juice cocktail
⅔ cup diet lemon-lime or club soda

1 lemon wedge
1 lime wedge

Fill 10-ounce glass with ice cubes; pour in juice and soda. Squeeze in lemon and lime wedges; stir to combine.

MAKES 1 SERVING

THIS SERVING PROVIDES: *1 Fruit*

PER SERVING: *51 Calories, 0 g Protein, 0 g Fat, 13 g Carbohydrate, 3 mg Calcium, 46 mg Sodium, 0 mg Cholesterol, 0 g Dietary Fiber*

Raspberry Fizz

Mary Anne has made, as she says, "the transition from a 'fat' cook to a cook of tasty, healthy meals" that fit the Weight Watchers Program. Her Raspberry Fizz was the result of experimentation to find a festive beverage to serve at holidays.

MARY ANNE ROBINSON · DAYTON, OHIO

1½ cups fresh or frozen raspberries
1 cup orange juice
⅔ cup pineapple juice

Two 12-ounce cans diet lemon-lime
soda, chilled
Mint sprigs for garnish

In blender, combine raspberries and orange and pineapple juice; blend until smooth. Strain into pitcher; slowly pour in soda. Stir to combine. Divide evenly among 6 ice-filled glasses; garnish with mint.

MAKES 6 SERVINGS

EACH SERVING (1 CUP) PROVIDES: *1 Fruit*

PER SERVING: *50 Calories, 1 g Protein, 0 g Fat, 12 g Carbohydrate, 14 mg Calcium, 34 mg Sodium, 0 mg Cholesterol, 2 g Dietary Fiber*

Malibu Cooler

Tending her roses is Judi's favorite relaxation. On hot summer afternoons, after puttering in the flower beds, she trades her pruning shears for a Malibu Cooler sipped on the patio chaise.

JUDI CAMPBELL · MISSOULA, MONTANA

½ cup grapefruit juice
⅛ teaspoon coconut extract
⅛ teaspoon rum extract

4 ice cubes
One 12-ounce can diet lemon-lime soda,
chilled

In blender, combine juice, extracts, and ice cubes; blend until ice is coarsely chopped, about 1 minute. Pour into chilled 16-ounce glass; stir in soda.

MAKES 1 SERVING

THIS SERVING PROVIDES: *1 Fruit*

PER SERVING: *54 Calories, 1 g Protein, 0 g Fat, 12 g Carbohydrate, 9 mg Calcium, 101 mg Sodium, 0 mg Cholesterol, 0 g Dietary Fiber*

Fruity Yogurt Milkshake

Diane runs a small country crafts business, making all the merchandise she sells in her store. She's also selling friends on her healthy lifestyle; inspired by her success, several joined Weight Watchers.

DIANE HANSEN · KANAWHA, IOWA

1 envelope (four ½-cup servings) reduced-calorie instant vanilla pudding mix
2 cups skim milk
2 cups strawberries (reserve 4 berries)

1 cup reduced-calorie nonfat strawberry yogurt
1 cup crushed ice

1. In blender, combine all ingredients at medium speed until smooth and frothy.

2. To serve, divide milkshake evenly among 4 chilled 10-ounce glasses. Garnish with reserved strawberries.

MAKES 4 SERVINGS

EACH SERVING (1¼ CUPS) PROVIDES: ¾ Milk; ½ Fruit; 25 Optional Calories

PER SERVING: 116 Calories, 7 g Protein, 1 g Fat, 22 g Carbohydrate, 236 mg Calcium, 417 mg Sodium, 3 mg Cholesterol, 2 g Dietary Fiber

Shown with Chocolate Raspberry Squares on page 285.

Iced Spiced Coffee

Becky first tested this recipe on New Year's Eve in front of a roaring fire. It was a hit then, and it's just as refreshing during the summer months.

BECKY MAGAZINER · RANDALLSTOWN, MARYLAND

3 cups cold brewed coffee
½ cup skim milk
1 tablespoon grated lemon peel
6 whole cloves

6 whole allspice berries
2 cinnamon sticks
Granulated sugar substitute to equal
   2 tablespoons sugar

In 4-quart glass measure, combine all ingredients. Let stand 1 hour to develop flavors. Strain into 2 ice-filled 10-ounce glasses.

MAKES 2 SERVINGS

EACH SERVING PROVIDES: ¼ Milk

PER SERVING: 39 Calories, 2 g Protein, 0 g Fat, 7 g Carbohydrate, 95 mg Calcium, 85 mg Sodium, 1 mg Cholesterol, 0 g Dietary Fiber

Root Beer Float

Whenever his taste buds call for something sweet, Robert splurges on this low-cal, low-guilt drink. He keeps a mug in the freezer so it's always frosted.

ROBERT APPLEGATE · GALT, CALIFORNIA

½ cup frozen vanilla low-fat dairy dessert

One 12-ounce can diet root beer, chilled

Place half the dairy dessert in chilled 16-ounce mug. Pour root beer over dessert. Scoop remaining dessert on top. Serve immediately.

MAKES 1 SERVING

THIS SERVING PROVIDES: 82 Optional Calories

PER SERVING: 82 Calories, 3 g Protein, 0 g Fat, 21 g Carbohydrate, 0 mg Calcium, 175 mg Sodium, 5 mg Cholesterol, 0 g Dietary Fiber

Hot Chocolate

From a medical technologist who admits she's not a huge fan of milk comes a delicious treat that heats up quickly in the microwave.

ROSA ANNA CANTU · SAN ANTONIO, TEXAS

2 teaspoons unsweetened cocoa powder
1 cup low-fat (1%) milk

Granulated sugar substitute to equal
2 teaspoons sugar
1 cinnamon stick

Stir cocoa and ½ cup of the milk in large mug until blended (small bits of cocoa will remain); stir in remaining milk. Microwave on High 1½ to 2 minutes, until hot. Stir in sugar substitute; add cinnamon stick.

MAKES 1 SERVING

THIS SERVING PROVIDES: *1 Milk; 10 Optional Calories*

PER SERVING: *117 Calories, 9 g Protein, 3 g Fat, 15 g Carbohydrate, 311 mg Calcium, 152 mg Sodium, 10 mg Cholesterol, 1 g Dietary Fiber*

Appendix

Metric Conversions

If you are converting the recipes in this book to metric measurements, use the following chart as a guide.

VOLUME		WEIGHT		OVEN TEMPERATURES	
¼ teaspoon	1 milliliter	1 ounce	30 grams	250°F	120°C
½ teaspoon	2 milliliters	¼ pound	120 grams	275°F	140°C
1 teaspoon	5 milliliters	½ pound	240 grams	300°F	150°C
1 tablespoon	15 milliliters	¾ pound	360 grams	325°F	160°C
2 tablespoons	30 milliliters	1 pound	480 grams	350°F	180°C
3 tablespoons	45 milliliters			375°F	190°C
¼ cup	50 milliliters			400°F	200°C
⅓ cup	75 milliliters			425°F	220°C
½ cup	125 milliliters			450°F	230°C
⅔ cup	150 milliliters	LENGTH		475°F	250°C
¾ cup	175 milliliters			500°F	260°C
1 cup	250 milliliters	1 inch	25 millimeters	525°F	270°C
1 quart	1 liter	1 inch	2.5 centimeters		

DRY AND LIQUID EQUIVALENTS

TEASPOONS	TABLESPOONS	CUPS	FLUID OUNCES
3 teaspoons	1 tablespoon		½ fluid ounce
6 teaspoons	2 tablespoons	⅛ cup	1 fluid ounce
8 teaspoons	2 tablespoons plus 2 teaspoons	⅙ cup	
12 teaspoons	4 tablespoons	¼ cup	2 fluid ounces
15 teaspoons	5 tablespoons	⅓ cup less 1 teaspoon	
16 teaspoons	5 tablespoons plus 1 teaspoon	⅓ cup	
18 teaspoons	6 tablespoons	⅓ cup plus 2 teaspoons	3 fluid ounces
24 teaspoons	8 tablespoons	½ cup	4 fluid ounces
30 teaspoons	10 tablespoons	½ cup plus 2 tablespoons	5 fluid ounces
32 teaspoons	10 tablespoons plus 2 teaspoons	⅔ cup	
36 teaspoons	12 tablespoons	¾ cup	6 fluid ounces
42 teaspoons	14 tablespoons	1 cup less 2 tablespoons	7 fluid ounces
45 teaspoons	15 tablespoons	1 cup less 1 tablespoon	
48 teaspoons	16 tablespoons	1 cup	8 fluid ounces

Note: Measurements of less than ⅛ teaspoon are considered a dash or a pinch.

Since 1963, Weight Watchers has grown from a handful of people to millions of enrollments. Today, Weight Watchers is a recognized leader in the weight control field. Members of all ages, from youths to senior citizens, attend weekly meetings virtually around the globe. Growing numbers of people enjoy our expanding line of convenience foods, bestselling cookbooks, personal planners, exercise audiocassettes, fitness videos, and *Weight Watchers Magazine*.

The recipes in this book represent the best from our vast Weight Watchers family: the delicious foods cooked at home by staff and members throughout North America. These recipes all fit the current Weight Watchers Food Plan; they're nutritious, easy to prepare, and home-kitchen tested. We hope you'll enjoy this cross-country sampler of recipes for all seasons and occasions.

Acknowledgments

For their tireless energy and enthusiasm in screening, testing, developing, writing and checking, designing and creating this book, we thank Patricia M. Baird, M.A., R.D.; Lynne S. Hill, M.S., R.D., L.D.; and Linda Rosensweig; Lee Haiken and Mary Novitsky; Shelley Stansfield and K. C. Witherell; Helen Fixler and Susanne Speranza.

Index